DEAD RECKONING

DEAD RECKONING

A Therapist Confronts
His Own Grief

David C. Treadway, Ph.D.

BasicBooks
A Division of HarperCollins*Publishers*

All clinical case material in this book consists of composite characters drawn from various clinical cases. Characters and incidents described are not based on any one particular case, and actual patient names have been changed.

Copyright © 1996 by David C. Treadway.
Published by BasicBooks,
A Division of HarperCollins Publishers, Inc.

FIRST EDITION

Designed by Elliott Beard

Library of Congress Cataloging-in-Publication Data

Treadway, David C.
    Dead reckoning : a therapist confronts his own
grief / by David C. Treadway.—1st ed.
        p.   cm.
    ISBN 0-465-00728-7
    1. Grief.   2. Bereavement—Psychological
aspects.   3. Death—Psychological aspects.
    4. Grief therapy.   I. Title.
BF575.G7T74   1996
155.9'37'092—dc20
    [B]   96-3842

96 97 98 99 00 ❖/HC 10 9 8 7 6 5 4 3 2 1

To Kate
for being my lifeline and best friend

To Dad, Jon, Lauris, and Jim
for being my partners in the journey

To Dr. Barbara Greenspan
for her gentle hand and the missing key

CONTENTS

ONE

David, sailing, 1956

SMALL CRAFT WARNINGS
July 1955

I CAN'T WAIT TO GET HOME. I STILL CAN FEEL THE SALT ON MY sunburned face as I charge up the hill on my bike with my sail bag over the handlebars. My legs are pumping hard. I turn onto Pleasant Street and speed past the crawling cars and the flood of tourists spilling over the sidewalks.

I can't wait to tell Mom about the moment we passed *Sea Devil*.

Sandy Bay was covered with dots of white sails as all the fleets raced in the last day of the Cape Ann Regatta. It was blowing hard. Already two boats had flipped. The remaining thirteen little Turn-abouts were strung out along the course. Each of them was filled with two little kids in orange life preservers hiking out on the windward rail. We slogged along in the blustery 19-knot southwester, taking in great dollops of water as we heeled way over in the puffs. Small craft warnings had almost caused the committee to cancel our race, but they relented in the face of our strenuous pleading.

My brother Jimmy and I were hanging on for dear life. We were the youngest crew in the race and it was the first year I owned my boat. I had just turned ten. All season long we had been soundly trounced by everyone, including the girls.

But as we rounded the last mark, we were in second place and catching *Sea Devil*. I couldn't believe it: Phil Jones's boat was always faster than mine and he had won most of the races in our class all summer.

Headed toward the finish line, we were neck and neck. He was still ahead, but slightly to leeward. I had his wind; slowly but surely, we stole by him. Jimmy and I glanced at each other in disbelief. We didn't say a word. We drove for the favored end of the line. The gun sounded and it was over. We won.

Coming around the corner onto Pleasant Street, I see my house, the narrow tall Victorian that looks like a Charles Addams cartoon. Our summer home is in the middle of Rockport, Massachusetts, and it's the tallest building in town. From the widow's walk you can see the water. I always go up there to check out the conditions before heading down to the harbor.

Finally I'm home. Rushing up the driveway, I see my mother in our backyard working at her easel. Her back's to me and she's sitting on her little artist's stool. She's wearing her blue denim smock and a red kerchief to keep the hair out of her face. She's painting as usual.

I want to run to her, but stop to catch my breath. Then I casually walk up behind her. She doesn't hear me coming. She's really concentrating. It's funny how she almost looks mad when she's working hard. She's finishing up an oil painting of the yacht club I just left.

"Hi, Mom."

She glances up at me. "How long have you been standing there?" she asks, quickly turning back to the canvas. "Not long. That's really a good painting of the club," I smile at her.

"That's sweet of you to say, David."

I pause for a moment, holding my bubble of excitement. "Guess what, Mom? We won today."

"That's nice," she replies without missing a stroke.

July 1962

Mom's in bed all the time now. She reads novels, sleeps, and sometimes just lies there like a lump, staring into space. She hardly ever gets up, although she still makes it to art class.

Dad and I are the only ones living with her at West Cedar Street in Boston this summer. We sold the Rockport house years ago because of financial pressures. The parents never said anything, but I know sending us all to fancy private schools has been a killer.

Mornings are hard. Dad and I take her up a breakfast tray before leaving for work. We're always hoping to leave her smiling. Sometimes we dance into her room doing a kind of Crosby and Hope soft-shoe routine or croon a schmaltzy tune like "When Irish Eyes Are Smiling." We must look pretty silly to her. Sometimes she smiles, but mostly she just looks away.

I don't know what's really going on. Dad says she's "under stress" or she has a "nervous condition." He warns me, "Your mother needs her rest."

I don't know what he's talking about; seems to me that she's resting round the clock.

Since she never wants to eat meals, Dad and I go out to dinner without her. He doesn't like to cook and I don't know how. We go to this cheap steak house around the corner. He talks to me about Mom and about his worries. I listen. Sometimes I offer advice, which he politely ignores. Giving him suggestions makes me feel important anyway, more like a grown-up.

Earlier tonight, I even tried to help Mom, but it didn't work out so well. I suggested something brilliant such as "Why don't you and Dad try to talk about what's wrong?" She just turned away from me and said coldly, "Why don't you mind your own business?"

Her words slapped me. I went to my room. I felt so small.

She's probably right. It's none of my business. But I wonder what I should have said.

July 1967

Kate and I are ghosting along slowly in the fog. There's hardly a breath of wind. We left the red nun #2 an hour ago on a course of due west magnetic. We're not really lost yet, it's just that we should have heard the bell off of Misery Island by now. We hear the crash of breakers to our right and left, but we can't see a thing. We're enshrouded in wet folds of gray.

It's been two summers since my mother killed herself. Dad's already remarried, and Kate and I just got engaged. This is Kate's first sail. She's scared and I'm pretending to be calm. But I haven't been sailing since I was thirteen and I don't know these waters.

This little Rhodes 19 sloop that we rented doesn't have any instruments except a compass, so we are keeping close track of our course and time. I factor in the effect of the tide by watching the direction the currents pull on the lobster buoys. We're feeling our way from buoy to bell, using the traditional technique my grandfather taught me. It's called dead reckoning.

We sit utterly still and listen hard for the reassuring clang of the bell.

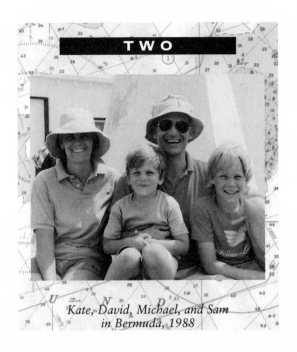

Kate, David, Michael, and Sam
in Bermuda, 1988

QUICK SKETCHES

July 1990

THE DAY'S SCHEDULE LOOMS LIKE A SQUALL LINE ON THE
horizon.

I'm back to back with clients and teaching until 3:00 P.M.
Then I have to scoop up the boys, pack, meet Kate at the airport,
and we're off to Evanston, Ilinois, for the weekend.

Kate comes out of the bathroom. She is dressed for work in
the black short-sleeve summer dress she often wears to the hospital. I'm used to seeing Kate in black. It's becoming on her. It
goes well with her lovely silvery brown hair and her bright blue
eyes. This morning Kate looks tired and sad.

"You don't really want to do this weekend, do you?" she asks
softly.

"Well, quite honestly, I don't want to go very much. But I think it's important for you."

"I feel selfish dragging you and the kids along."

I take her in my arms. "Hey, it's okay. Your boys and I will pull ourselves together. We can make this work. Don't feel guilty, okay?" As I stroke her cheek, her face softens.

She's right about this trip. I don't want to traipse out to Evanston to visit her parents' graves. It certainly would never occur to me to visit my mother's grave, even though I've suggested that grieving ritual to clients for years.

I don't want to deal with Kate's grief anymore. Kate's father died when she was fourteen. She still misses him to the marrow of her being. My mother died when I was twenty. I've never missed her for a moment. I feel mean being so unresponsive to Kate's pain. Or maybe I'm afraid to encounter my own. Ever since the hypnosis workshop in the spring, a dam inside me has been crumbling.

At the workshop, I volunteered to be a guinea pig for the hypnotist. She put me in a trance and tried to lead me back into some pleasant memories. All that came to me was seeing my mother after winning the race, a flash on that awful last summer home and the time Kate and I got lost in the fog. I began to cry in the middle of the trance. This was definitely not part of the plan. The hypnotist tried to pull me back into the present, but I was being swept along by waves of emotions about these images. They were more than memories. I was transported back in time. And yet I didn't know what I was crying about.

Coming out of the trance was embarrassing. Suddenly I was facing a roomful of colleagues who were looking sympathetic and concerned. I just wanted to get out of there.

I didn't say much to Kate about the episode. I haven't even told her how much I miss her mother, much less talked about my own. It's easier to slip into my familiar therapeutic role and comfort her. But soothing her doesn't seem to comfort me anymore.

"Well, it's time to wake up the kids," I say, pulling away from the embrace abruptly.

After we launch the children, we go about our day. Kate commutes to Massachusetts General Hospital, where she works as a general internist, and I head to my office off the kitchen where I practice psychotherapy. She treats everything from head colds to the terminally ill, and I minister to the heartache and turmoil that lurk inside many marriages and families. We spend our days up to our elbows in the pain of people's lives. Sometimes it's intense, rewarding work. Then there are days we're so overwhelmed by it all that we have nothing leftover for each other and our two boys. For fifteen years we've fantasized opening a low-key joint practice on the coast of Maine. We've jokingly called it Kate and Dave's Head and Body Shop. But we know we're not going anywhere.

9:00 A.M.

A year ago Mark and Lynn Sullivan's youngest daughter, three-year-old Melissa, drowned. She wandered into a neighbors' yard and fell into the pool. When they were struggling with their intense grief, they read somewhere that a high percentage of marriages break up after the death of a child. They had vowed to beat the odds. They went into therapy and tried to grieve their immense loss, without blaming each other. It didn't work. Their marriage began to die anyway. That's when they came in to see me.

Unfortunately, I didn't have any profound wisdom or healing balm that revived them. Now, Lynn is ready to separate. Mark doesn't want her to go. He cries and she gets impatient. We talk about how to tell the kids. We talk about visitation.

The couple lapses into a long and painful silence. Mark and Lynn sit stiffly on either end of the sofa. They don't look at each other. Lynn seems to be looking at the bookcase next to the sofa. She keeps twisting her fingers in her lap. Mark stares at the floor.

The couple waits for me to say something. I am their last hope. I force myself to step into the silence.

"There's really nothing to say," I begin haltingly. "There are no words that I know that will truly soothe the tearing pain; no words that can heal this wound. I don't know; maybe separating is the only way for the two of you to face going on in life without your daughter. For some couples, it is just too hard to confront every day the haunting loss they see in each other's eyes. Sometimes people in their grief just rip at each other because they can't bear it any longer. I hope you two won't shred each other by rushing into divorce. There's an old expression in A.A. that I like: 'Give time, time.'"

I pause. They stare at me with tears in their eyes. Have I just been blathering at them? I feel as foolishly useless as the Wizard of Oz. Sometimes words don't help. Maybe I should have simply trusted the silence.

10:00 A.M.

I have ten minutes to make some phone calls before going over to the Extern Therapist's Training program that I codirect. As I reach for the phone, my mind flips back to the Sullivans. What does a coffin for a three-year-old look like? How do you stand up while you watch it being lowered into the ground?

I remember my father on his hands and knees putting the cardboard box with my mother's ashes into the ground. It was cold. The ground was frozen. The cemetery people had managed to dig a small hole with a jackhammer. My sister and I stood silently, watching my father on his knees and watching the box disappear into the earth.

I was as frozen as the ground. I still am. I pick up the phone quickly. I'd always rather focus on my clients' problems.

The last message is from Cindy Knowlton. I'm beginning to worry about her. Cindy is a bright, chipper woman. She has two kids under six and her husband just ran off with his hairstylist after emptying their joint bank account. At first, she joked about her plight at the hands of "yet another worthless man." "This is all preparation training for becoming a hard-drinking and hard-hearted country and western singer," she had said with a tough smile in our first meeting.

The therapy had seemed as if it would be relatively straight-forward. Her bitter anger and deep sadness were appropriate responses to her situation. Yet there was something off about her. Underneath her wisecracking facade, she seemed extremely insecure and brittle. She always came to her sessions as if she were going to a job interview. She dressed up in chic suits, perfect makeup, her blonde hair carefully wound up in a French twist. Not the typical getup of a full-time housewife. In our last session, she confessed that she had always assumed her husband would leave her. "Who wouldn't leave your average run-down, ugly milk cow as soon as he got the chance?" she said with a hard smile. I was struck by the sharpness of her self-deprecation in contrast to her skillfully presented beauty.

Her call is a chilling one. "Hello, David, here's a message from the universe that I thought might give you a chuckle. I saw a bumper sticker that said, PROTECT THE PLANET: KILL YOURSELF. You might want to warn your more emotionally challenged patients about it lest they take it to heart. Just kidding. I'll see you on Monday."

It's already 10:55, but I have to call her back. She has an easy bantering style of relating, so her black humor isn't shocking. But something in the tone of her message makes the hair on the back of my neck stand up, a clinician's clue. I'm probably overreacting, but you never know. I try her number. Naturally there's no answer.

11:10 A.M.

By the time I get to the institute, my trainees are already behind the one-way mirror and the video camera is on. We see families as a team, with one of the trainees doing the interviewing and the rest of us observing behind the mirror. At the end of the meetings, I meet with the family.

The father in this morning's family is a dangerously out-of-control alcoholic who won't come to the sessions. The whole family is discouraged, particularly the older daughter, Kristin. The therapist, Carol Blaine, is trying unsuccessfully to motivate them.

"He's hopeless anyway," says Kristin, the thirteen-year-old, angrily. "I don't see why we bother coming. Nothing helps."

"We can't give up, Kristin. Your father needs all of us," says Carol. "Alcoholics do go into recovery. You have to remember that it's a disease just like cancer. People can be cured."

"Most people die of cancer," retorts Kristin.

"That's not true, actually," Carol rebuts. "People do recover from cancer. It depends on which kind."

Behind the mirror, the other members of the team are becoming restive. "Maybe we should stop this. Carol's just arguing with the kid. Maybe we ought to get her to engage the mother in talking with Kristin."

"Don't panic, guys," I say to the five members of the team in the darkened room. "Let's be patient."

There is stifled laughter from the group.

"I know, I know, I'm not exactly famous for patience myself. Well, for once, I think we ought to wait."

Maybe I was willing to wait because I've been distracted by intruding memories. When did I give up on my mother? I must have been about the same age as Kristin. I remember deciding I didn't care anymore. That was a long time before she died.

At the end of the session, I meet with the family to encourage them to do an "intervention." This is a dramatic technique of bringing in family members, friends, and relations and helping them learn how to confront an alcoholic in a loving and supportive way. I wish it had been available to us back in 1965. I'm sure it would have saved my mother's life.

I try to engage Kristin, but she stonewalls me. She's not taking any candy from therapeutic strangers. "You don't know my Dad!" she says bitterly.

My trainees are waiting for me to pull a rabbit out of the hat. But I don't have any therapeutic magic today. It's a minor accomplishment just to get the family to agree to come back for another session.

2:00 P.M.
———

Bill and Sarah Dunbar are in for their first session. They are an attractive, motivated, personable couple with two school-age kids. As they chat with me, they never look at each other. Sitting side by side, they manage to appear as far apart as those people in split-screen television interviews. Bill and Sarah are probably having difficulty with intimacy and, most likely, sex. There's something about the way they avoid eye contact and seem so physically distant.

Later, I begin to zero in on the problems that bring them to my office.

"We don't seem to make the time for each other the way we used to," Sarah quickly jumps in. "I know everyone says this, but we don't know how to communicate."

They give me the usual reasons they can't make time for each other: the kids, work schedules, house projects, sick parents, and so on. It sounds painfully familiar.

Kate and I often joke about the long stretches when it feels we are just ships passing in the night. Sometimes it's not funny. Sometimes it seems so hypocritical to be helping couples become more intimate in the midst of muddling through my own marriage.

"You're just not really there," Kate has often complained. Throughout our marriage, Kate's emotionally direct and open manner has been hard for me. I grew up in a family in which no one ever said how he or she felt. I've always been jealous of her blunt sureness. Once I teased Kate that her version of Descartes's famous dictum "I think, therefore I am," would be "I am; therefore I'm right." She laughed readily and agreed.

I used to claim that I didn't know what she was talking about when she accused me of "not being there." But I do. I've been going through the motions for a long time, just as I was prepared to do again on this weekend trip to Evanston. It's harder for me to be intimate with my own family and friends than it is to be close to my clients. It's easier to immerse myself in my patients' feelings than to be in touch with my own.

The Dunbars' session goes well and I look forward to working with them. It might be a routine case of midlife marital malaise, but I suspect there's probably a deeper, more complicated hurt in each of them. It's hard to tell whether our therapy will skim along the surface or slip below into colder, darker waters.

After they leave, I pause before hurling myself into getting the boys ready for the trip. It's been a hard day. I'm flooded with the heartache and frustrations that people pour out to me. Sometimes I feel so unworthy of their trust. It's difficult enough to manage my own life, much less help anybody else. But I love these people who troop in and out of my office. Their courageous struggles move me. I want to take care of them, embrace them, succor them. Some days we make a truly healing connection. Other times, I feel like a salesman pitching pop psych Pablum. Yet, they keep coming. Their presence is a gift to me.

After racing through downtown traffic, the boys and I arrive at the airport, only to discover that the plane will be delayed. This is fortunate because Dr. Kate is also late. We would have missed our flight.

As I try to keep Sam and Michael entertained, my mind flips back to my client, Cindy, and her bumper sticker joke. I wish I could have gotten through. Her call probably wasn't a veiled suicide message, but what if it was?

"Calm down, David, for God's sake," I mutter to myself.

"What did you say, Dad?" asks Michael, looking up from his Garfield book.

"Nothing, Michael, I'm thinking out loud."

"That's weird," says Michael as he walks over to the candy counter. He's twelve and just coming into the age where it's embarrassing enough just to be seen with one's parent, much less one who is talking to himself.

I go to the phone booth to dial Cindy's number. I'm undoubtedly overdoing it, but I'd rather err on the side of caution.

"Cindy, this is David. I don't mean to be a worrywart, but your funny message sounded as if it was maybe your subtle way of letting me know that you're really having a rough time. I just thought I would check in."

"Christ, Doc, where's your sense of humor? I thought you'd get a kick of it. Don't call out the men in white coats on me yet. I'm okay," she says quickly with a slight slur in her voice. "I got to go. Dinner's on the stove and the inmates are banging their cups."

"All right, Cindy, I'll let you go. See you Monday. And keep your eyes out for those EASY DOES IT and ONE DAY AT A TIME bumper stickers," I add teasingly. Cindy's been drinking heavily since her husband left and I've just started to talk with her about A.A.

"Take it easy, yourself. It's the weekend."

Making the call seems silly instantly. I meant to be responsive, but it was a little much. She didn't think she was making a suicide threat and didn't expect to hear from me. You know you're overdoing it when your client reminds you that it's the weekend. And it was certainly not the time to be making references to her drinking, even in a light tone. On the other hand, I can't ignore that she already has a buzz on at the dinner hour. I'm still nervous about her.

By the time the plane takes off, we're all a little tired and frazzled. I catch myself being impatient with Kate for being late and with Sam for complaining about the seating arrangements. "Stop being such a jerk," I chide myself. Lately I've been snapping at the kids again. My anger used to explode out of me. Once when Michael was little he literally shook with fear while I was yelling at him. The image of his scared little face is seared in my brain. I've been blaming my recent agitation on my work load and chronic back pain. But I suspect these are just minor scratches.

I need a drink. This is great: here I am worrying about Cindy's drinking and I can't wait to have my own. I don't like the way I use alcohol. I'm always concocting rules and strategems to keep my drinking at a maximum level of five drinks a week. This is very light drinking. Yet being a specialist in the substance abuse field and coming from a family riddled with alcoholism, I know that my relationship to alcohol is dangerous. It's not the amount of alcohol. It's the amount of time I spend worrying about it. It's how easy it would be for me to drink more than I do. It's about the instant relief I find in a glass of cabernet.

Kate tries to be cheerful. She's obviously feeling guilty about dragging us along on this trip. I feel bad for her. She's had a hard day too. One of her favorite patients, whom she's been taking care of since her internship days, finally died. She's also worried about leaving the animals and the house. She worries about a plane crash, too. Kate's a comprehensive worrier. She considers all possible disaster scenarios.

"I'm really glad we finally got the wills signed," she says out of the blue.

"Katie, you're forgetting we brought the kids along. If the plane goes down, they won't be around to collect their inheritance," I tease. "Maybe we should have made funeral arrangements too. I hate to leave things to the last moment."

"Oh, shush," Kate reaches for her book. She's unamused by my attempt at repartee. Throughout our marriage, I've been the playful one while Kate's carried the anxiety. Over the years she's helped me become more responsible and I've helped her lighten up. But not today.

As the Delta 747 glides over the Boston skyline, Kate points out her office building to the children. I look for the lights on Beacon Hill. It's too dark to see my childhood home, one tiny little house among all the miniature doll houses passing beneath us.

Passing over West Cedar Street, I can almost see myself as that little boy from long ago, in tie and coat and maroon Dexter School cap, grabbing his green bookbag and rushing to the door. I don't remember my mother being with us at the beginning of the day. Perhaps she had already begun to stay in her bedroom, lying so still under the covers with the shades down and the door closed.

"Stop fiddling with the window shade," I say a little too sharply to Sam, then bury myself in *Time* magazine.

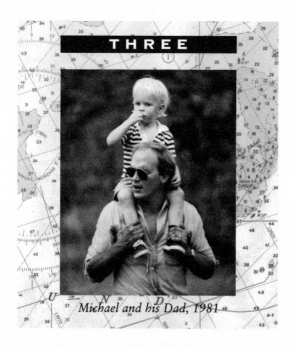

THREE

Michael and his Dad, 1981

JUST BEYOND THE
SURF LINE

SATURDAY MORNING KATE TAKES US ON A TOUR OF HER NEIGH-
borhood. It hasn't changed since she was a child. The home she
grew up in is a sprawling white house surrounded by wide
porches. The four of us stand in front of the house for a long
time while Kate shows us where she played hopscotch, where she
swung on the porch, and the place in the yard where she buried
dead animals.

I have only a handful of memories of my childhood tucked
away in my mind like some faded black and white pictures discarded in a drawer. I don't look at them very often. Kate considers my lack of interest in my childhood as evidence that I'm cut

off emotionally. My standard defense is to claim that I worked out those issues in therapy during my twenties. But I know it's not true. There's still an old ache that wells up inside me. It's there when I murmur soothing words to my clients as they find their tears. By connecting to them, I find myself.

The boys are fidgety. I'm hot and sticky, but doing my best to stay engaged. This is so important to Kate. None of us has mentioned her mother or tomorrow's trip to the cemetery.

Late in the afternoon, we adjourn to the Evanston beach on Lake Michigan, where Kate spent every day all summer long. The boys play in the water while Kate and I share the skimpy hotel towel. I am leafing through a tourist book about New Zealand and she is reading a novel.

I turn the page. There is a shot of a boat sailing alongside a cliff at night. A full moon floats high above the mountains in the background. The sheer cliffs tower over the sailboat. The sloop is on a close reach, working its way just beyond the surf line where the waves begin to break on the submerged rocks. It's heeling way over, laboring hard against the wind. At the masthead, there is a little spot of red, the port-side running light. The boat looks like a tiny and fragile toy. It seems much too close to the rocks.

"How about this one, Kate?" I ask.

She glances at the picture of the boat against the cliff. "I have to admit it's very pretty," she says. She starts leafing through the New Zealand book.

I look out at the water. Michael and Sam are playing in the gentle surf. My two towhead boys. Michael is a bright, anxious boy who takes life very seriously. He's shy around other children, but doggedly pursues school and social success despite his discomfort. In the family, where he feels more secure, Michael's funny, bossy, and outgoing. Sam's a bubble. He seems to float along with good cheer and equanimity. Actually Sam's easygoing quietness masks a more complicated internal life that he doesn't have the words for. Temperamentally, Michael seems to be a clone of Kate and Sam's definitely a clone of me.

It's fun watching the two of them playing together. They're

almost six years apart so they don't have many of these moments. I wonder how long it might be before Michael decides he is entirely too grown-up to play with Sam.

Sam seems too far out. He's in almost up to his neck, and he can't swim at all. We should have brought his life preserver. Maybe I should get him to stay closer to the beach. But he's having such a good time with Michael.

Kate looks up from the book and glances out at the boys. "Are you watching Sam?" she asks.

"Of course I am. He's okay."

"I just remember the time a boy drowned here when I was Sam's age. I remember the mother getting out of the police car and running to where the boy lay. Then she just collapsed on the sand and began howling like a wounded animal."

The image of the boy drowning at this apparently safe beach chills me. I'm not used to being afraid. Sometimes I force myself to imagine the death of one of my sons. I couldn't handle it. I'd become a dry husk, a dead soul. No wonder that couple whose little girl drowned couldn't go on.

I quickly go back to my New Zealand book. The lush pictures of mountains, prairies, rivers, lakes, and beaches are all compelling. It's clear that Kate's upset, but she really doesn't want to cry. She buries her head in her book. I should be encouraging her to open up, but I just don't want to plunge into her sadness. I'm having a hard enough time keeping a lid on my own.

Out of the corner of my eye, I watch the kids while my mind wanders toward my New Zealand plan. One more big sailing project. Probably the last one. The thought of crossing the Pacific doesn't frighten me at all. The idea of getting away on my boat excites me and, paradoxically, calms me down.

My first boat was an ugly light green and rather incongruously named *Typhoon*. We bought it secondhand and I never did manage to change the color or the name. Every morning, all summer long, calm or storm, I would get up and go down to the harbor, row out to my boat, and set sail. I remember the excitement the first time I went far enough out so that the land was lost in the haze and I was completely alone on the water. I used to daydream idly about heading east and sailing my little boat across the Atlantic to England. I went so far as to wonder how I would stow the necessary food and water and what it would be like to be in a storm in a 9½-foot boat.

I turn to Kate and ask, "Did I ever tell you about the time I sailed my boat the 15 miles from Rockport to Marblehead? I was a year younger than Michael, and my brother was only nine."

"Only about a hundred times," Kate replies.

"I appreciate your interest. But really, I'm not even sure my parents knew about us doing it. I don't know what's worse: that my parents would have been so off in their own world that they didn't know, or that they had given the trip an okay. I would never in a million years let Michael do that. It was nuts."

"I don't know why you still sound surprised about your parents' detachment. As far as I've been able to tell, they were never very involved with your childhood."

"I know, and your parents were so wonderful."

"Don't be a jerk."

"Sorry, that was a dumb crack. I just don't like thinking about how it really was growing up."

Many years later, I finally did sail my 33-foot sloop across the Atlantic to Scotland and back. That was eight years ago. Now I am working on a new dream: sailing to New Zealand. In 1996, when Michael has finished high school and Sam's in the eighth grade, I want us to take a year off and sail to New Zealand. It will be the last time we can all be together as a family before Michael slips away into adulthood.

I've been toying with this idea for a while, but its coming together this weekend. There's nothing I like better than having a new plan to mull over. It's always been a surefire fix for the emptiness lurking just beneath the surface of my normal upbeat persona.

Later, I call my answering service. No messages, but three hang-up calls came in like waves at 3:45, 3:46, and 3:47. Not likely a wrong number. My stomach tightens. I can't think of anyone who would make a hang-up call.

Maybe Cindy was tempted to leave another "funny" message? Is she in trouble? I imagine her sitting with the phone in her hand, listening to my machine voice, then hanging up with a flush of embarrassment. It would be hard for her to call if she really needed me. On the other hand, maybe she was upset by our talk, and my wisecrack about A.A.

Michael interrupts me, "Dad, can I talk to you while Mom's in the shower?"

"Sure, Mike, what's up?"

"I don't want to hurt Mom's feelings or anything, but I don't see why we had to come here."

"I know, Michael. But you have to understand that this weekend is really important to your mother. Your Mom went through a very rough time last year with Fran's death, and she misses her terribly. I think she needs a little support from all of us. I'm counting on you to help out."

"What am I supposed to do? I don't even think about Franmother anymore. I can barely remember what she looked like. Am I supposed to be feeling all sad?" Michael asks earnestly.

I reach over and put my arm around him. "You don't have to feel sad. You just have to be easy on your Mom this weekend and go along with the program."

"What about you, Dad? Do you miss Franmother? I never see you get upset about it."

"Well, I don't cry as easily as your mother, but I do miss Fran," I say glibly. "Anyway, it's time for you to go to bed."

As I tuck Michael in, I remember how much Fran loved the boys. If she had lived, there would have been many nights that she would have been putting them to bed, reading a story and kissing them goodnight.

Sunday, 6:00 A.M.

It's still dark. Michael said that he wanted to get up and run with me. I try to wake him without disturbing Sam or Kate.

"Michael, Michael, let's go. Time for running."

The lump in the bed doesn't stir.

"Come on, we only have a little time," I whisper urgently.

"Do I have to go?" Michael asks.

"No, of course not, it's just that you said that you would."

"I'm tired, Dad. Can we go later?"

"No, we can't go later. We won't have any time. Look, skip it. I just thought you wanted to go running with me. I'm going to go and you sleep in. It's all right. It's no big deal."

My feet hit the pavement. I can't find a rhythm. My breathing is already labored. I'm mad at myself for being hurt that Michael didn't want to go running. The sight of a playground reminds me of Michael and the day we tackled the challenge of the slide.

It was one of those endless Saturdays when he and I were alone for the weekend because Kate was on call at the hospital. Michael was three.

"It's just you and me, Kiddo," I said cheerfully as I bundled him up, "but we're going to have a great day. We're going to the park, then we'll stop and have lunch, and then maybe we'll go to the aquarium. How about that for a day?"

"But I want to watch more cartoons. I don't want to go to the park. It's too cold," he whined.

"Well, tough nuggies, little guy," I said, running over his resistance with my enthusiasm. "When I was a kid, my parents didn't care how long I watched cartoons. But you're stuck with a parent who wants to be with you."

He didn't have a clue what I was talking about, but I was trying to distract myself from his whining. I always started off our excursions determined not to be impatient.

I held his hand tightly when we crossed the empty street.

"Today might be the day. You just might be able to do it today. What do you think?"

"Do what, Daddy?"

"The slide, silly." It bothered me that he was scared to go down the slide. Lots of other kids his age seemed to do it fearlessly. "I know you can do it. It'll feel great after you do."

"I don't want to," he said.

"Don't decide now. Let's wait until we get there."

Once we got to the park, we went over to the bottom of the slide. The strain of the challenge was getting to both of us.

"Look, Michael, just try it once. I promise you won't have to do it again if you don't like it. Watch me." I climbed up the slide and, like an awkward Gulliver in the land of the Lilliputians, I sat at the top while Michael watched from below.

"See, this is great! You could do it sitting in my lap. How about that? He-r-r-r-e, I come," and off I went down the slide.

"Now, come on, let's try it," I said, beginning to force the smile.

Micheal started to cry. I turned on him and said in a cold whisper, "You don't have to do the slide. Just stop crying, or else we'll go straight home and no more TV for the day."

The threat worked, and he wandered off snuffling to climb on the alphabet animals. I retreated to the bench and pulled out the paper while surreptitiously glancing at the other mothers to see whether they had witnessed the scene. I imagined with a shudder what my clients would think if they could see Dr. Treadway in action.

It was during those difficult years of Kate's residency that I did the transatlantic trips. Michael spent much more time with his babysitters than with both of us put together. So, in addition to Kate's being away on call every other night, I left home for a month at a time, two summers in a row. Michael was only a toddler. It was a terrible time for me to be leaving my family, but I had committed to the trip and had been preparing for it way before Michael was born. It had been a lifelong dream. It's only in recent years that I've fully recognized how selfish I was then.

It must have been brutal for Michael having me be gone that much when Kate was working eighty hours a week. The second summer, I took the boat from Scotland to Spain, where Kate and Michael joined me for ten days before I headed back to the States. Kate told me that when she and Michael left Madrid and flew out over the Atlantic, Michael stared out the window at the ocean for hours. He was hoping to see his Daddy's black boat so he could wave good-bye. However, when I pulled into Rockport Harbor a month later, Michael held onto Kate's leg and wouldn't come near me. He just kept saying, "Go away, Daddy, go away."

I wince with the sudden memory of the story about my little brother Jimmy's response to my parents the morning after they returned from their two-month trip to France. He was just about three, and when he saw them at the breakfast table, he ran to our nanny crying because he didn't know who the "strangers" were. The story's always told in our family as a joke.

I promised myself that I would never lead as self-centered a life as my parents, but in many ways I have. No wonder Michael didn't want anything to do with me when I got back from the Azores.

And I also promised that I would never demean my kids the way my mother did, but sometimes I have. For years when Michael had trouble sleeping at night and was frightened, I would patiently try to help him settle down and relax. I would sing to him and rub his back. But if it didn't work, I would suddenly snap at him out of frustration. The family psychologist was woefully inept at helping his little boy go to sleep, and then I blamed him for my failures.

I reassure my clients that all parents are inadvertently hurtful to their kids: that good parenting isn't protecting children from life's pain; it's being there for them when they're hurting. But talk's cheap. I hate the ways I've harmed my kids.

I'm awash with self-loathing. My legs feel leaden as I slog along the sidewalk.

Then the situation with Cindy pops back into my head. I ought to check my service again. She frightens me. I've dealt with dangerous clinical situations for years, but I feel differently about her. Lots of clients have suicidal feelings, but it takes a certain cold anger to kill yourself. There's something about Cindy that makes me feel she could do it.

Thinking about her distracts me. It's funny how my mind always slips back to my clients when I'm uncomfortable with myself.

I never do find a good running rhythm. I just work up a sweat. The sun rises over the lake with the promise of another sweltering day.

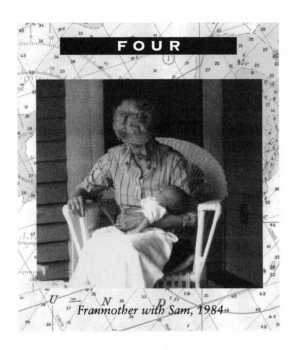

FOUR

Franmother with Sam, 1984

RED RIGHT RETURN

LINED UP IN OUR PEW ON OUR KNEES, WE LOOK LIKE A NORMAN Rockwell print: a dad, a mom, and their two handsome boys. Just being in church usually transforms me into my slouching adolescent self back in my boarding school chapel. Kate has always taken comfort from the familiar rituals. The spectacle usually irritates me.

Yet, this morning, there's a haunting beauty in this kneeling gathering. The parishioners seem bound together by their frailty and their fear as they open their hearts in silent prayer. How many thousands of generations before them have dropped to their knees, seeking a glimpse of the light in the darkness? I've always felt dismissive of this spiritual neediness, but now I wish I could wholeheartedly join them.

I was in church a few months ago, singing a hymn that we used to do in elementary school assembly: "Oh, God our help in ages past, Our hope in years to come, Our shelter from the stormy blast and our eternal home." I suddenly caught myself yearning for a God I could believe in, for a God who would provide shelter. For a brief moment, I felt the presence of such a God. Then suddenly I was angry. I imagined saying directly to God, "Why the hell did you let my mother die? She turned to you for help, you son of a bitch!"

I was stunned by the intensity of the emotion. Decades of comfortable atheism seemed to have washed away like a sand castle in the rising surf. Suddenly it was just God and me. I was helplessly angry and felt very young.

Maybe that's partly why I agreed to join the men's prayer group that Father Mark was forming at our church. But I don't think so. I let him talk me into it because he's such a good friend. He's helping me take the boat down to the Virgin Islands next spring, and I didn't want to hurt his feelings. We're supposed to meet in a couple of weeks. I can't imagine what it will be like to sit around with a group of guys and talk about prayer and our supposed relationship to God.

"And we would especially remember Frances M. Kennedy, whose family has given the altar flowers in memory of her on this, the first anniversary of her death." The minister's mention of Fran snaps me back to the present. I squeeze Kate's hand. I haven't been thinking much about Fran. As usual, the depth of Kate's grief has distracted me from my own feelings. Throughout our marriage Kate has always been able to express her feelings openly while I have hidden behind my role of providing a shoulder to cry on. At the funeral last year I just stared at the casket, imagining what Fran's body looked like locked inside it. I did my job of keeping the kids in line and taking care of Kate. Twenty-five years ago, when I was twenty, I functioned dutifully at my own mother's funeral. Jimmy and I were the ushers. Many people complimented us on our composure and consideration for the mourners. I was an empty suit.

My sister, Lauris, did all of the emoting for my father, my brothers, and me. It was too much for her and her mind snapped. She spent the next twenty years in and out of mental hospitals. For years, my mother had carried the stress and pain between her and my father. She was the one with the worries, the headaches, and finally the pills and the booze. She used to call Dad "the handsome man with the happiness neurosis." In my family, dealing with emotions was women's work.

And now here I am self-centeredly distracted, while Kate is weeping beside me.

Fran loved me. It took a long time for me to know that. Besides Kate, she was the only one whom I had wanted to read my first book while it was still in progress. She seemed interested in me for my sake rather than for her own benefit. I basked in her concern.

I became engaged to Kate a year after my mother died and my family fell apart. Our senior year in college. We were kids. It turned out to be the best way to get adopted. Fran always knew I needed a mother, and she was probably daunted by the responsibility. A few years back, she gave me a small embroidered pillow for Christmas. It said, "Behind every successful man is a surprised mother-in-law."

That our marriage is a success is a surprise to everyone. Kate had a reputation for being aloof and very proper and I was unfortunately renowned for being a wastrel and a womanizer. Our early years were an unmitigated disaster. Looking back now, we joke that the only reason we stayed together was that we were too neurotically dependent on each other to split up. Besides, neither of us was prepared to face the wrath of Fran.

The true bond that held us together despite our struggles was our mutual understanding about having lost a parent. Although I couldn't touch my grief about my mother, holding Kate while she wept for her Dad soothed both of us. She felt nurtured and I felt strong. It was a good match. And we've always been best friends. It feels as if we've grown up together.

At the end of the service, Kate, the boys, and I wait behind an elderly woman at the votary table. Kate lights a candle for Fran. She pauses, and then lights another for her father. I watch her silently pray over the two tiny flames side by side.

I linger in front of the flickering candles. The impulse to light a candle for my mother startles me. First the match won't light after repeated strikes and then I can't get the wick going. It takes three tries to get my little flame lit.

Rosehill Cemetery covers a huge area with a population in the thousands. We are looking for S 5. It doesn't take long. Kate remembers the way from the burial last year. We stop alongside a tree.

KENNEDY
JOSEPH C.
1905–1961

FRANCES M.
1913–1988

"Where exactly are they?" asks Michael.

"Well, they're right in front of you, between about where we are standing and the headstones," Kate points. "Mother is right along there and Daddy is over here."

After a while, Michael goes off looking for unusual tombstones and Sam chases after his balloon. Kate and I sit together facing the graves. I put an arm around her and she leans into me.

"I don't know why I'm crying," she says. "Somehow I kept feeling this whole weekend that I was coming here to see them. I guess not so much Daddy anymore, but I just can't believe that I'm never going to see Mother again. It makes me feel so alone. I know that you'll think this is silly, but it makes me feel as if there's no one to take care of me."

"I'm here," I whisper gently. I put my arm around her. It's a relief finally to be fully responsive.

"I know that, but it's not really the same. I would always call Mother up at the end of a trip like this and she would want to know all about it. I don't have anyone to call."

We lapse into our own silences. I don't know whether anyone in my family has ever been to visit my mother's grave. I have a vague memory of going with Kate many years ago while on a trip up to Vermont to visit with Fran. Lauris must have gone at some point.

I don't know about Jimmy and my older brother, Jon. We've never talked about it.

I watch Sam, in his T-shirt and his shorts, exuberantly running through the graveyard, chasing his balloon. In the distance, Michael is hiding behind a big tombstone. He's probably pretending to be lost and waiting for someone to look for him. Kate's lost in her own reverie.

It's hot. I glance at my watch.

"I'm thirsty," says Sam.

"Wait a sec, Sam." I turn to Kate. "What do you think? Do you want us to give you some time alone? You could stay here and be by yourself. I'll take the boys to get a soda," I ask, both wanting to be genuinely helpful and selfishly looking for an excuse to get a break from this scene.

I gather up Michael and Sam. The car seats are scalding hot from the July sun. As we leave, I watch Kate in my rearview mirror receding among the tombstones. (Which of us will be the one to drive away someday?)

Joseph's Family Restaurant is a classic greasy spoon. The boys and I order up a huge amount of food. It's all terrible. They don't eat theirs and I fulfill my reputation as the family garbageman. I stuff myself. It doesn't help. I feel full and empty at the same time. Sam watches Michael play an arcade game. My mind wanders back to that last year with Fran.

After Fran's lung surgery, we decided to build an addition on our house so that she could move in with us. Fran waited patiently for almost a year while the work was done. None of us expected her to have a severe relapse just before she moved in.

Kate would be fine for stretches and then she would come undone. Once I found her sitting cross-legged on the floor of her office, weeping while she read over a letter that her father had sent her when she was thirteen years old. I sat next to her and put my arms around her. "I still miss him," she said; "I wish he were here."

"When I'm teaching about grief, I often quote the line from the movie *I Never Sang for My Father,* 'People die; relationships don't.' I know it might sound dumb, but sometimes I tell my clients to write to the dead parent. It might help," I said.

"But you've never done that with *your* Mom."

"Well, I don't miss the lady either," I retorted.

Kate did write the letter. She told her Dad all about Fran, our children, even her horse. She ended it with a poignant P.S.: "By the way, Daddy, you should know that my name isn't Kathy Kennedy anymore. It's Kate Treadway. But it's still me."

She wept while she read it to me. For a moment, I was jealous of her pain.

July 2 was a Thursday last year. It was the moving day. That morning Kate and I walked through her mother's new rooms. The shiny hardwood floors, the brick fireplace, and the cream-colored walls looked warm and inviting with the bright morning light streaming through the windows.

"I think her sofa should go here under the bay window," said Kate. "That way she can watch the boys playing in the yard."

Her eyes filled. "Do you remember the day we put up the walls? Everybody was hammering and banging away, even Sam. It was so much fun." She looked out the window. "I just don't want this to be happening. I'm not ready. I don't want her to die."

Fran looked haggard. Her extremities were thin and fragile. The veins in her hands bulged thickly under her translucent skin. Her belly was distended with fluid and tumor. The doctors said she wouldn't last much longer, but she was determined to move into the apartment we had built for her. It was almost as if she had been holding off dying until she could move in.

She sat outside in a rocking chair under an umbrella and directed the flow of her possessions like a general sending troops into combat. This lamp for the bedroom, that chair for the living room, and please be careful with the china. I watched her from the kitchen as she gave orders. In spite of her fragile appearance, she was still in charge, as all of the precious pieces culled over a lifetime of making homes were marched into our house, her new home.

Kate's brother, Stephen, and his family spent the weekend with us in a frenzied rush of unpacking boxes, arranging furniture, and hanging pictures. The rooms began to look like Fran's. Even the smell of the rooms was reminiscent of the New York apartment's. Fran took to her bed as soon as we had it set up. She was exhausted.

In the beginning, we kept pestering her about what belonged where. Toward the end, we simply decided among ourselves. "Let's not bother her," we said. "She's tired."

She didn't really care whether the good Oriental rug should be in the living room or the bedroom. She was dying instead.

"Have you talked with her yet?" Kate asked on Sunday night. It was clear that Fran was going downhill rapidly.

"No, I don't know how to get into it. I mean, what do you say? 'Gee, Fran it looks like you're dying faster than we expected, and I just want to say I love you before you start to lose it mentally?' Seriously, I really don't know what to say. You're a doctor. You deal with this stuff all the time."

"Well, you're a therapist, for God's sake. What would you tell one of your clients?"

"What's that got to do with this?" I said, only half-kidding.

Kate just rolled her eyes at me.

On Monday night, I took a tray of food in to her while Kate was in the kitchen talking with the doctor. It was the first time I had been alone in the room with Fran. She was lying flat in bed with her eyes closed. For a moment, I thought she was dead.

"Fran, I brought you some food," I whispered.

She opened her eyes slowly. It took her a moment to focus. The pain medication was making her quite fuzzy.

"Where am I?" she asked.

"Here, Fran, in your bedroom."

Her eyes searched the room as she took in the mixture of new space and familiar belongings in different arrangements.

"Of course, how silly of me." Fran gathered her social self and sat up a little in the bed.

"I brought you some juice and some toast."

"I can't eat anything, but I'll take some of the juice."

"How are you feeling?"

Fran pondered my question for a bit and then said, "This medication seems to slow everything down. I hope I don't have to keep taking it so much. Where's Kate? She knows—." She paused and looked over at the bureau. "I think it would be better if that lamp were over on the other side of the bureau."

"I'll move it for you,"

"Thank you, David," she said.

I blurted out, "You don't need to thank me, Fran. I need to thank you. I need to thank you for all the love you've given me. For treating me like a son. You've always been there. Even when our marriage was a mess, I always felt you loved me for me. I love you and I'm going to miss you, and I just wish we had more time."

"Oh, David, don't be silly," Fran said.

She let me hug her. It was my last conversation with her.

Kate came upstairs to wake me at two o'clock Wednesday morning. She'd been sleeping on a mat at the foot of her mother's bed.

"Come on, you've got to help. Mother has to go to the bathroom and I can't get her there by myself."

I got on my robe and went to Fran's room. She was hunched over on the side of the bed. Her bare feet didn't reach the floor. Kate and I each took an arm and helped her stand up. She let out a soft moan with the effort of each step. In the bathroom, her reflexive modesty made her resist taking down her pajama bottoms.

"Do you want me to leave?" I whispered to Kate.

Kate shook her head.

"It's okay, Mom. Let me help you," Kate said gently. Then she pulled down Fran's pajamas and we steered her toward the toilet bowl.

"I can't," moaned Fran.

"Yes, you can. Let's not make a mess."

Fran collapsed onto the toilet seat with a groan.

Kate bent over her mother and rubbed her neck. Fran wept and finally peed. I watched Kate the doctor and Kate the daughter, gently nursing her mother. I was proud of her.

Kate could tell that Saturday would probably be the last day. She called Stephen and Jo and made sure that they came out early in the morning. We all sat by the bed as Fran's lungs filled up. Her breathing became slower and slower. She struggled with each breath. We held her hands and sat in silence punctuated only by her raspy sucking on air. Her face looked dead but her lungs wouldn't let go. I wondered whether this was what Mom looked like during those days that Dad kept vigil and she lay there with the machine breathing for her.

Nobody knew what to say. Finally, I surprised myself by suggesting that we read from the Book of Common Prayer. We read the Twenty-third Psalm and prayers for the dying.

"The Lord bless you and keep you. The Lord make his face to shine upon you, and be gracious unto you. The Lord lift up his countenance upon you and give you peace, both now and evermore."

Near the end her breath came in slow, tiny sips. "It's time to let go, Mother," Kate said softly.

Then Fran was gone. We held hands and said the Lord's Prayer. We wept together. For a second, I thought of my mother's last moments when she crawled into bed and closed her eyes, her belly stuffed with Seconal.

When the boys and I get back to the cemetery, Kate's cleaning the headstones with her handkerchief.

"I don't know why they're so dirty," she says.

"Must be because they're close to the road. Most of the others aren't so bad. Cars must splash on them when it rains. I don't think cleaning them will really help much," I say, being more rational rather than responsive.

We leave the boys in the car for a minute while Kate and I stand by the graves alone. I hold her in my arms again. For a moment, she's just a hurting little girl. I hug her with all of my heart.

"Sweetie, your folks are so proud of you and they're still with you," I whisper in her ear.

At the airport, Sam trips and bursts his balloon. He flies into a tantrum of tears. I try to calm him down by holding him in my lap and rocking him, but he is inconsolable.

I hand Sam over to Kate and go to call my service again. There's one message.

"Hi, Doctor T., it was me hanging up on you, but don't worry, I was only feeling a tad down at the mouth. I wasn't thinking about doing anything foolish just yet. I was going to accuse you of sending brigades of A.A. people after me because everywhere I've driven lately I'm seeing their silly slogans. Anyway, I decided you probably wouldn't think it was very funny. But this morning I worried whether you'd get upset by the hang-ups and I thought I ought to confess. Anyway, to cut a long story short, no emergencies here. See you tomorrow."

Cindy's tone is cheerful, but the message is unnerving. It's hardly reassuring being told I needn't worry about her doing something foolish "just yet."

I'm not going to ask Kate what she thinks. I don't want to sound paranoid and she's got enough on her mind. But I am going to talk directly to Cindy about suicidality tomorrow.

Later, on the plane, I feel an undercurrent of excitement as the New Zealand plan takes shape in my mind. It reminds me of the delicious pleasure I had as a child whenever I got caught up in a new dream. I always looked forward to getting older and bigger. I was consumed with plans about what I would do when I was a grown-up. The future was my favorite hiding place.

"Kate, you know I'm serious about the trip to New Zealand. We'll spread it out over a number of years. We already have the plans to take the boat down to the Virgin Islands this year. We'll just head down for the Panama Canal rather than bring it back."

"Do I have to agree to this right now, or can we take some time to think about it?"

"Sorry, I was just trying to chat," I say defensively.

"You always want to talk about these kinds of incredible plans at the worst times. This has been a hard weekend. I'm exhausted and I just want to get home."

"I'm sorry," I say, instantly contrite. "I'm just tired and agitated. And I'm beginning to worry about this client of mine who seems to be more and more suicidal. That sounds like an excuse, but it's true."

"I'm sorry about your client, but I just can't think about a big sailing trip right now," says Kate, turning back to helping Sam with his puzzle.

I look out the window. I watch the blinking red light at the end of the wing in the dark. It reminds me of a harbor buoy flashing its endless warning: red right return, red right return.

The stewardess brings dinner and the kids bicker about who should get the last Salisbury steak. I pick up the New Zealand book. The picture of the sailboat under the lee of the cliff grabs me again. The boat definitely seems too close in. To my surprise, I notice my cheeks are wet. Recently, I've had tears come into my eyes when I'm not aware of any particular emotion. Kate calls them my "borrowed tears."

Fran's face comes into my mind. I really do miss her, more than I ever did my own mother. I can't even remember what my mother looked like except in pictures. Thinking about her makes me angry. I was actually relieved when she died. And in the past twenty-five years, I've barely given her a second thought. Am I really that cold?

When clients ask me why they don't miss a dead parent, I help them gently and slowly confront the pain buried underneath their apparent detachment. But I'm just not ready for such high-risk excavation. I'd have to bore through thick layers of bedrock and shale. Sooner or later, I might hit an underground lake of sadness. I sense it's there. It's in most of my clients. I'm no different. I don't know whether I want to find it even though I've witnessed many of my clients' profound healing experiences. Maybe I'm really afraid I'd come up empty. A dry well.

Kate's probably right about my tears. For a long time I've suspected that while I sit safely in my therapist chair as my clients' pain spills over, they're doing the grieving for me, too. Maybe I have been borrowing their tears.

I look out the window at the flashing red light and the reflection of the tired and tense middle-aged man staring back at me. The plane pushes eastward into the enveloping night.

FIVE

The Sandy Bay Yacht Club
by Martha Treadway

THERAPIST, HEAL THYSELF

October 1990

I AM DRESSING UP FOR THE DAY. I PUT ON MY BLUE-STRIPED shirt with the red foulard power tie and my charcoal gray workshop suit. I pause in front of the mirror. My hairline has receded significantly, my blond hair is actually quite gray, and my brow is lined with furrows from what Kate calls my "therapist's look." I look every bit of forty-five. Nevertheless, the man in the mirror appears trim, confident, perhaps even distinguished.

I catch myself smiling at my image. It's an old habit.

When I was eleven or twelve, my sister and her friends used to tease me about how I could never pass a mirror without pausing to check myself out. I was always considered vain. My mother's particular talent as a parent was to make each child feel special. She was the sun in our little solar system. When she deigned to smile on any one of us, we basked in her warmth. She would bind us to her with a conspiratorial intimacy. The "special quality" that my mother bestowed on me was my good looks. I wish she had chosen my personality or intelligence. But she chose my face.

In retrospect, it's no surprise that I grew up living the credo "Look good, feel good." I remember the summer I was working in the State House as administrative assistant to a legislator. There I was, a nineteen-year-old in a three-piece pinstripe suit, briefcase in hand, jaw square, shoulders back, striding purposefully through the corridors of power. A woman representative whom I was friendly with came up behind me one morning and whispered playfully in my ear, "Playing governor today, David?"

I was then. Maybe I still am.

Kate walks in and says, "What are you dressed up for? Are you doing a workshop today?"

"Yeah, I've got a seminar this morning," I reply, but that isn't why I've dressed carefully. I know that I've really suited up for my first interview with Barbara Greenspan. Barbara was our couples therapist for a few visits when Kate and I went through a rough period again several years ago. We had become so swamped by our professions and our children that our relationship had dissolved into nothing more than a frantic, poorly run small business. We definitely needed help rekindling a romantic spark.

It seems ironic to watch myself dressing up for my first session with Barbara the same way that my client Cindy does for me.

Cindy's situation has deteriorated since last summer. She's seriously depressed and using antidepressants hasn't helped at all. Now she's talking openly about suicide. She's also drinking heavily and refusing to go to A.A. or even consider a hospitalization. The case feels completely out of control and I'm scared. I try to convince myself that I'm on top of the situation, but who am I kidding? I should be getting help with the case, but I haven't talked to anyone. I'm hiding it and I know better. I've been avoiding the obvious connection to the way it was with my mother in the last years, but I can't.

"What's the workshop about?" asks Kate, pulling me back from fretting about Cindy.

"Intimacy, sexuality, and gender. Just what I want to be talking about today. How do I look?"

"You look fine. How do you feel?"

"Horrible."

"What's going on?"

"I'm agitated about my suicidal case. She's becoming more and more dependent on me. I'm seeing her three times a week. I talk to her on the phone. I can't get her into inpatient treatment. She has no friends or family. I'm it. She keeps telling me I'm the only reason why she's still alive. And she's got two young kids at home."

"Why don't you hospitalize her?"

"It's not that simple. She says that if I force her into the hospital it's the same as signing her death warrant. It would be the ultimate betrayal."

"You can't listen to that kind of blackmail."

"Christ, Kate, you make it sound so goddamn easy," I snap back.

"Sorry, I didn't know you were in such a vile mood. Barbara has got her work cut out for her. Are you nervous?" Kate asks.

"Nope. I just can't stand the idea of going back into therapy. I think it's a waste of time."

"Is this what you tell your clients?" Kate smiles.

"Ease up, will you? I don't want your supervision or your teasing. The truth is that I'm afraid it won't really work for me and then what? Just because I can do therapy and teach others how to do it, doesn't mean I'm going to be able to accomplish anything myself."

Kate's face softens. She looks at me with genuine concern and moves toward me. I let her hug me. "I know you're feeling bad, but I don't know what to do," she says.

"I don't know what you can do either," I mutter while slipping away from her embrace. Kate pulls back and busies herself. The way her lips are pursed shows she's hurt, probably because I couldn't let her comfort me. I ought to say something, but can't make myself. She seems small and far away as if I were looking at her with the wrong end of binoculars. She's just trying to love me. But I can't let her in. I don't know how.

Ever since the beginning of our relationship, Kate and I have been able to feel close and connected when I am being nurturing toward her. But when she tries to comfort me, I tighten up and feel trapped. I'm like a frightened wild animal being petted for the first time. Even our couples therapy with Barbara didn't really change my reflex response. I just learned to manage it better.

I head downstairs to cook breakfast and make Sam's lunch. Life goes on.

I'm on the blue sofa where my clients usually sit, going over my appointment schedule for the day. I imagine the perspective my clients have of this office. My more discerning clients must note the haphazard array of furniture and the vaguely adolescent quality of the nautical themes on the wall. Many people comment on the framed Montaigne quote over the bookcase, "A sailor without a destination cannot hope for a favorable breeze," another Christmas present from Fran.

I am sure very few of them notice the collection of items on my messy desk. There's a broken spyglass that Kate gave me when I decided to sail the Atlantic, a Jew's harp given to me by a client who subsequently killed herself, and a small, curved piece of wood with an eye stamped into it that looks as if it could be either a fish or a bird. I made it in shop when I was eleven and gave it to my mother. It turned up in her things after she died.

Directly behind the blue sofa are windows that look out on my backyard. Sometimes I find myself surreptitiously watching my children playing on the swings in the middle of sessions. On the wall to the left of the sofa is the painting my mother did of the Sandy Bay Yacht Club where I learned to sail. No wonder it showed up in my hypnotic trance in Florida: it's in my peripheral vision all day long.

It's 7:55. Bill and Sarah Dunbar are already in the waiting room. I don't want to see them. It isn't their fault. They're great people and they've made a good start in therapy. I just don't want to see anybody this morning. I don't want to give a talk today about sex and intimacy, and I definitely don't want to go see Dr. B. this afternoon, no matter how well dressed I am for the encounter.

It's not even clear to me why I am going back into therapy in the first place. It's as if for years I've been in a hot-air balloon drifting along above the trees and now suddenly there's a tear in the fabric and I'm coming down. I feel as if I'm going to crash. But why? I have a good career, solid marriage, good kids. What's missing? It's not as if I was sexually abused or my marriage was falling apart.

The other day I saw a bumper sticker that sums me up: HAVING A GREAT TIME! WISH I WAS HERE. In the midst of a full life, I feel as if I'm missing in action. Is that enough of a reason for therapy? It's so easy for me to reassure clients that they don't need to be in the depths of despair to come into treatment, but I can't give that permission to myself. To me going back into therapy carries a whiff of failure and weakness.

Some people agonize over the decision to enter therapy. I did it impulsively. I just called Barbara a couple of weeks ago and said I thought I could use a little tune-up. We made the appointment. It seemed easy. It doesn't feel that way today. Maybe I'll get the flu.

Kate's relieved that I am going. She attributes my dark mood to the visit to Fran's grave; she thinks it stimulated my unresolved grief about my mother. I dismiss that interpretation as a classic case of projection. Kate has never stopped grieving for her father and therefore assumes that my underlying issue is my mother's death. Of course, she would say I'm just "in denial."

The phone rings. It's my Dad. He's depressed and needs to talk. It used to make me feel strong and important to be his confidant. Now I'm just impatient in that role. Can he tell? I wouldn't want to hurt his feelings.

My Dad's never recovered from what happened. He's on his third marriage and retired in Florida now. He puts on a good act, but he's still hurting. His wife, Peggy, is loving and understanding. She helped him build a workable life.

My clients in the waiting room are a legitimate excuse to keep the conversation brief, but guilt squeezes me anyway. I give him a little pep talk on what a good job he's done helping out my sister. I hope I don't sound patronizing.

Time to collect Bill and Sarah.

"Come on in, you two," I say. "Sorry about the mess," I add, embarrassed that my sons have left clothes all over the room from the night before.

"Oh, we don't mind," pipes up Sarah, smiling with cheerful well-mannered charm; "it just makes you more human."

Sarah and Bill settle onto the sofa. They are quite a handsome couple. Even in her late thirties, Sarah hasn't lost that fresh cheerleader look that often results from the combination of thick blond hair, bright blue eyes, freckles, and a perky smile. Bill is lean with salt and pepper hair. His angular long face looks severe, but is frequently softened by a boyish grin.

This is our fifth session since last July. I am a little worried that we've been moving too quickly. My relationship with them is still quite superficial, and I'm not sure that we've established the kind of emotional safety net that would make it possible for them to deal with much intense vulnerablity. My quick and direct style is one of my clinical strengths, but sometimes it gets me into trouble if I haven't been careful enough in building the therapeutic relationship.

The meeting begins well enough with a review of their continued progress in talking more openly and being more careful to show their appreciation for each other. I catch myself hoping it will be an easy session.

Fifteen minutes into the meeting, Sarah opens up a new topic. "Well, we certainly have something to talk about today."

"What's that, Sarah?"

"Bill's mother is coming for Thanksgiving, and he just dumps her on me. You plunk yourself down in front of the football games, and you really drop out of the family. You don't think the kids notice? Last year Bobbie said, 'Good-bye, Dad, have a nice trip,' when you turned on the first game."

"Come on, Sarah, it's not that bad. I just don't have anything to say to her."

Sarah turns toward me and smiles brightly. "Well, what do you think, David?"

"Now come on, Sarah. Being a judge isn't in my job description. I think it's up to Bill," I reply judgmentally. The couple hasn't really changed much, even though they were getting on so much better. Bill is still the "designated problem" and Sarah continues to try to enlist me in the effort to fix him. I haven't decided whether to address the underlying pattern of their relationship. They seem comfortable in a quasi-mother-son dynamic. Could Sarah tolerate it if he became more adult and assertive? If he ever addressed his unresolved feelings about his own mother, who deserted their family, he might be less tolerant of Sarah's dominating tendencies. Would she ever risk dealing with her stuff with her Dad? Maybe they could both shed their childhood curses. But what if one did and the other didn't?

Bill cut short my musing. "The less I have to deal with my mother, the better, as far as I'm concerned. I stopped having any feeling for her when she left us while I was a kid."

"How long was it before she reentered your lives?"

"Well, she always sent us Christmas and birthday cards. But we didn't actually speak to her for two years. Then one Christmas she called. My father and my brother wouldn't speak with her. They just handed me the phone and sat there watching while I talked with her. The minute she heard my voice she began to cry. She started telling me how much she missed me, and loved me, that kind of stuff. She never said a thing about leaving or about the woman she was apparently living with."

"Have you and your mother ever talked about this? It sounds as if it was profoundly hurtful." I'm caught off guard by this new information about his mother.

"Of course not, and I've never met her lady friend either. When she comes to our house she comes alone, thank God."

Bill's voice drops to a near-whisper. His head slumps forward, and he has tears in his eyes as he talks.

"It seems you may still have some tough feelings about your Mom."

Listen to yourself, David. You're so quick to encourage him to deal with his relationship with his mother. What about your own? I'm going to have to bring this up with Barbara this afternoon. For years I've been able to deal effectively with my clients' deepest vulnerabilities without getting caught in my own. But lately my emotional responses in the middle of sessions have distracted me rather than moving me closer to my clients.

I feel impelled to see whether Bill can go a little further.

"Bill, if you could talk to your mother about all of this, what would you want to say? Pretend for a second that she's right here, right now. And tell her what you would like to say after all these years."

"I don't know that I can do this, but I'll try."

"Take your time, Bill, this is hard," I respond. "Just close your eyes and imagine her sitting in this white chair across from you. Don't worry about getting it right; just say whatever is in your heart." I'm leaning forward in my chair. I'm a little taken aback by how eager I am for him to get into this stuff.

Bill closes his eyes and begins haltingly, "I don't understand why you left. We were a good family. What was the matter with us? Why didn't you tell me? I could have understood. You always complained about being the only woman in the house, but were we that bad? Were we bad enough that you decided you liked women better? What was the matter with us?"

Bill sobs heavily. Tears well up in my eyes. He talks like a little boy. My mother never left a note either. No explanation. I wish I could have talked with her. Was it really so bad? What was so wrong with us?

I fight back my tears. This is neither the time nor the place. I must regain my focus on Bill. "Have you ever thought it might be a good idea to talk directly to your mother about some of this?"

"I couldn't do that."

Even as I say it, I know it's a premature suggestion. But I can't stop myself. I don't know where it's coming from. I keep at it. "Well, I know it would be very difficult. Maybe you should consider asking her to do it in here. I often meet with my clients and one or both of their parents."

Bill stiffens. "I don't think I'm ready for this, Doctor Tread-way."

"There's no rush, Bill," I backpedal quickly. I know I'm in trouble when a client goes back to the formality of calling me Doctor Treadway. Bill's just taken a huge step and all he needed was for me to acknowledge his vulnerability gently. Here I am dramatically upping the ante and proposing a direct confrontation with his mother. My timing's way off.

I decide to switch gears and focus on Sarah as a way of taking the heat off him. "Listen, Bill, we all have to deal with our unresolved issues with our parents. In one of our earlier sessions, Sarah acknowledged that part of the reason she has difficulty trusting you and being intimate with you is because of her Dad. Right, Sarah?"

"That's true," Sarah replies. She looks startled by the change in topic. "But I've dealt with my relationship with my father in individual therapy years ago. I think Bill just doesn't want to recognize that he's transferred a lot of his negative feelings toward his mother onto me and onto women in general."

"Damnit, Sarah, you are not the shrink here," Bill snaps. "If you're going to set yourself up as the high priestess of mental health, I'm out of here. Why don't you and the doctor have a consult on my case and let me know what your findings are?"

Sarah looks as if she's been slapped. The color drains from her face and then she begins to cry.

Bill is sitting straight as a board. He has a hard set to his jaw and his arms are crossed. He's staring at the wall.

Normally, this kind of blowup can lead to a productive confrontation, but I'm speechless. Suddenly I feel the way I did when I was trying to talk to my mother decades ago. I don't know what to say. I feel small and inadequate. This mess feels as if it was all my doing in the first place.

"I think I made a mistake pushing so hard into this stuff about your mother, Bill. Then suddenly shifting the focus over to your relationship with your Dad must have felt pretty abrupt to you, Sarah. I was off the mark with both of you."

There's only a slight response to my apology. The session just goes on and on. I can't get them to talk with one another. They won't even look at each other. I offer them another session that week. They say they'll let me know. I recognize that I am working too hard, but can't stop myself. I'm not even sure they'll come back at all. Nothing I say seems to help. They aren't listening. They're just waiting to get out of the room, away from me and away from each other. They seem utterly helpless and alone. So do I.

SIX

David in clown suit

TALKING THE TALK

THE AUDITORIUM IS FULL OF CLINICIANS. PEOPLE ARE STILL FILING in with coffee and notebooks in hand. I feel a typical rush of nervousness during the introduction.

The audience claps expectantly as I stand in front of them with a microphone and a smile. What am I doing up here at the podium about to teach these people about couples treatment after the mess I made out of the session with Bill and Sarah? What would they think if they knew that later on this afternoon I'll be headed off to my own therapy appointment?

I give them a beaming grin and launch in. "Anyway, to get us started today, I'm going to begin by asking a few questions. Feel free not to answer any question that might be embarrassing. But first, how many of you have had, currently have, or would like to have a sexual life?"

Surprised laughter. Everybody's hand goes up.

"How many of you are completely comfortable with the quality of your sexual intimacy?"

Nervous laughter, and some people bravely raise a hand.

"Good for you folks. Most of us are not quite sure, are we? Here's another question for you. How many of you are comfortable bringing up sex and intimacy with your clients?"

Most of the audience raise their hands.

"Do you ever find yourself doing a little covert comparison? It gets a little difficult when a couple wants to work on a level of intimacy that my wife and I aren't managing too well. You know how that goes."

Rueful chuckles. And we are off. I always try to engage the audience personally right from the beginning. I begin to feel my tightness lift as I slip into my old familiar role, buoyed by the warmth of their initial response. Someone once called me the Johnny Carson of family therapy training; unfortunately, I'm not sure that it was meant as a compliment.

I ask the audience to break into pairs and address some questions on how their personal experience with sex and gender issues affects their work as therapists. The room explodes into a cacophony of noise as they all talk with each other.

It's good to sit down for a moment. Lately I've been like Willy Loman getting by "on a shoeshine and a smile." Just the week before when I was doing a day-long workshop in Chicago, I caught myself checking the clock to see how much more time I had to go. It was only 10:25 A.M.

The session goes well. At one point, when someone asks whether all my cases are successful, I talk briefly about my earlier couple session, and how overwhelmed I was. It helps therapists if the designated experts acknowledge their own limitations. Several years ago I did a demonstration interview that was a disaster. The audience loved it and we learned from my mistakes.

This group likes the videotapes and there's an easy dialogue between us. I feel confident and comfortable as I bask in their warmth and acceptance.

Later in the session, I talk about how much we, therapists, satisfy some of our own intimacy needs in our relationships with our clients. "Therapy gives us a kind of safe intimacy. We engage in an intense emotional relationship with our clients, and yet they pay for our time. We encourage them to pour out their hearts to us, but we keep strict control over what we choose to share of ourselves. Unlike in most normal relationships between equally vulnerable people, we have most of the benefits of intimacy and few of the risks.

"Also, many of us come from pretty dysfunctional families ourselves. A good part of our identity is derived from our role as caretakers to other family members. Sometimes I think the only difference between me now and when I was a kid trying to give my parents ad hoc marital therapy is that nowadays I have a higher success rate and I get paid. The role hasn't changed much.

"The key question for all of us is how much are we dependent on our need to be needed? I had a rather surprising revelation about this issue in my own family several years ago.

"For years, I had been the in-house therapist in my family. I was always the one expected to manage my sister's mental illness, Dad's marital difficulties, and my brother's alcoholism. Ironically, when I finally announced in a martyrish, self-pitying way that I would no longer continue in the role of family therapist, they all said, 'Fine.' And everyone has been much better ever since. That's more than a little disconcerting. I have discovered that, without my role as designated savior in my family, I have felt much more insecure and uncomfortable. It's as if I've lost my place at the table."

I often tell stories in my teaching about the craziness in my family. It makes it easier for other therapists to weigh their own baggage, which they carry into their work with clients. Sometimes there's a certain disingenuous quality to my being so open with audiences. It doesn't feel right to talk about my family as if they were just one of my more difficult cases. But today, it's genuine. I definitely feel as insecure and uncomfortable as I say I am.

Near the close, I decide to do a hypnotic exercise that helps therapists stay centered in their own life while being so intensely connected to their clients. My motives for doing this are a little self-serving. I need the exercise as much as they do.

I begin speaking softly and slowly. "Before we end today, I would like you to shift gears mentally for a moment. I'd like you to move around in your seat until you can find a comfortable and relaxing position. As I begin to talk to you, you can listen intently or you can just let your mind wander wherever it pleases. You can listen with your eyes open, or, if it's more comfortable, you can listen with your eyes closed. What I would like you to do is to bring an image of yourself as a child under the age of twelve into your mind, so that you can literally see that child."

Pause. I watch as members of the audience begin to do their own inward searches.

"Where do you see that child? In your bedroom, in the yard, with your friends, or alone? What is the child wearing?

Pause. I try to pace the exercise so that all of them have time to recall themselves fully as children. For some people, just the act of going back into childhood is emotionally powerful.

"I would like you to look at this child with the special knowing that you have of everything this child has gone through. No one will ever know this child as well as you do. You know how hard this child tries, how scared and lonely this child may feel sometimes; and only you know what secret worries are there as well as those secret dreams.

"Look at this child with your special knowing. . . . And then I would like you to consider what you would give to this child if, for just a moment in time, you could go to this child as the adult that you are now and give the child whatever you wanted to give, based on your understanding of what that child truly needs."

Long pause.

I pace up and down in front of the audience. Most of them are slumped in their seats with their eyes closed, while others are sitting stiffly upright and staring straight ahead at me. Tears are running down some faces and some hands are reaching into purses for tissues.

Then suddenly, I can see me, a little boy in his white T-shirt and jeans. He's alone in his little Turnabout, his hand on the tiller of his boat, his eyes raised to check out the set of the sail.

At the end, I ask the audience what they would have wanted to give to their childhood selves. Many people report that they wish they could give that child a simple hug, a hug that might express the reassurance, love, and acceptance that they needed when they were young. I could have used that kind of hug. I could use one today.

After the workshop, many of the participants gather around me. They just want to say a word of appreciation, shake my hand, or ask me to autograph my book. One woman asks me for a hug. The feeling from the earlier session with Bill and Sarah lifts like a morning fog burned off by the rising sun. I'm completely relaxed about the upcoming session with Barbara. For the moment, I am all that I appear to be.

I follow Barbara into her office. She's taller than I am. I hadn't noticed it before. Maybe I am just feeling smaller. I head for my old position on the couch.

"My individual clients usually sit over here," Barbara points out a chair by the window.

"I don't know if I'm entirely ready to be an 'individual client.' " I smile as I shift dutifully to the new chair.

"I imagine it feels different to be here by yourself," Barbara says as she sits across from me, crosses her legs at the ankles, and folds her hands in her lap. She looks straight at me, fixing me with an intent gaze and a warm smile.

"I'm not uncomfortable being here, if that's what you mean," I reply, though I can't match her steady gaze. I'm actually quite nervous. Much more than I expected to be. But I'm not ready to tell her that.

Barbara has soft curly gray hair that falls to her shoulders, brown eyes that convey warmth and acceptance, and an easy, natural smile. Yet her attractiveness doesn't compromise a strong presence and sense of purpose.

The couples work Kate and I had done with Barbara had been effective, but I wasn't at all sure she'd be able to deal with me. I could talk a good game in therapy while always maintaining a safe distance from exposing too much vulnerability. I wasn't sure how to be genuinely vulnerable even if I wanted to be. To paraphrase the saying from A.A., I could talk the talk, but I didn't know how to walk the walk.

I don't know where to start. I notice the plants by the window. Clearly the colorful collection of small delicate flowers are there to provide a benign distraction for the scurrying eyes of my anxious predecessors.

"If I were your supervisor, I would tell you to watch out for this guy. He's going to try to stay in control the whole time," I say, to break the awkward silence with an attempt at some humor.

Barabara smiles. "Thanks for the tip, but whatever it takes for you to feel okay about being here is fine."

I shake my head slowly. "I'm not sure when it started. Last summer we took a trip to Evanston to visit Kate's parents' graves. It was a very emotional weekend for Kate and I couldn't connect. It's as if I'm swimming around in my own fishbowl and the rest of the world is just a blur of color and shapes outside the thick rounded glass. All I could think about was myself and getting through the weekend. Kate's pain was mostly a problem that needed to be managed.

"On the other hand, just this morning, I was in a session where I was helping a client deal with stuff about his mother, and I was almost in tears myself. It's been like that a lot lately."

"Your tears are close to the surface in your work. This seems to be uncomfortable for you, particularly when you couldn't be fully present on that weekend with Kate."

Barbara is carefully reflecting to me what she's hearing. I find it unsettling to be therapized. Part of me wants to tell her not to bother with the "active listening" technique. Yet her presence is strong and gentle. I still can't make steady eye contact. I glance at her extensive bookshelves and wonder whether she has a copy of my book.

I blurt out my tale of woe as she listens intently. Reviewing my stress, feelings of emptiness, and depression seem like whining. People are starving to death every minute, and I'm fussing over some emotional hangnails. To make matters worse, everytime

Barbara responds, I can't resist correcting her. By the end of the hour, I'm slouching down in the chair and staring at the floor. There is a long silence. It seems odd that I can't bring myself to talk about my worries about Cindy's suicidal stuff. I don't want Barbara to advise me about how to manage the situation or tell her how scared I am. But what the hell am I here for, then?

"I don't know what to say," I mumble defensively.

"Take your time. There seems to be a lot that has been stirred up for you. There's no hurry."

"Well, the fact is, it seems as if I'm just role playing. It doesn't matter what I'm doing: father, husband, therapist, mentor, whatever. Maybe even in here, too. I just put on the appropriate face and persona for the occasion as a woman puts on makeup or, better yet, as a clown paints on a smile."

The image makes me chuckle. "That brings up a strange connection. You know what I have beside my bed? I have a little picture of my younger brother and me encased in one of those inverted fishbowl paperweights. Anyway, I'm about six years old in the picture. And I'm dressed up in a clown suit and I have this smile plastered on my mouth with a big gash of lipstick. Yet the boy in the picture isn't really smiling. It's more like he's trying to smile. I don't know why I have that by my bed. Isn't that funny?"

"It doesn't seem funny. You look as if it makes you sad to think of that boy in the clown suit." Barbara leans forward slightly.

I quickly sit up and look away. I remember the hypnosis workshop last summer. The sadness came up from a place inside me that I didn't even know was there, and it was so humiliating bursting into tears in front of the audience. I'm just not ready to fall apart in front of Barbara.

"You know," I say, summoning up my best workshop smile, "I've been spouting off at you about trivial midlife malaise and I haven't said anything at all. Besides I can't keep from smiling at you like a deranged game show host."

"David, you've told me a lot today. You may not be ready to let out where you are on the inside completely, but it sounds like a scary and lonely place. And don't worry about the smile; perhaps it's been protecting you for a long time."

I sigh heavily. I'm relieved we're almost done and yet I'm glad I came.

The traffic on the way home is bumper to bumper. Normally, I would start getting agitated or throw in a tape to distract myself. Instead I start mulling over our session. I'm struck by her comment about how my smile protects me. She's more right than she knows.

I learned about smiling before I was six. I always wore a smile and everyone always smiled back. But no one ever saw me at all.

Suddenly I flash on those early April days under the pine trees back in Sturbridge before we moved to Boston. I must have been five or six. There would still be patches of snow. The ground was wet and squishy. The air had a chill in it, but the sun was warm on my face as I walked down the hill to the pine trees. I would find a place where the pine needles were dry. Then I would lie on my back and watch the clouds move across the sky. I would breathe in the tang of the pines and listen to the wind rustling through the branches. It always felt good to be alone. It made me feel big and little at the same time. I didn't need to smile.

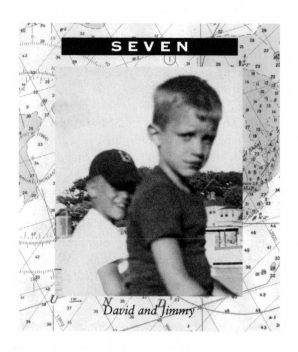

SEVEN

David and Jimmy

LITTLE BOYS

November 1990

IT'S LATE THURSDAY AFTERNOON. THE PALE LIGHT IS DWINDLING into winter darkness. It's cold. The trees have a bare skeletal look after yesterday's storm. The orange and brown remains littering the lawn demand attention. I'll have to devote Saturday to the raking. I'm supposed to work with Michael on the go-kart project over the weekend. This will be another delay.

I can see Michael on the swings out of the corner of my eye as I look directly at Cindy on the sofa. In spite of the encroachment of winter, Michael still retreats to the swings every afternoon when he returns from school. Sometimes he stays out there for a half an hour or more, swinging and listening to his Walkman. It's his time to be alone. He's about to turn thirteen; I wonder how much longer he will allow himself to enjoy the swings.

I tune back into Cindy. She's sitting in front of me in an elegant gray wool suit, ivory silk blouse, and string of natural pearls. Her makeup is fashionably muted. Her painted nails match her pink lipstick.

"I don't know if I can keep doing this. I'm nothing. I can't be with my kids or my friends. Last night I was just horrible with Jack. I literally yanked him up the stairs, just about pulling his arm out of his socket. He doesn't deserve this. He's just a little boy. They would be better off without me."

Her eyes fill with tears. She looks at me for reassurance with a pleading glance. She's sitting on her hands, her knees are pressed together, and her feet are turned toward each other so the tips of her shoes are touching. She looks so young.

"Cindy, you're going through a bad time. All of us screw up with our kids sometimes. There's no way that the kids would be better off without you. You've been a good mom to Jack and you will be again," I say, hoping to be gently reassuring. I'm trying to sound as confident and convincing as I used to be.

"So you agree with me that I'm worthless as a mother now," Cindy came back at me. "It doesn't matter anyway. My kids should be with their father and their new mother."

"God, Cindy what are you talking about?" I blurt out. "You think your kids are going to be better off if you're dead. That's nonsense. If you kill yourself, your kids will spend the rest of their lives wondering what the hell they did to drive you over the edge."

The stunned look on Cindy's face makes me realize I've been almost shouting at her. What am I doing? Is this about her or my mother? Her kids or me? Is this desperate unreachable woman in front of me what my mother was like?

"I don't mean to come on so strong," I quickly apologize; "I guess I'm really frightened that you think the kids would be better off without you."

"It's okay," she says reassuringly. "At least I know you care."

Great. Who is taking care of whom, I wonder? We stumble through to the end of the session. I slump in my chair. I've got to break through the impasse we're in or she's not going to make it. I used to be able to treat these cases with the right mix of deep care and commitment and a certain measure of disciplined detachment. I don't know where that's gone. This case is a mess. She's filled with self-loathing and hopelessness and I'm just desperately blathering at her.

I glance back out the window to see whether Michael is still swinging, but the swing set is lost in the gathering shadows.

I've got a list of phone messages a mile long and only a half-hour before my visit to Barbara. I'm supposed to call "Twenty-Twenty" about doing a show on treating emotional abuse. I feel like such a fraud. I'd rather talk to the boatyard in Bermuda about the boat. I reach for the phone to call Bob Macmaster, the yard manager.

"Hi, Bob. This is David Treadway. Quick question. When you guys inspect the rigging for wear, do you use that red stuff on the turnbuckles that shows up the smallest cracks?"

"It depends on whether the boat is going offshore for an extended period."

"Well, I'm headed down to St. John in the Virgin Islands in March, and I'd like you to go over the rigging with a fine-toothed comb. I'm always a little paranoid about losing the mast."

"Don't worry, Doc, we've got plenty of time to get your boat ready. We'll take good care of her."

Why am I so worried? I've been sailing oceans for years and here I am anxiously fussing with the yard four months before a trip. The passage to St. John should be an easy one, about twelve days of mostly trade-wind sailing. The trip across the Pacific to New Zealand will be a much bigger test of boat and crew. Besides, the boat's in excellent condition, considering it's more than twenty years old. Actually, since it was built in '66, it must be twenty-five years old now.

That's odd. My mother died in '66. It's strange to think of the *Crow* being built at the same time and not very far away from where my mother was being buried in western Massachusetts. I never connected the two events before.

Then I decide to call Mark, my minister and crew member. "Hi, Mark. Have you cleared your schedule for the trip down to the islands?"

"Absolutely, Cap'n Dave. It's in my book and I'm looking forward to it. But how about you? Are you going to make the meeting this Sunday?"

"God, I was supposed to call you, wasn't I? I'm going to be there, but frankly, given my attitude to the whole God thing, my going to an 'Episcopalian men's prayer group' seems like a major leap of faith. To be honest, I'm mostly going because you asked. And besides, I'm a little curious what a collection of aging preppies will have to say about their spiritual life. I can't imagine it."

"Well, if it's any comfort, I don't think anyone in the group is all that certain about 'the God thing,' as you so delicately put it. We'll just be trying to find our way together rather than each of us doing it alone."

"Well, maybe that's why I let you talk me into it. I'm tired of trying to figure out everything on my own. Frankly, I'm a little bored with my own ideas. And I look forward to being just a group member and not the leader. Anyway, I've got to run; I've got my own lost sheep due in the waiting room in a few minutes."

I notice the little lie I told Mark about having to see clients as I head for my car to go to Barbara's. Why should I be so ashamed of being in therapy that I'm hiding it from a good friend? Yet another item on the Chez Barbara menu.

I spill onto my chair in Barbara's office like a dumped bag of dirty laundry. This time I can't wait to talk about Cindy. I guess my trust level in Barbara has increased or my desperation has worsened. Or both. I hate exposing how scared and helpless I feel about Cindy. I feel so little.

"God, I'm glad to be here. I'm treating this woman who is in serious trouble and I'm not getting anywhere. I feel as if I'm just hanging onto her ankles to keep her from jumping off a cliff. And sooner or later, she's going to leap anyway. The situation has been getting progressively worse for months.

"I'm used to being able to manage these situations with a real emotional connection to the client while maintaining a good measure of clarity and calm. I never used to be afraid. And it's not like this is the first suicidal case I've ever encountered.

"I know you're going to try to get me to see a connection between my feelings dealing with her and what it was like for me with my mother. But that's not what's been bothering me," I say, emphatically trying to steer Barbara away from the obvious. Watching myself play peek-a-boo as a client is an eye-opener. I bet she can see right through me.

"Anyway, no matter what else was going on in my life, being a therapist was my anchor to windward. I had confidence in myself and, furthermore, I liked the kind of person I was. I always felt buoyed up by my clients' responsiveness to me."

"And now, sometimes, you feel unsure of yourself?" she asked.

"I don't know what I am anymore. I used to be able to rise to the occasion, a cool hand in a crisis. It is the role that I played when my family fell apart. I actually liked everyone's relying on me."

"Being able to handle crises in your family was one of the ways that you were able to manage your own pain and confusion."

"You're right. It makes me wonder whether my whole career as a therapist isn't just perpetuating the same role. It's definitely easier being the Doc than being the patient."

"It's not always so easy in one's own family, is it?" Barbara says, redirecting me back toward my family.

"I don't know if I want to deal with my past. What can I say? My mother was a drunk and then she killed herself. My father and sister both had nervous breakdowns after the funeral and were hospitalized. My older brother, Jon, who became an alcoholic when he was fourteen, disappeared back to Florida, and my younger brother, Jim, and I were the only ones left standing. I was twenty. Suddenly I was the head of the family.

"Every weekend I would skip my Friday classes at Penn, leave Philadelphia, and drive to New York. I would visit my sister, who was on a locked ward at Columbia Presbyterian, where she had gone to nursing school. Then I would get back in the car, drive up to Boston, and visit my father at McLean Hospital. Then I drove back to Philadelphia on Sunday. One time, I left Boston about 3:00 A.M. I made it from downtown Boston to downtown Philadelphia in five hours flat."

"It's hard to imagine what that must have been like for you. It sounds as if you were speeding through quite a lot."

I don't know what to say next. I've been just speeding though the telling of this stuff, too. I glance at Barbara, who is waiting patiently.

"This is hard," I pause. I'm back in my slouch again. "I'm ashamed about how I responded back then. I actually used my family's mess to cut corners at school. It was gross, but I would tell teachers about my mother's death in order to take makeup exams, skip class, explain missed assignments. You name it. Women professors really went for it in a big way. I even used the story to get a sympathetic response from girls. It worked like a charm. I was a jerk back then."

"It sounds as if it was the only way you knew how to tell anyone what was happening in your life."

"You think it was my way of trying to connect? I don't. It seems pretty manipulative and cavalier. Maybe you're being too generous. Sometimes I feel that I'm doing the same con job on you that I did back then. Making a pitch for sympathy."

"Maybe you're being too harsh on that young man who had no one to turn to, no one to talk to."

"I couldn't have really talked to anyone, anyway. Actually, I was pretty numbed out long before my mother died.

"I guess this is where I really have to dig in. It's funny, I've worked with the survivors of a suicide and they're always frozen. They're caught between their rage toward the murderer, their grief for the victim, and their guilt for being an unwitting accomplice.

"I understand this stuff up here," I say, tapping my forehead, "but I am still completely frostbitten in here," pointing to my heart.

"It's important to warm up frostbitten skin very slowly and carefully. Maybe now you're more ready to bear the feelings that were too much for you back then?" she asks intently.

"I hope so."

"Perhaps we need to go through the whole story slowly and take our time with each piece of it."

"Of course you're right, but my first thought is, 'No way,

José.' I guess we might call that resistance. Aren't I a prize to work with?"

Barbara pauses. Then she looks me straight in the eye. "I won't pretend this is easy, David, but I want you to have a chance to do this work. I think that there's a part of you that's been waiting for a long time."

It's hard for me to take in what she said. I can't think of a quip. I look away.

It's pouring rain as I work my way home in the traffic. It rained hard that first morning after I got back to Boston and woke up with the shock of remembering that Mom was dead. The rain beat against the windows as I looked out at the gray sky and the black slick streets. Later that day a relative referred to the rain as "God's tears." I almost punched him.

The session with Barbara was draining. I couldn't let her know how cold and detached I feel toward my mother. I didn't want to disappoint her. I want her to like me. But I am so angry. Just thinking about my mother reminds me of the stuff I wrote back in my twenties. I used to call my poetry the "dead poems." I still know them by heart.

TO MOTHER

You squat on my days
like some obscene hen
smothering her young.

Sometimes I think
that you forget
that you're dead.

It's been twenty years since I wrote that. Nothing's changed.

The minute I walk into the house, Michael is after me. "Are you ready, Dad?" he ask eagerly.

"Hold your horses. I've got to check for messages."

"But you said we would work on the car as soon as you got back. I've been waiting," Michael whines.

"Dammit, Michael, just give me a few minutes, will you please? I have to make a few calls."

"All right, don't get all mad. I was just asking."

"You're right, Michael. I'm sorry. It's been a long day."

This is the problem with having my office at home. I finish the day loaded up with all the painful feelings that my clients have expressed in the past eight hours, and then I jump down the throat of one of my children. As far as parenting goes, the expression "I gave at the office" is altogether too accurate: My clients get the best of me. Too frequently, I serve my children leftovers. It doesn't help matters to add a trip to the therapist's office, where I feel like a kid myself.

Then I think of Cindy trudging through her evening ritual, wine glass in hand. Is she snapping at her kids at the table the way Mom used to snap at us? Maybe she's already retreated to her bed complaining of a headache. It was a relief that Barbara let me sidestep this issue in our session today, but I can feel the pressure building. Treating Cindy stirs up stuff that I thought was as dead as my mother.

I watch myself give in to my own need for a glass of cabernet. Tonight was supposed to be an abstinence night, but sometimes I cheat on my own rules.

On the TV, there's a special on the Battle of the Bulge during World War II. I watch my father's generation of men slogging through the snow and desperately digging foxholes in the frozen ground. One old man weeps as he describes trying to kill his buddy quickly so that he wouldn't slowly bleed to death. Another describes how often the new recruits would be blown to bits before anyone even learned their names.

I watch the faces on the screen. They're just boys.

What the hell do I have to complain about? Compared to what those guys went through, my life's been a breeze.

I flip off the TV, fight the temptation to have another glass of wine, and go look for Michael. He's ensconced in front of a video game, happily blasting away at thousands of enemy soldiers.

"Michael, let's get to work. How about it?"

"Can we do it later, Dad? I really want to win this game."

"For God's sake, Michael, what is this? Punishment because I wasn't ready earlier?" I say, trying for a light touch.

"Dad, why are you always being a psychologist?"

I burst out laughing. He has me dead to rights. "Okay, Mike, you got me. Dr. Dad will close up shop for the day. I promise. Finish the show and then we'll go to work."

Later, we go out to the enclosed porch off the dining room where we keep the soapbox racer we're building from scratch. The porch is strewn with tools, parts, and other odds and ends. I have never been skilled with my hands, and this idea of building a go-kart with a mounted engine is way over my head. We are making it up as we go along, and so far the project has been an unmitigated disaster. I don't know what I am doing and keep having to redo completed steps because I have inadvertently made the next step impossible. As much as I try to include Michael, unfortunately his role is often reduced to handing me tools and stoically tolerating the agitation that seems to accompany my every move.

"Can we do the wheel tonight, Dad?" Michael asks.

"Sure, Michael. I think it's going to be something that you can do a lot of, too. We need to drill a few holes, screw in the turning blocks along the sides, mount the panel with the wheel on it, and hook up the lines. What do you think? You want to start with some drilling?"

"Can I use the power drill?"

"Sure, let me just get the right drill bit and make sure it's in tight. You've got to be really careful. It's not a toy."

Coming across as a wise old craftsman makes me laugh. I never learned any mechanical skills as a child. It must have been somone observing our family who made up the old joke "How many WASPs does it take to change a light bulb? Two: one to mix the martinis and one to call the electrician." It wouldn't have occurred to me to expect my father to help me on a project. He was rarely home, and when he was, the adults led quite separate lives from the children. I developed my sense of competency through sailing.

My younger brother, Jim, was enterprising enough to teach himself how to fix and build things. When he was about eleven, he built a soapbox racer with a lawn mower engine. I was always jealous of his talents. Here I am, thirty-one years later, trying to build my own.

As I tighten in the drill bit, I say to Michael, "You know, your Uncle Jim built one of these things all by himself when he was your age. Isn't that something?"

Michael doesn't reply. Damn, he probably feels belittled by my comment. I'm such an idiot.

When Sam asks to help out, Michael pretends to threaten him with the electric drill.

"Michael, stop that! I told you that it wasn't a toy!"

"I was just kidding around, Dad. It's not even plugged in. See? Did you have a bad day with your clients?"

"Now look who's playing doctor," I smile. "Michael, you drill the holes. Sam, you can help put in the screws."

"He can't do that. He's too little," Michael quickly retorts.

"I know he doesn't know how to do it. But I'll bet his big brother can teach him," I say, using a little therapeutic manipulation.

Michael grins, turns to Sam, and says, "Get a screwdriver out of the toolbox. We'll do a practice one."

The boys begin to work together. They remind me of Jim and me painting the rust-red bottom of my Turnabout in the backyard in Rockport. Suddenly, I can hear the deep mellow sounds of my grandfather's cello. He always practiced out on the porch at dusk, and the music spilled into the yard, lending a slightly melancholic air to the coming of evening. "The little boys"—that's what they called Jim and me—would be clutching at the last bit of daylight in order to get on the first coat. We knew that when the music finished, it would be too dark to continue. The long summer day would be done.

I watch my sons. Their backs are to me. The two blond heads are almost touching as they lean over the car. And I can see the other "little boys" from long ago. The sweet ache of the cello floats in the air. My heart swells with a rich sadness. It feels surprisingly good.

EIGHT

Martha Treadway, 1961

TIME FOR YOUR TEARS

I AM STANDING IN THIS LARGE EMPTY ROOM THAT HAS NO rugs or furniture. It looks like a family room the day after the movers came. The darker rectangles of paint on the wall indicate where the pictures must have hung. At the other end of the room my brother, Jim, and my sister, Lauris, are standing next to each other and are talking to someone. I can't see who they are talking to, but they seem quite excited, as if they were talking to someone they hadn't seen for a long time. Slowly, it dawns on me that they might be talking to our mother. But I can't see her or hear her voice. I keep looking in the same direction they are, but I can only see an empty wall. Somehow I don't feel that I can interrupt this conversation to ask them where she is. I just listen hard and keep looking for her.

All of a sudden, I can see a pair of woman's shoes. They are scuffed black flats with a beaded gold design on the toes. I can see the bare ankles and calves. As I slowly lift my eyes, I come to the hem of a black wool skirt that falls just below the knee. Suddenly I know these are my mother's legs. I recognize the shoes. She wore them when she was working in the studio. I jolt my head up to see her face, but she's not there. I quickly glance back to find the legs, but they're gone too.

I wake up, crying.

It's 5:45 in the morning. The tree branch outside my window is heavily laden with the first snow of winter. As I walk out in my bathrobe and slippers to get the paper, it's cold and still. There's just a hint of light in the eastern sky. It reminds me of dawn after a long, cold night-watch at sea.

It's Michael's birthday. He's turning thirteen. We're giving him the day off from school and a CD player.

Walking back into the house, I remember with a jolt the dream about my mother. It seems so pathetic to me that I can't even see her in my dreams. All I can see is her legs. It's as if my memories of her have been obliterated from my brain by laser. I don't have a clue when her birthday would have been or exactly when she died. I wonder whether Dad's biography of Mom has the dates in it. It must. I'll look it up and get it straight once and for all.

My father has been working on a biography of my mother for the past year. He has sent me numerous chapters, but I have only glanced at them. I have been annoyed that Dad seems to be more concerned about telling his story than actually recording Mom's. I've also recoiled from my old role of being a cheerleader for Dad. He's clearly wanted approval for his effort and I've found myself resisting being supportive. I've been puzzled by my response. It makes me feel stingy and churlish.

It's no wonder I don't want to deal with this stuff with Barbara. I'm not grieving my lost childhood, missing my mother, or yearning for a strong father figure. I'm just a pissed-off, sulky adolescent. "The hell with both of them," I say to our old Lab, Copper, who seems to think she's being offered seconds on breakfast and enthusiastically wags her tail.

The day's starting on the wrong foot. I don't want my foul mood to get in the way of our celebrating Michael's birthday. I decide to stop in his room on my way back upstairs. This might be one morning he won't resent being awakened early. He's really excited about the possibility of getting that CD player.

I look over at the jumbled covers on his bed and there are only a few wisps of blond hair emerging from the pile. I suddenly remember Michael when he was three and four years old. I used to wake him up every morning with a song and a tickle. He'd always look so cute as he fought to stay snuggled down in his bed when I pulled back the covers and gave him nuggies.

I can see that sleepy little boy padding off to the bathroom in his green cotton PJs as if it were yesterday, and yet that little boy is gone forever.

I sit down next to him on the bed and begin to sing softly.

> *Good morning, birds; good morning, bees*
> *blades of grass, and leafy trees, trees, trees.*
> *Good morning sky, good morning sun,*
> *and all the little things that run, run, run.*

I reach under the covers to give him a tickle as I sing and Michael growls from his lair, "Don't even think about it, Dad. Touch me and you're dead."

"Lighten up, Mike. It's your birthday."

"Right, Dad, and my first birthday request is you don't sing to me and you don't tickle me."

"Well, all right, hotshot—but can I give you a birthday hug? Or are you too old for that too?" I look forward to his opening my present, a T-shirt that says, "Cheerful morning people should be shot."

"If you insist," he grumps condescendingly.

He's lying on his stomach with his head buried in the pillow face down, but I hug him anyway. I catch a flash of that beaming smile that I remember so well. It makes my morning.

My first appointment is Bill and Sarah. Much to my surprise, they've been doing much better since the disastrous session several weeks ago, when I pushed Bill too hard about dealing with his mother. I don't know why I am still taken aback by this phenomenon. I often tell my students not to trust the sessions that feel great and not to be surprised if the awful ones lead to something useful. Sometimes a crisis prompts people to make positive changes. Unfortunately, it can just as easily go the other way. Therapists ultimately have very little control over what happens.

Bill and Sarah have made real progress, while Cindy is still hanging on by her manicured fingernails. Yesterday she told me that I was the only reason why she just didn't end it all. She meant it as a compliment, but it felt like a noose tightening around my neck.

In the last few sessions, with much trepidation, the Dunbars have begun to explore their difficulties with sexuality. They've talked about their disappointments and frustrations. Bill complained that Sarah treated sex like a chore, like "doing the dishes or the laundry." He told her that he feels she's turned off rather than flattered by his sexual desire and that really hurts his feelings.

Sarah has talked about the pressure she feels to perform sexually and how impersonal it is. "I feel as if it doesn't have anything to do with me. It's just sex for sex's sake."

Slowly, they've begun to move beyond hurt and blame to talking more about how much they had enjoyed sex when they first met and fell in love. They seem to be getting much closer.

I've been feeling comfortable working with them, although I'm aware that I tend to avoid bringing up their issues with either of their parents. It isn't clear whether their unresolved grief about their parents will have to be dealt with directly in therapy. Given how ambivalent I'm still feeling about dealing with my past, it doesn't surprise me that I'm undecided about them.

As they come into the office, I can see that they are tense and distant again. They look dejected and they're back to sitting on opposite ends of the sofa with their bodies turned away from each other.

Uh, oh, I say to myself. Caught off guard, I blurt out, "What happened to you guys?"

Amid some tears, recriminations, and downcast looks, the story haltingly emerges. They'd been feeling so much closer that they decided to have a romantic evening in a local hotel. Bill tried to surprise Sarah by giving her some sexy underwear for the occasion. Sarah was acutely uncomfortable dressing up in the black lace teddy that Bill gave her. She tried to act pleased, but when he asked her to model it for him, she was overwhelmed with embarrassment. She burst into tears and retreated into the bathroom. Their romantic evening degenerated into an awkward and sullen distance. Bill felt rejected and angry. Sarah felt humiliated and guilty.

As they each report their versions of events, they seem to be caught in a barbed wire tangle of bad feelings. They both look to me for some kind of redeeming response.

My heart goes out to both of them. I remember a time when I couldn't respond to Kate's shy attempt at a sexy overture. It hurt her terribly and it took a long time for us to repair the damage.

"It seems that both of you were surprised and hurt and the more you try to explain yourselves to each other, the more you seem to feel attacked. This is the hard part of our work. Opening yourselves up means risking being hurt. Being intimate frequently doesn't feel good and doesn't feel safe. Would you try something that may feel kind of gimmicky and awkward? It may help you reconnect even when you feel battered and bruised. Sex and romance are easy when the feelings are right. The real dilemma for all of us is finding a way of reaching out during times like these. Who is ready to go first?"

"I don't know what we're doing, but I'll do it. What have we got to lose?" Bill says with a shrug.

"Okay. Bill, you turn so that your back is to her and you, Sarah, move over closer to him so that you can massage his shoulders. As she massages your shoulders, Bill, you can allow yourself to feel the warmth and gentle pressures of her fingers kneading at the tension in your shoulders, and you can still be fully concious of your anger and disappointment about what happened. Sarah, I want you to know that as you gently massage him, it is fine for you to continue to feel some of your frustration and defensiveness. You can touch and be touched in a loving way while still being caught in all these rotten feelings."

This exercise works well when I have a strong sense that a couple wants to reconnect but is jammed up by trying to talk about their feelings. As the fox teaches in *The Little Prince,* "Words are the source of misunderstandings." It's essential for couples to learn that they can stay in touch with each other even when they are experiencing angry feelings. This is easy to say but it took Kate and me a couple of decades of trial and error to learn how to stay connected when we were hurt and angry.

Initially, Bill and Sarah seem tense and tentative, but slowly Sarah becomes more absorbed by the effort to give a good massage and Bill seems to be relaxing and enjoying himself. After a few minutes, I ask them to switch places. I give them the same caveat that they simply accept their negative feelings while giving and receiving this touch.

Shortly after Bill begins massaging her shoulders, tears start running down Sarah's cheek.

"Do you want to talk about what's going on?" I ask Sarah as gently as I can.

"I was just remembering my Dad. Sometimes when he was drunk he would get sloppily affectionate and he would want to hug me or give me back rubs."

"Do you want me to stop?" asks Bill.

"No, it feels nice." Sarah breaks down in heavy sobs and leans back against Bill. Amid bursts of tears, she presses on, obviously needing to talk about it. "He'd come into my room at night for what he called 'cuddles' and he would just reek of alcohol. He would hug and touch me. It felt so awful. I just lay there. I turned to stone. It was so horrible. I didn't know what to do. Sometimes, his thing poked at me. It was hard and I didn't even know what it was at first. Oh, God, I can't believe this really happened. Once he sprayed his stuff all over my nightgown. It was disgusting. I never thought I would tell anybody this. I hated him."

She breaks down again. Bill wraps her in his arms and she cries hard for a while.

I feel deeply moved. It's not unusual in this day and age to be dealing with incest issues in therapy, but rarely does someone who has never talked about it have a flashback in a session.

"Take your time, Sarah. You've just said a whole lot. That must have been a terrifying experience."

Sarah sits up and pulls away from Bill a little. She reaches for her purse to find some tissue.

As she daubs her eyes, she looks at me and says almost apologetically, "Well, it's not really incest. He never actually did that much besides rub up against me, and it only happened a few times that I can remember. Anyway, it's twenty years ago. I should have gotten over it by now."

She turns to look at Bill and in a very soft, young voice, she asks, "Are you mad at me?"

"Oh, God, no. I'm not mad. I understand and I love you," Bill says gently. They embrace. I just sit there in silence, watching, feeling the privilege of bearing witness to such a moment. I feel so sad for the young girl who had her childhood torn away from her. It's not a surprise to have her minimize her Dad's behavior and even begin to blame herself. The cruelest damage of incest is that children often blame themselves. They think that they brought it on or should have been able to stop it.

Bill and Sarah break from their embrace. She turns to me and says, "I'm glad this happened; I never thought it would. It hurts, but it feels better."

I smile at her. I watch her reach for Bill's hand.

"Sarah," I say gently, "your courage in letting yourself deal with the the horror and shame you experienced touches me deeply. It will take time for you really to work through this material. But healing is possible for you and the two of you together. I'm really glad that you can let Bill comfort you. You deserve his support."

They smile at each other. After several missteps and awkward moments in our work, the three of us finally seem joined in a common bond. We are like mountain climbers tethered to each other at the waist by our common rope. We are taking turns being strong and steadying the rope for each other as we practice climbing the face of the cliff, one step at a time. Today was Sarah's turn, but Bill's time will come. And I am being challenged right along with them. Guides have to climb the cliffs, too.

On the way over to Barbara's, my mind's darting about like a bird trapped inside a small, dark attic. I'm agitatedly debating what to talk about. The session with Bill and Sarah has me all stirred up. In an odd way, I feel jealous of them and what they were able to accomplish today. But something about Sarah's stuff about her Dad really got to me.

Suddenly I remember my mother's coming into my room late at night to tell me to go to bed. I was about thirteen. I was working out with my weights, and I was only wearing a jockstrap. I stopped when I saw her and went to cover myself. She said, "Don't stop, let me watch you exercise. I can't believe how much you've grown." She stood in the doorway. I felt her eyes on my crotch. I did some arm curls and tried to ignore her and my growing erection. I felt horrified and thrilled at the same time.

Christ, I hadn't thought about this in years. That was the same damn year she gave me bikini briefs for Christmas and suggested that I model them for her. And I did. I paraded in front of her like a fashion model. I was just Michael's age.

As Barbara sits down, I pour out a torrent of words. I tell her about Bill and Sarah and how moved I was. But I skip over the connection I made to my mother's inappropriate interest in my body. In my mind, it's easy to dismiss that brief episode compared to what happened to Sarah. Then I jump to talking about not being there enough for Michael when he was little.

"That little boy that I could cuddle in my lap is gone, Barbara. I'll never hold him in my arms again. This hulking thirteen-year-old is like a different kid."

"The little boy is still inside your growing son. He still needs you, just like there is a little boy inside of you who still needs you."

Her comment reminds me of my dream. I recount every detail of seeing my brother and sister talking to my mother with me standing far away and only being able to see her lower legs.

"But the amazing thing is, they really were her legs. I recognized the shape of her calves, her ankles, and even the black flats. It was her. I felt so eager to see her and was bitterly disappointed that I couldn't see any other part of her. I feel this way about my whole past. I can't see anything. All I have is a smattering of memories that don't mean much to me, but it's particularly true about my mother. She's not there. She never existed. I don't even remember her birthday or the day she died. It's time I let myself remember this woman. I've been numb for so long. I wish I really felt something about her. I don't care what."

"Yet you said you woke up crying from your dream. You were feeling something then."

"It was strange. Mostly I was just missing her." I pause and look down at the floor. Suddenly my emotional intensity just disappears. I smile at Barbara and wisecrack, "Trust me, this was unusual. I don't normally do grief. Missing dead parents is Kate's department.

"Kidding aside, Barbara, the feelings just evaporate. I get close, but I can't stay in them. It's such classically male behavior. You know, 'Big boys don't cry' and all that nonsense. The only time I remember crying about my mother was when I was writing the epilogue of my book and that came as a complete shock to me.

"You've got a copy of it over there. May I look at it? I'll read you what hit me so hard."

Barbara goes to her bookshelf. She quickly locates my book and hands it to me. I feel myself tensing up. I turn to the last page. "It's the very last paragraph. It just came out of me. Here it is:

"Well, Mom, the book's done. It's called *Before It's Too Late*. I wish you could read it. Actually I don't care that much about you reading the book. I just wish you were here."

My eyes fill up with tears. Then I'm sobbing, my head in my hands. I feel so sad and so little. I don't say anything for a long time. Finally, I am able to reach for the tissue box and wipe my face. I smile at Barbara, who is leaning forward in her chair.

"I don't know where these came from. I only cry at movies," I joke.

"Maybe it's time for your tears," Barbara replies softly.

When I try to describe how powerful the session was to Kate, it sounds like melodramatic psychobabble. I'm back inside the prison of my words.

"I read the last paragraph from my book to her and bawled."

"She must have been surprised to see you cry."

"I doubt it. I suspect she knew it was coming. It probably surprised her that it came out of reading from my book. I'll bet that was unusual. Somehow my emotions weren't blocked when I read out loud."

I paused. For years, I've been able to rattle on about my mother and my family's story as if I were reviewing a case study. But writing the story and then reading it out loud might bypass my automatic dissociation.

"That's it, Kate. I think I just figured out how to work on this stuff. I'm going to write about it."

"About what?"

"About my family, my childhood, but mostly about my mother. I don't even know the woman. Maybe that's the way I can get back some of my feelings and memories. In fact, I'll try to get everyone else in the family to do some writing, too. Dad's already done most of his biography of Mom, even though I haven't really read it. Lauris has been writing about her for years. I'll see what I can get Jon and Jim to crank out. Maybe their memories will help me find some of my own."

I toss and turn long after Kate's sound asleep. I'm excited about this writing project. It hits much closer to home than my original idea of keeping a journal about sailing to New Zealand. I'm too pumped up to sleep. Maybe I'll start by reading a little of Dad's biography, which is buried in my office closet. I put on my robe and head downstairs. It's almost midnight. I tiptoe through the pitch-black kitchen trying not to wake up the dog.

As I pick up Dad's manuscript, I see underneath it an old medical record. I'd managed to forget I even had this. It's a copy of my mother's records from her various admissions at Massachusetts General. Kate got them years ago, when she was an intern, because she was curious about whether my mother ever really had a chance for recovery after she overdosed. I had only glanced through them at the time. Then I promptly forgot them. I put down Dad's biography and pick up the charts.

Name: Treadway, Martha C.
Address: 22 W. Cedar St.
      Boston, Ma.

5-21-63

The 1st MGH admission of this 45 y.o. married white female, mother of 4.

Patient's presenting complaint: "I'm just trying to escape."

Assessment: The patient has been in fairly good health all her life and has entered the hospital now for a number of reasons. She has been very upset over the winter about moving from the family home and trying to set up some new hotels (husband's business is the "Treadway Inns").

Off and on Mrs. Treadway has had a host of vague physical complaints and has consistently sought medical workups which have always tested negative for physical symptoms. She reports some diarrhea over the winter which she attributes to tension, "lost my nerves, am drinking too much, etc." She acknowledges a real concern about her use of alcohol and reports that she drinks upwards to eight "hotel sized" drinks daily.

This patient is a very tense individual who says that her "perfectionism" causes an undue amount of distress and contributes to her abuse of alcohol. Fundamentally, she keeps a sound body by a lot of tennis and other sports, but she persists in obsessive worries about her health. She also expresses particular tension about never having any time for herself. She's an accomplished painter, but feels thwarted most of the time because she cannot get any freedom from assorted duties. She describes her duties as "Particularly burdensome due to my notion that everything I do has to be just right."

The second admission was in June 1965.

Fundamentally about as detailed in 5/21/63 note. A highly sensitive perfectionist who has constant emotional distress both on the basis of family problems and her own inherent difficulties.

The main complaint is aching of the legs. Patient reports intense discomfort in her legs that can only be temporarily relieved by hot baths and constant motion. There are no physical or neurological indicators. The syndrome of "restless legs" is mostly seen in patients with acute emotional problems. Mrs. Treadway would seem to fit this category, I am afraid.

During the physical exam, Mrs. Treadway repeatedly massaged her legs. She could not lie still, as her legs were constantly in motion. She apologized profusely for being a "bother" and the "messy" hospital bed.

There's much more, but I have to stop. My eyes are blurred with tears. Who was this poor woman? She sounds so pathetic. I didn't know her at all. I reach for the tissues that I always have in my office for my clients. As I wipe my cheek, I remember Kate's crack about my "borrowed tears." These tears aren't my clients' anymore. These tears are mine.

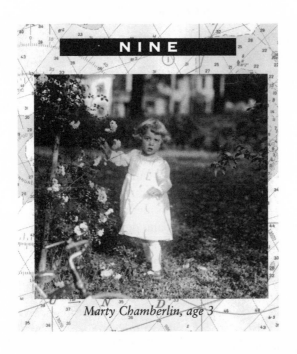

NINE

Marty Chamberlin, age 3

FEY

March 1991

I'M LATE FOR MY LUNCH WITH AUNT JANE AND I CAN'T GET Cindy out of my office. At the end of the hour, she's collapsed like a rag doll. Suddenly she sits bolt upright and looks me straight in the eye. Her face is streaked with tears and eyeliner. She gives me a hard bitter smile.

"I know it's late. I've used up my rented hour and I'm sure you have more important things to do. I'll get out of your way."

I'm torn. I feel like saying, "You're right, I do have better things to do." Yet I ache for her. She needs to keep testing my commitment and caring because she feels so scared and so alone. I try to find an authentic middle ground. I lean toward her and say gently, "Yes, it is late and time to end, but I am here and I'm not going to quit on you. I have other things I have to do, but none more important."

"You get an A for effort, Doc," she wisecracks with a flash of the sardonic humor that I haven't seen in months. She blows her nose, pulls herself together, and gets up to leave. "I don't know what's the matter with you. I would have quit on me a long time ago. You're some kind of nut."

"It takes one to know one," I tease her back. We made it through another one. Working with her is like riding out a night storm at sea. Wave after wave crashes down on the boat as we slog our way to windward. Sometimes her despair breaks over both of us. We feel swamped and dead in the water. But then we shake it off, the wind fills the sails again, and we shoulder into the next wave, pressing on into the blackness.

Speeding down Route 128 toward the Pillar House, I can't get Cindy out of my mind. I don't know whether she's going to make it. I'm scared. I finally talked to some colleagues about it and they were reassuring, but I've lost my confidence. One of the odd consequences of my therapy with Barbara is that the more vulnerable I become the less sure I am in my work. Being in the patient role makes me appreciate differently how raw and needy some of my clients are. Sometimes I catch myself desperately needing Barbara's reassurance just as Cindy needs it from me. I feel the weight of Cindy's heart in my hands.

What was it like for my mother's therapist? Dad called her on that last day. He told her that Mom seemed even more depressed than usual. Apparently, her doctor reassured him that she had an appointment with Mom for the following day. At the time of the call, Mom was lying in a coma, dying.

As I pull into the Pillar House parking lot, I notice how much the white clapboard colonial building reminds me of the Publick House, the inn my parents bought and ran during our years in Sturbridge. I suspect I picked this place more for nostalgia than for convenience.

For weeks, the therapy with Barbara has felt stalled as I've talked about working on connecting more emotionally to my mother by interviewing family members and going over their journals. I've slipped back to talking about emotions rather than feeling them. Barbara's been patient and persistently defused my repetitious self-criticism.

As usual, the February anniversary of my mother's death would have come and gone unnoticed except for my sister's phone call. Lauris never forgets. She cried about how much she misses Mom and I tried to be gentle and supporting. This year, she asked me directly whether I miss Mom. Normally I would dodge a question like that, but I decided to tell her the simple truth. "I don't miss her. I wish I did. I'm trying to learn how."

This lunch today is a big first step.

Jane flashes me a broad smile as I walk in the door. She's a bubbly youthful sixty-five-year-old with a twenties-style bob of blond hair only slightly streaked with gray. She swallows me up in a hug and says, "Oh, dearie, I promised myself I wouldn't cry, but I'm so happy you wanted to talk about your Mom. She was such a star. She lit up my life. I miss her every day. She was the best friend I ever had." Then she burst into tears.

In years past, I would have become instantly annoyed with Jane's blubbering and regretted the whole idea, but I find myself hugging her back. I still have no idea what made my mother so special to her.

The restaurant is filled with fashionable suburban ladies. As I follow Jane to our table, I imagine how natural it would have been for my mother and Jane to be having this lunch.

"Of course, I'm biased," Jane admits; "I completely adored your mother. She was the most glamorous, beautiful woman I've ever known. She and your father together were such a dashing couple. They took Boston by storm. Their dinner parties were the talk of the town. She was the only hostess who ever seduced Tom Lehrer into playing for the fun of it at a private party. She crowded all those proper Bostonians into that basement room around the piano and led us in a whooping chorus of 'Be Prepared: It's the Boy Scout Marching Song.' We laughed and played til dawn. Your mother hung the moon. She was so fey."

"What do you mean by 'fey'?" I ask.

"Oh, you know, she was an artiste. She had flair, but she wasn't at all self-centered. She had the knack of making everyone feel special. When she talked to you, she made you feel like you were the center of the universe.

"Since I was eight years younger, Marty was almost a big sister and mother to me wrapped up into one. She tutored me in the art of becoming stylish. She had such an eye for color that she always looked dramatically original. Of course, your mother was such a perfectionist that she ruined Lauris, but her criticism always helped me. She wasn't simply 'in' fashion. She 'was' fashion. Lauris could never keep up with that."

"What happened with Lauris?"

"Poor Lauris couldn't quite get it right. Your mother had a sharp eye and was always trying to improve Lauris. It must have been hard being the only girl. I'm sure Marty didn't fuss over you boys."

I can't imagine my mother fussing over any of us. But it sounds like getting her attention was no prize. I catch myself being put off by Jane's adulation.

"What was it like with her in the last few years when she was really falling apart?"

"None of us knew. I was her best friend, and she didn't utter a peep of complaint except when she went into the hospital for her stomach ailments. Your mother was as tough as nails and always wore a smile. We didn't have a clue how desperately unhappy she must have been."

Jane daubed at her eyes with her napkin. "I'm still in a state of shock. I miss her so much."

I avoid eye contact and look down at my plateful of food. I can't eat.

I summon up my warmest smile. "I'm so glad you're willing to talk about this. What about Dad? Did he really understand what kind of shape she was in?"

"Well, your father, God bless him, tried so hard to protect your mother. He completely covered up for her. He never told anyone but me about her little experiment with an overdose the summer before because he didn't want to embarrass her. It's the same reason why he didn't call anybody while she was in the coma. He didn't want anyone to know so that she wouldn't be humiliated if she came out of it."

"I think those days alone with her on the respirator was what drove him around the bend. It was so awful. He was in trouble the day after she died. He told me he saw her picture in the travel section of the *Globe*. There was a photo of the backs of two women in bathing suits walking the beach in Antigua. Your father showed it to me and announced happily, 'There she is. I knew this was all a mistake. I'd recognize her rear end anywhere.'" Jane begins to weep again.

"Janie, it's okay, we don't have to go over everything today."

"No, I want to. Don't mind my tears. I've never talked about your father to any of you because I didn't want you to be ashamed of him. His mind just snapped like a toothpick. A few days after the funeral, he went competely gaga. He thought he was the Messiah and tried to heal everyone he could put his hands on, even the taxicab driver on the way to the hospital. When we arrived, he tried to bless the psychiatrist. Needless to say, it wasn't difficult to get him admitted."

Jane stifled a chuckle. "I don't mean to laugh. But it was all so bizarre. I remember it like it was yesterday."

I flash on my first visit to Mclean Hospital. I took Dad to lunch at this same damn restaurant twenty-five years ago. I had completely forgotten.

My father had been in the hospital for a week. They had knocked the delusion out of him with drugs, but he was still manic. They signed him out to my care for two hours. Right after we sat down, Dad cornered the poor waitress.

"This is my son David. He's up from Philadelphia to visit me because I'm in the mental hospital. I've had a nervous breakdown, you know, because my wife, Martha, committed suicide. But they've let me come to your beautiful establishment because my son is here and he's watching over me. You remind me of my dear wife in her youth. I'm sure she would have liked you. Martha worked with the waitresses back at the Publick House when we first started out. You've heard of the Treadway Inns—"

Dad prattled on. He even told his story to people sitting next to us. I shriveled. The lunch lasted forever.

"Would you order me some coffee, Jane? I need to use the

head." I beat a hasty retreat. Now I've got a taste of why I've been avoiding all this. I feel like throwing up.

Returning with a little more composure, I ask her what she remembers about me back then.

"I always lumped you and Jimmy together as if you were twins. You both seemed to have everything going for you: terrific private schools and a great social life. And you were such handsome boys. You were perfect at the funeral. I remember you at Trinity Church all dressed up in your suits. I was so proud of you."

"Part of the reason why I wanted to talk with you is that I barely remember that time. Do you have any sense as to how I handled it during those days?"

"You seemed so self-contained, like you didn't really want or need anyone else. I felt much closer to Jon and Lauris. You seemed very much in your own orbit, not quite in the 'cuddle.' "

"What do you mean by the 'cuddle'?"

Jane's eyes filled. "Oh, here I go again. You don't remember. It was one of your mother's favorite expressions. Being in her inner circle meant that you were part of the 'cuddle.' I remember when I went off to Austria to work, your mother said to me these parting words: 'Now, Jane, dearie, I am giving you a part of me just like it's a baker's yeast, so that when you get there you'll have a piece of the cuddle and you'll be able to make your own.' "

Mercifully the lunch draws to a close. I leave Jane with a bouquet of gratitude and a big hug. I'm as shell shocked as I was at my mother's funeral. The handsome boy in the grown-up suit, not quite part of the "cuddle."

I'm late getting back for my appointment with Bill and Sarah. They're doing well and I always enjoy my hour with them. Their therapy is almost complete. We never did much work on Bill's relationship with his mother. But they seem to be doing fine anyway. It makes me wonder all over again whether I really need to do this grieving work. My mother's been dead for a long time.

I smile at myself. I know why I'm backpedaling from dealing with my mother. The lunch with Jane shook me. Jane's face lit up while she talked about Mom. But for me her glowing anecdotes about the charming and charismatic Martha Treadway may as well have been about a stranger.

Bill and Sarah are already in the waiting room as I race into the house. But I'm not ready to switch gears. I'm still lost in thoughts about the luncheon. I can't believe the possibility that Mom "experimented" with an overdose and nobody did anything. I'm going to have to ask Dad about that. And what the hell did Jane mean by fey? My Random House dictionary gives me some chilling definitions.

Fey: 1) Doomed, fated to die. 2) An apprehension of death calamity, or evil. 3) Supernatural, unreal, enchanted. 4) Being in unnaturally high spirits as were formerly thought to precede death. 5) Whimsical, strange, otherworldly.

TEN

Marty Chamberlin, age 16

THE SNOW ANGEL

SATURDAY. I'M BUNDLED UP IN A PARKA, SKI HAT, AND GLOVES. There are some tiny green shoots in our garden that suggest spring is on the way, but winter has not relinquished its hold. Despite the beckoning sun and the bright blue sky, there's a brisk cold northwest wind.

"Where are you going?" asks Kate as she checks out my winter garb.

"I'm headed out to the porch to finally start reading my family's stuff. I have Dad's, Lauris's, and Jim's writing about Mom."

"Why are you going outside? It's freezing."

"I need to be alone. Besides the air has a hint of spring to it. It feels like going out to my backyard in Sturbridge when I was a kid."

I pick up the old family albums first. There we all are: Martha and Dick Treadway and the four children, Jon, Lauris, David, and Jim. We seem to be happy and carefree, an all-American family. Dad used a family picture in his successful campaign for the State Senate. We were also one of the early families who used a family picture for Christmas cards. We even posed for a *Look* magazine photo spread on Thanksgiving. They dressed us up in Puritan garb and we were seated around a table laden with a turkey and other food. They had us piously sitting with our hands folded and our heads bowed: very Norman Rockwell.

Pictures conceal as much as they reveal. There's nothing in these bright sunshiny faces that gives any hint of the gathering shadows that lead to the shattering of this family.

I put down the album. There's no meaningful epiphany. It could have been anyone's family album.

I pick up Dad's biography of Mom first and begin to read.

Dad

In 1957, I was elected to the Speckled Band, which meets annually to celebrate the memory of our Master, Sherlock Holmes. In toasting him, Douglas Lawson said, "For three hundred and sixty four days and eighteen hours, we live in a world of unreality, but for these next six shining hours, we live in the real world, the world of Sherlock Holmes."

Why do I start a biography of my late wife with a reference to the author of elaborate mysteries? The reason is simple. For those of us who loved her, the death of this beautiful person will always be a mystery. To coin the cliché, "she had so much going for her." She was so gifted and so loved.

In sorting out the pieces of this puzzle, I realize that my approach is more emotional than intellectual. I am acutely aware of the unhealed and still painful bruises that I haven't been able to sublimate or finally cure some 25 years later.

I am indebted to my children, Jon, Lauris, David, and Jim who have contributed personalized anecdotes and insight to this biography. These loved ones, who knew her best, all remember a strong and quite remarkable woman. They were as mystified as was I when she committed suicide.

Dad is surprising me. His frank acknowledgment of his wounds and his mystification about Mom's suicide are touching. Blaming Dad for it all has been a cheap emotional trick that I've indulged in for years, but it's time to stop holding him at arm's length by picking at his flaws. I just want to get to know his story.

Dad

Martha was the family star. Not only extremely bright in school, she excelled as a gifted artist and avid skier. I would guess that Martha was one of the 10 best women skiers in New England. She even decided to include ski jumping in her repertoire. With considerable courage, she went off the Dartmouth jump, landed on the back of her skis, and cracked her head on the ground. She had to have fluid and blood drained from her cranium. A subdural hemorrhage gave her dreadful headaches.

This sobered her, and thereafter she lost some of her ebullient joie de vivre. Subsequent doctors speculated that this accident and the metal plate they had to use in her skull may have been a contributing cause to her recurring depressions. I do know the headaches were in existence when we got married, soon after Martha turned 19. But I was shocked when my mother said to me, "Isn't it a pity, Dick, that you're going to marry a semiinvalid?" Little did she know what a marvelously energetic woman I was about to acquire."

The idea that Dad was going to "acquire" a wife is striking and so's his mother's "pity."

Times have certainly changed. I pick up the photo album and here is an ancient picture of Mom on skis. She looks about sixteen. She's bundled up in bulky clothes with a wool watch cap pulled down over her forehead. With a broad infectious smile and big brown eyes, she appears to be flirting with the camera. I'll bet it wasn't one of her parents snapping the picture.

Skiing in the thirties was an unusual adventure. No lifts, no trails, just put the long heavy wooden skis on your shoulder and slog up the hill. The leather boots would freeze. The woolen clothes would become soaked and cold. It was not a "girl" sport. Ski jumping would have been the most daring and adventurous activity of all. What did she feel like going down the runway? Was she terrified? Or was she grinning with an "I'll show you guys" exuberance?

She taught us all to ski when we were practically still babies. We loved it. Suddenly I can remember the backyard in Sturbridge. Mom held us between her legs on our tiny toothpick skis and we would swoosh down the little slope and fall with a great crash in the snow. It was how she taught us that falling was fun and certainly nothing to be afraid of. I remember those great plops in the snow greeted with hoots of laughter by all. I wasn't ever afraid. It was fun to fall, cradled in her arms.

Finally, the first blush of dawn after a cold night at sea. My Mom's arms around me. I'm beginning to feel her.

Dad

Martha was 5'3 and ½" with a slim figure and big luminous brown eyes. Many years later, her painting mentor and friend, John Follensbee, remembered saying to her, "Marty, you have a three-point look. You look at me, look down, and look away. It is quite coquettish and captivating. Yet, I have spent many a night wondering what you really are thinking. I suspect that no one will ever know."

I was attracted to her by her innovative sense of humor, her ability to laugh at herself, and her ebullient personality. To put it simply, she was fun.

We spent that spring getting further acquainted and imperceptibly, but forcefully, falling in love. Each day in the bucolic town of Hanover followed one another in an unbroken chain of joy and beauty. I felt that I was the luckiest man in the world, which I suspect is not an uncommon feeling for someone in love.

May 8, 1937, was a corker of day. We were married in the austerely white Dartmouth chapel by Martha's father who was the school's chaplain. A good bit of the leadership of the college was there, including President Hopkins, which certainly made the bride and groom swell with a sense of importance. The floral arrangements in the church showed the mark of Martha's artistic background. Allowing for my natural prejudice, it was without question the most handsome wedding that I ever attended. The truth is we thought we were the cat's meow.

There's a picture of them on their wedding day. Mom looks radiantly beautiful. She wore an unusual, yet elegant lace wedding gown and Dad was tall and strikingly handsome in his dark suit. They seem young, eager, and confident; ready to set forth and conquer the world.

Mom was the talented and beautiful professor's daughter and Dad was the dashing "big man on campus." They were the shining stars of their ambitious families. They appear confident and capable. They must have assumed they were embarking on a life of adventure and success.

Dad is seventy-eight years old now and living in Florida with his third wife. He married an old family friend only nine months after Mom died. Then ten years later, after that relationship didn't work out, he married again. The wedding that he so lovingly describes took place fifty-four years ago. Mom killed herself in 1966.

For years, Dad has worried about his terrible memory. Yet, these moments from long ago seem as alive and vivid as a bouquet of freshly picked flowers. I'm beginning to understand his need to write Mom's story. He just wanted to hold her one more time.

But I still can't get a sense of my parents as people. It all seems too charming and easy. I decide to go inside and call up Mom's brother, Roy. We used to call him Uncle Tiger. He was a minister like his father. Tiger had an infectious gentle smile and he always made me feel I mattered. My first cruise on a sailboat was with Tiger and my grandfather. We sailed down east to Boothbay, Maine. Tiger made sure that I had some significant work to do, so that I would feel like a full-fledged crew member, and not just a kid.

Thinking about Tiger reminds me of Pop. I haven't thought about my Mom's dad for almost two decades. He was tough. I can see him with pipe in hand wearing his sailing hat with the broad plastic visor. He had a craggy face that looked like the weathered granite rocks of Maine. It was a hard face, but capable of breaking open into a broad smile when he was pleased with you. I remember him at the tiller of our 18-foot Cape Cod Knockabout, the *Dart*. His eyes were always fixed on the jib as he worked the boat up to windward. If we were about to make a maneuver, I'd be perched nervously amidships with the jib sheets in hand. Pop did not suffer fools gladly. I'd carefully review the steps he taught me so that I wouldn't screw up when he called, "Ready about! Hardalee."

I wonder whether Mom was ever frightened of Pop. Both Tiger and Dad report that Mom was always his favorite. Although he was a stern taskmaster with his two sons, he tended to let his beautiful, spirited daughter get away with murder. I wonder how much of her virulent perfectionism developed in response to her being undeservedly indulged. Perhaps she felt unworthy of his special treatment or maybe she identified more with his own self-critical bent.

My grandparents lived with us in the summers for most of our childhood. They were both very close to my mother and father. But the special bond was between Pop and my Mom. For years they took painting classes together, critiqued each other's work, and helped each other prepare canvases and frames.

How did Pop feel the day Dad called him and said, "Skipper, Martha died this afternoon; she took an overdose of pills; there was nothing the doctors could do"?

That proud old man. He died a year later.

I haven't seen Uncle Tiger for years and I've never talked with him about my mother. He's surprised but seems pleased to chat about her. He describes his younger sister as being hell on wheels: a completely ebullient, devil-may-care little girl.

"How about as a teenager, was she boy crazy or rebellious?" I ask him.

"Well, during her early teens Marty was sort of taken up by

Rollie Stevens. He was a young medical student who came to live with us when Martha was about ten or eleven and he fell passionately in love with her. In fact, he proposed marriage to her when she was thirteen."

"You're kidding. What did your parents think of that?"

"Well, everybody loved Rollie and treated him like he was one of the family. I think my folks thought that he and Martha would just grow out of this romantic entanglement in due time."

"It must have been hard for her to manage the romantic attentions of a twenty-year-old when she was just going through puberty."

"I don't think anyone was particularly worried at the time. She was beautiful and always attracting wolf whistles from the Dartmouth boys. She seemed to like it."

Tiger seems so casual in dismissing the impact on a little girl of this intense romantic connection with a grown man living in her house. I shudder to think what might have really happened.

"You know, David, I remember one story that I'll never forget. Marty must have been ten or eleven. It was late one winter afternoon; we had been building forts all day. The light was beginning to dwindle and it was getting cold when she decided to make a snow angel. Marty was bundled up in a baby blue snowsuit and a bright blue wool cap pulled down over her ears. She was cute as a button. I can still see her falling back on the snow spread-eagled and then sweeping her arms up and down to make the wings. When she got up, she reviewed her efforts. She was dissatisfied. The snow had been too hard for her to leave much of an impression. I remember Dad calling us in, but Marty was stubborn. She wanted to make a perfect snow angel, so she just stayed out there well past dark looking for the right patch of snow.

Next morning, she proudly displayed twenty or so snow angels dotted around the yard. She marched me over to the big pine tree. 'And this one here,' she said triumphantly, pointing to the silhouette in the snow, 'is perfect!' "

Just then, my younger son, Sam, marches into the room and interrupts, "Watcha doin', Dad?"

"I'm on the phone," putting my hand over the receiver.

"Mom had to go out. I'm bored." He holds up a football. "Can we play catch?"

"When I finish this call." I know I won't be able to stall Sam long enough to get into Tiger's reflections about Mom as an adult, so I arrange to talk another time.

I bundle Sam up in his parka and a ski cap because it's still quite cold, a little early for football. But Sam's excited about it. Last fall we played a lot of catch and he even began to learn some pass patterns as we pretended our little backyard was a football field.

We head out back. On the way I stop at my chair to resecure Dad's manuscript.

"What is that?" asks Sam.

"It's a book about my Mom that your Granddad wrote."

"Did he know your Mom?" Sam asks innocently.

"Of course, he did," I say with bemusement. His question shouldn't surprise me. It's not Sam's fault that I never talk about my mother and we hardly ever see my father and my stepmother.

"Granddad used to be married to my Mom, who died a long time ago."

"Why did she die?"

What do you tell a six-and-a-half-year-old? How did the proud little girl lying on her back and sweeping her arms in the snow become the limp woman with the tube shoved down her throat and air being pumped into her lungs?

"My Mom had a mental illness that caused her to think that everyone would be better off if she weren't around anymore. So she decided to take her life."

"Was she right?"

"Right about what?"

"Was everybody better off?"

"No, Sam, that's what's so sad. It was her illness that made her think that. She was totally wrong. It was terrible for all of us. I still miss her."

"Did you cry like Mom did when Franmother died?"

"Well, ah, no. I was too shocked. Hey, look, you still want to runs some plays?"

"Sure."

"You remember the little slant pattern that we did last year. Let's do it. Hut one. Hut two. Hike."

Sam tears downfield. I loft the ball. He catches it on a dead run and cradles it in his arms.

"Touchdown!" he shouts as he crosses our imaginary goal line.

Perfect pass. Perfect catch.

ELEVEN

*Family publicity photo in
Sturbridge, 1951*

HAPPINESS PILLS

April 1991

THE COFFEE'S HOT. THE KIDS ARE GONE. I'VE STOLEN THE NEXT
two mornings from my clients. I'm ready to plunge deeper into
the Treadway story. I don't remember anything about the Sturbridge years and yet everyone in my family talks as if those times
were our golden era, the Treadways' version of Camelot.

Dad
In 1946, Martha was 28 years old, handsome and confident, as she faced the challenge of a new hotel and a new community. We moved to Sturbridge, Mass., and bought the Publick House, an old tavern that had originally been built in
colonial times.

Throughout the late '40s, Martha developed her leadership role in the management of the Treadway Inns. After all, she had good taste, considerable experience as a decorator, and a fine sense of public relations. She even hired a cosmetic consultant to show our waitresses how to make themselves more attractive. Martha was always careful of appearances.

On the domestic front, we bought a stunning nine-room house on the top of Fisk Hill. The property was originally built in 1786 with an attractive barn and extensive pastures. I remember carrying Martha over the threshold the day we moved in. She was holding her purse as well as baby David when I swooped her up. She screamed to be put down, but I knew she really liked it. Of course, Jon and Lauris were properly mortified by our childish exuberance.

My daughter Lauris seems to have the most memories of Martha during those glorious Sturbridge years. She said, "Mom's playfully free spirit led us into games and fun beyond our wildest dreams. Later she would lead us over the furniture and under anything in the house, no holds barred. Barefoot and with abandon we followed our leader, laughing, giggling, tickling, tripping, falling; all fun!"

Martha was unquestionably one of the most creative or imaginative persons that I or my four children had ever known. When they were very little, Lauris recalls them all sitting around the kitchen table and gambling their pennies on a betting pool called "when will Daddy come home?" Martha's playful sense of imagination inspired the children. Lauris also tells the story of her putting some of her M&Ms into a bottle and calling them "Happiness Pills," which she sweetly offered when Martha had an episode of the "Sads." But, I'm getting ahead of my story, as the Sturbridge years were pretty much depression free for Martha.

Games of "when will Daddy come home?"; Lauris's giving Mom "happiness pills"? It's hard to read this without wondering about the magnitude of Dad's denial. What was Mom's case of the "Sads" all about?

Dad

Our time in Sturbridge were also financially worry-free years. Martha should have been living a carefree life. Unfortunately, this was not the case, as she worried unduly about a number of things. Martha was a perfectionist and rarely did things happen with the meticulousness that she expected. She could be completely undone by a soup being slightly over-salted for a dinner party. So, despite her outward show of confidence, she had a great deal of anxiety and insecurity. Unlike most of our swell Sturbridge friends, we weren't born with proverbial silver spoons in our mouths. It was as if she always felt she had something to prove.

Also, Martha was intensely self-critical. Nothing she did was ever good enough. She was horrified when she accidentally dropped a hot ash from her cigarette on David's cheek. She decided to quit smoking on the spot. I applauded her commitment, but, having never smoked, I had no idea what a tremendous and difficult decision this would turn out to be.

One afternoon, Martha broke six weeks of abstinence by smoking a cigarette in the car. I grabbed it from her mouth and threw it out the window. If I had not been driving, she would have tried to physically beat me up. She sobbed the rest of the way home. For the first time I began to understand the breadth and depth of a truly addictive personality. In retrospect, it casts some light on her later addictions.

So this is Dad's analysis of Mom. He seems to be looking for an explanation for Mom's difficulties that is buried deeply in her personality, far removed from any possibility that he had any role in her subsequent downfall. He ignores the implications of his grabbing her cigarette and throwing it out the window.

Damn, I can be so smugly judgmental. Dad has filleted his soul with guilt over his role in Mom's demise. I ought to be able to give the poor bastard a break.

But blaming is so easy. My knowledge of how frequently families turn on each other after a suicide doesn't prevent the typical response. My need to point the finger, to assign blame, is compelling. Am I trying to deflect my anger from being directed at the pathetic broken soul who crawled into her bed that last time? Or is it just a self-serving side step from my own guilt?

> *Dad*
> During these Sturbridge years, I would describe Martha as a heavy, enthusiastic party drinker, about average for our contemporaries, and would have been surprised if anyone had raised any questions about it. We were basically quite confident in ourselves and our lives. Our only real concern was about our eldest son, Jon, who seemed to be an overly aggressive and anxious boy. Martha was frequently critical of my laissez-faire approach to discipline. She was very frustrated that it was hard for me to summon much enthusiasm for spanking Jon when I got home at the end of a long day.
> The school finally convinced us to take Jon to a therapist because he seemed to have such difficulty socially and academically. The therapist said to us bluntly, "Your son's not the problem, I need to be meeting with the two of you." His proposal came as a shock and we declined the doctor's invitation as gracefully as possible.

That psychiatrist made a classic mistake. "Imagine bringing your child to a therapist," I always ask my trainees. "How would you feel if some shrink you just met decided that your kid wasn't the problem? You're the ones with the problem! Always accept the couple's initial focus on the child's difficulties; mobilize the parents around learning how to help their child more effectively. Build on the parents' strengths rather than expose their weaknesses. Just being in your office is stigma enough. Put yourself in their shoes."

The clarity of twenty-twenty hindsight. Jon needed help. My parents cared enough to take him to therapy. Maybe they could have actually learned how to work together differently if they had been engaged in helping Jon rather than being blamed for his problems.

Supposedly Jon and Mom were always fighting. When he was around, Dad would either ignore them or step in as the peacekeeper. Undoubtedly, Mom felt undercut by Dad's treating her and Jon like squabbling siblings. Maybe she was expressing some of her resentment of Dad's career and venting her anger on Jon. Maybe Dad was covertly supporting Jon because he was afraid to tangle with Mom directly. Dad's always been a conflict avoider. The possibilities are endless. Could they have been helped? They knew enough to see that Jon needed help. They wanted to be good parents. It sounds like a garden variety family therapy case.

I look around my office and think of all the families like mine that have paraded in here. After all, my first book, *Before It's Too Late,* was devoted to the principle that you can help this kind of family before catastrophe hits. If I had been the therapist, could I have helped the Treadway family? Would I have been able to spot Mom's depression? What if the new happiness pills, Prozac and Paxil, had been available instead of just bourbon and Valium? Maybe she'd be alive today.

Out the window, I catch a glimpse of the sun in the trees and remember the last line of Hemingway's *The Sun Also Rises,* Jake Barnes's harsh response to Brett's belief that maybe it all could have worked out fine: "Isn't it pretty to think so?"

I say it out loud and taste the bitterness.

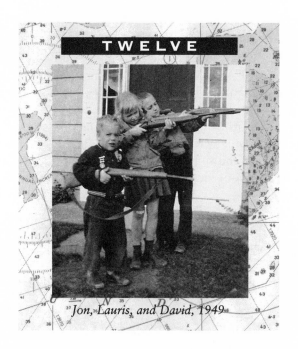

TWELVE

Jon, Lauris, and David, 1949

THE FISK HILL CAVALRY

YESTERDAY'S SHARP SLICE OF "IF ONLY" STILL HURTS. AND YET I'd rather have this heartburn than the dull numbness that I've been wrapped in all these years. I feel an urgency to press on into my mother's story.

This morning I've scheduled a call with my older brother, Jon. He says he's not going to write anything, but he's willing to put in his two cents worth over the phone. Tomorrow I'm going over my younger brother Jim's contribution.

My brothers think I'm slightly nuts to be pursuing this project. In my family, grief has been women's work. Lauris has always played the role of the professional mourner. Yet behind my brothers' bantering facades is a willingness to pitch in for my sake. It's an odd role reversal. I suspect their support has always been there. I've just never asked for it.

Jon lives in Florida now. I don't see him much. I'm nervous about our call. For the last thirty-five years, Jon has been caught in the grip of alcoholism. For a long time, he's been just another family problem to manage. In my role as family shrink, I would advise Dad about how to respond to Jon's drinking. I'd tell him to stand up to Jon and stop bailing him out financially. I would tell him to be more of a disciplinarian just like my mother did. Dad never followed my advice either. But he always asked for it and thanked me profusely. The game doesn't change, just the players.

I used to tolerate Jon. I'd get on the phone with him and he would blather on about his latest "get rich quick" scheme and I would pretend to listen just as I did when my sister was being psychotic. I usually timed the phone calls to coincide with a football game on TV. Often, I managed to slip in a pep talk about the importance of his dealing with his drinking. That's when he politely stopped listening to me. Maybe he had the game on, too.

Just after I started seeing Barbara last fall, I was leading a workshop about alcoholic families. A therapist volunteered to talk about her difficult relationship with her alcoholic brother. She was complaining that he was always in "denial" about his drinking and constantly rebuffed her help. She was frustrated that he was always "resisting" her love and concern.

I gave her my standard message: Maybe it was time that she stopped waiting for him to change, and changed the way she related to him first. I told her to stop acting like his parent and try relating to him more as his younger sister. I suggested that sometimes she should try asking him for advice on her life rather than always telling him how to live his. She looked shocked. "How could you say such a thing?" she challenged. "What would you do if you had an alcoholic brother?"

She stopped me cold. "I do have a brother who is an alcoholic," I said quietly. Then, in front of one hundred and fifty people, I heard myself say, "The truth is that I don't follow my own advice. I either don't deal with him at all or I nag him about his drinking. It's been too painful for me to really to try to relate to him. Maybe it's time I practiced what I preached."

I talked it over with Barbara and decided to radically change how I related to Jon. I forced myself to open up to him about my own life. I talked to him about my struggles rather than lecturing him about his. Much to my surprise, he responded with genuine interest and warmth. I began looking forward to our calls.

Feeling closer to Jon made me heartsick about his slowly slipping further down into the quicksand of alcoholism. Simply ignoring Jon's deterioration seemed like a crime. I knew I didn't want to be at Jon's funeral someday, wondering what I might have said.

I wrote him a letter a couple of months ago.

February 15, 1991

Dear Jon,

Lauris reminded me that we just passed another anniversary of Mom's death and uncharacteristically I found myself trying to pay attention this year. After really being depressed last fall, I've gone into therapy for myself. Naturally, I'm faced with coming to terms with Mom and the history of our family one more time. I hate it. I feel that there still is a black shroud of defeat, disease, and despair that is draped over my life despite my many outward manifestations of success. I was shocked to discover that I even feel guilty about Mom's death.

I feel a similar guilt about not being able to do anything about your slow and painful suicide. It's clear that you're being sucked under by the same disease process that killed Mom and it tortures me that I can't prevent it. Mom's death was a surprise. This time I get to watch. It's just a bowl of laughs.

This is an "I surrender" letter like the ones I tell my clients to write. I love you very deeply and I truly believe that you could recover from your addictions, but I am powerless and I have to surrender on the notion that I can make a difference. Even writing this letter has the quality of one more try to have an impact.

Obviously, you're aware that Dad's the only one who has any real leverage over you and it's clear he doesn't have the strength to threaten you into treatment. He's afraid that you would put a gun to your head if he pushed hard. Since he's wracked with guilt about Mom, the thought of you killing yourself eviscerates him. It scares me too. It even makes me nervous to write this letter and my fear certainly blocks me from letting loose with some of the damn anger I feel about the whole situation.

When you come down to it, there's not much to say.
Jon, I love you. I hope you choose life.
I'll still love you if you don't.
I'll pray for you. Will you pray for me?
Saddle up Joker, I'll get Lady. It's not too late to go for a ride.

> *Love,*
> *Your little brother, David*

Jon never responded to the letter and we've only talked a couple of times since. Yet he agreed to this phone interview about the family. We still haven't mentioned the letter. It makes me nervous about this call. Plus I've never really talked with Jon about our childhood. I don't know if we'll be opening a Pandora's box.

Everyone remembers Jon as an out-of-control tyrant. But I loved him deeply even though he scared me. I was like a pathetic mongrel always ready to greet a swift kick with a wagging tail.

Jon was the dominant child in the family throughout my childhood. He was a scrawny, combative kid. He stood up to Mom, intimidated the babysitters, and cowed Lauris, Jimmy, and me. Perhaps he filled the space left by my Dad's being away so much. It seemed like he was the king of the hill in Sturbridge. I was proud to be in his entourage.

I pick up the phone with some trepidation, but, much to my surprise, Jon seems enthusiastic about talking over the early years.

"The time in Sturbridge were the only good years of my life," Jon says unequivocally.

Jon's fifty-one. He left Sturbridge thirty-eight years ago when he was thirteen: 1953. The blunt acknowledgment of the barrenness of his whole adult life chills me.

"Just tell me about it, Jon, any way you want to."

"For me, the biggest thing was the horses and the barn. It got so the parents never even came into the barn at all. It was my domain. Do you remember the Fisk Hill Cavalry? Me on Joker, you on Lady, and Rory, from down the street, on Starfire. Even Jimmy rode along on his bike."

I wonder whether he remembers I made a reference to our cavalry in my letter. I watch myself switch to another topic. "Anyway, what do you remember about Mom and Dad?"

"Mostly, I remember that they couldn't ever agree about what to do about me. Mom and I would have been fighting all day and when Dad would finally come home late, as usual, she'd want him to punish me. He'd either try and cajole her out of it or go along in a halfhearted way and give me a token scolding. It was almost like there was a conspiracy between Dad and me. It would make her furious."

"What was the main thing that you did?"

"I just about ran the whole show back then because I wasn't afraid of Mom like the rest of you. I was the boss. Mom must have felt sorry for me. I was a disaster at school so she tried to make up for it at home by letting me have my way about stuff. It got to be so that I wouldn't take no for an answer. Besides, I was her first. She always let me know that I was extra special: special joy, special headache."

"Do you remember the hanging incident?"

"You mean when I wanted to try out the noose I had made, and I had you and Jimmy lined up at attention in the barn watching me throw the rope over the rafters? Sure, I remember you panicked when I had you up on the stool with the noose around your neck. You took off and we didn't see you for a long time. You know, I wasn't really going to do anything. I just wanted to see what it looked like."

"It didn't feel that way to me. I ran into the woods and stayed there for hours. Don't you remember calling into the woods and inviting me to come out to play soldiers with you? I could hear you, but I vowed I was never coming back. I don't think I came back until it was dark, and by that time I was more afraid of the woods than I was of you."

"Were you really that scared I would hurt you?"

"I was scared out of my mind." And suddenly I'm there again. It's raining. The woods are wet. As the light fades, the tree trunks look like shadowy cloaked sorcerers. I keep hearing the rustling of leaves and the crack of branches. He's out there. He's going to get me. I want to go home.

Jon breaks into my flashback. "Well, David, this may seem a little belated, but I'm sorry. I didn't mean to frighten you that much."

The sincerity of Jon's voice reaches me. My eyes fill up. For years I have simply dismissed the hanging episode or his shooting me pointblank with a BB gun as standard childhood mishaps. I've never acknowledged to myself how frightened I was.

"Thank's for saying that. Believe it or not, after all these years, it matters a lot to me. More than I knew."

There's an awkward pause and then I jump back into my interviewer role. "Another thing I wanted to check out is that I have a vague memory of chasing after you as you walked down the road toward the Donaldsons' house. You were running away from home after having a big fight with Mom. I was pleading with you not to go. I remember that there had been a big scene at home and that you had threatened Mom with a knife. Is any of that true?"

"Nope. I certainly never attacked her with a knife. I just showed it to her once when we were fighting. And I don't remember you following me when I ran away. I only ran once or twice anyway.

"One time I ran into the woods and they came out looking for me. They kept calling me. Finally I got bored of hiding and circled around and snuck back into the house. I was cold so I took a bath. Boy, were they pissed when they found out. I guess you could say that I wasn't exactly the easiest kid in the world to manage. I'm glad I never had children. I wouldn't want to have me for a kid, that's for sure."

Jon's sharp self-deprecation slices through me. He wasn't such a bad kid. He was a willful, headstrong little boy who felt very insecure in the larger world of school and peers. He fought mightily to be powerful and important at home. "I don't know,

Jon. I think you're being too harsh on yourself. If Mother and Dad had been able to pull together they could have managed you okay. Every kid tries to divide and conquer. It's not your fault that you succeeded. They were the grown-ups."

"I thought you were supposed to be retired, Dr. Treadway."

"Give me a break. I just think you're a little too critical of yourself. You can't take all the credit for screwing up the family. We all contributed. It's not all your fault that you got away with murder back then."

"Maybe not, but it all changed when we moved to Boston and they shipped me off to Governor Dummer. I guess they just didn't know what to do with me. I was about thirteen, and I wanted to stay in Sturbridge so badly that I asked if I could live with another family instead of making the move. They didn't really consider it. I think the worst thing was when they sold the horses without even telling me. That was Dad. He said he didn't want to upset me.

"Once I was at boarding school, I was a complete zero. I never really made Boston my home. It was more like a hotel. I lived out of my suitcase. That's really when I started warming my bones with good old Southern Comfort."

"Were you really only thirteen? That's just Michael's age."

"Well, I was actually fourteen by the time I became a regular drinker. Drinking used to be the only way I could get to sleep back then. I always could handle it though. I'd never really get drunk."

"You know, even after all these years of hearing horror stories about teenage alcoholics, I never really thought about how young you were. You must have felt so lonely and sad."

"Come on, it wasn't really such a big deal. Besides I didn't start drinking up at school during the week until I was fifteen or so."

Jon's cavalier responses cued me that he didn't want to delve into his own adolescent pain. I shifted the subject to lighter terrain. "Do you remember introducing me to bourbon? You poured me a tall glass full; no ice, no water. 'Neat,' you called it. Said it would make a man out of me. I got so drunk I puked my guts out. I must have been about thirteen myself. It was a helluva initiation into manhood."

"I'm sorry I did that. Maybe I just wanted some company down there in my basement apartment at West Cedar Street. Although I never used to mind drinking alone. By that time, Mother had become a pretty good drinking companion anyway."

I glance at the clock. Time's run out. There seems like a lot more than we could talk about. I try to thank him, but he brushes me aside, saying, "It's no big deal."

After the call, it's hard to get Jon's story out of my mind. It must have been devastating for him to lose his home, his horse, his school, and his family when he was shipped off to boarding school. In Sturbridge he was the center of the family universe. Boston never became his home. The bottle did.

And it's truly odd that we managed to have this whole conversation about our childhood and still avoid talking about the damn letter. But that's the slippery dance of mutual avoidance that my family has always practiced. I feel like trying to break the pattern even though I've got clients in the waiting room. I grab the phone.

"Hi, Jon, it's me again."

"Oh, God, why don't you go pick on your patients."

"Seriously, it's high time we cleared the air about that letter I sent you. Even though I meant every word, I didn't want it to be hurtful."

"Hey, don't take offense, little brother, but truth is, I didn't let it bother me much. I figured you were just doing your job."

"My job! That's great. Well, screw you and the horse you rode in on, then."

"Well, at least I could always stay on one."

"That's a goddamn low blow. You're the one that made that stupid pony of mine so mean."

"Hell, no, Lady was a natural born bitch."

We both burst out laughing, probably our first belly laugh together in thirty years. A frozen knot of tension between us seems to loosen. Suddenly we start reminiscing about the bad old days.

"Hey, when was the last time you thought about that trip to

California? You remember screaming along through Nebraska, drunk as skunks, and shooting at road signs?" I say, slipping into my old reprobate role.

"Don't forget, Dr. Treadway, you're the one that shot the last few rounds straight out the window. You could've killed somebody. That wouldn't look too good on your resume."

"Thanks for reminding me. But that was a wild summer, especially after I blew all my money in Reno."

"Yeah, right, I couldn't get you out of there until seven o'clock in the morning."

Our conversation flows for the first time in years. I selfishly let my clients wait. What the hell. The Fisk Hill Cavalry rides again.

Kate's always engaging me in rerooting flowers and bushes in our garden. She digs them up carefully and then finds just the right spot for them. It's my job to dig the new hole, mix in the fertilizer, and do the daily watering. Yesterday's call with Jon still makes me smile. I feel as if we just transplanted our relationship with a load of cow manure and a lot of water.

Today I'm working with Jimmy's letter. He's been very supportive about this project even though he tends to avoid dwelling on the painful parts of our history. He's just the opposite of Lauris, who lives in the anguish of the past. True to being a middle child, I'm divided down the middle. Most of my adult life, I've denied any connection to my past. Nevertheless, just coincidentally, I've spent twenty years helping people resolve their deepest childhood wounds.

Jimmy and I were almost like twins. Just a year and eleven months apart. Today, he is a powerful executive in the hotel industry. He's the one that's carried on the family tradition. He brings a rare blend of intense drive and self-deprecating charm to his work. I remember visting him at one of his hotels and being awed at how well he knew each employee. He has the gift of making everyone who works for him feel important.

Jim took the task of recounting his life in our family to heart. The day after I asked him, he called in his personal secretary and dictated his story for an hour and a half.

Then he called me. "My secretary will mail you my memoirs

about the family. You can do what you want with it, but I don't think it's very good. It was actually pretty upsetting doing it. Do you make your patients dredge this stuff up all the time?"

"No, I don't. Most people choose to leave well enough alone. I'm doing this for me."

"Well, it certainly didn't do wonders for me. I was breezing right along and the next thing I know I'm completely choked up in front of my secretary. By the way, have you gotten the airline tickets yet?"

The conversation quickly moved onto more comfortable terrain for both of us: our next year's ski vacation in Colorado.

I skimmed Jim's letter when it first arrived. I'm looking forward to digging into it.

Jim

This little story is in response to David's asking me to write something about my relationship with our mother. It's interesting how human nature plays tricks with one's memory. I find myself recalling my childhood days vividly, while February 1966 when my mother died is a blur.

Our house in Sturbridge was wonderful. As the youngest member of what ostensibly was a great big, happy family, I enjoyed a tremendous sense of place, and was usually quite comfortable in my surroundings. Of the adults in our environment in my earliest days, I was closest to our nannie, Alice Holland. Alice exuded goodness and comfort. Mom would breeze in and out of my life offering lots of love and attention, but on a fairly infrequent basis. I remember Dad and Mom's trips to France and long periods of time with just Alice and my siblings.

What I enjoyed most about Sturbridge were winter sports, skating and skiing; the horses; crystallized maple syrup on snow; and family gatherings and get-togethers, like Thanksgiving and Christmas, our ski vacations, and summer trips to Rockport.

Dad was a good guy but unfortunately, he wasn't around very much. Also, it was often difficult to get his attention focused on you. I felt very close to Mom, despite first Alice, then Emma, running interference for her. She wasn't around much more than Dad. But when she decided to spend time with us, she was always getting us involved in elaborate games of pretend that were lots of fun, at least most of the time. You wouldn't want to get on her bad side. She and Jon used to fight all the time.

But I remember her being so nice to me when I had the nightmares about the worms. I'd be screaming my lungs out and she'd come into my room and play doctor. She'd pretend to give me a shot to make the worms go away. One time I remember her putting me into the bath to wash the worms off. Overall, Mom invested enormous charisma and extraordinary talent in everything she undertook. I took it for granted at the time, but now I've come to really appreciate it. She was a very powerful character even for a three- or four-year-old.

Why can't I remember her? Jimmy and everyone else seem to have such a strong picture of her in their minds. I only sense a fleeting glimpse of her like the flash of seeing us all skiing in the backyard. Mostly, I can only imagine her from the pictures in the album. Did this woman ever tuck in my shirt? Comb my hair?

"A very powerful figure," Jim wrote. It's true. She dominated our life. Everything revolved around her when she was well and later when she was sick. But I can't see her. It's as if she was a black hole, holding us all in her gravitational field and yet invisible to the eye.

That's too harsh an image. It seems we were all happy back then. But I wish I had more memories. I'd like to remember her talking directly to me. I wish I could see her eyes looking at me. I'd like to hear her saying something like "David, finish your peas."

Going over these family versions of our time in Sturbridge feels like picking up shards of glass from a shattered mirror. None of these pieces fit together. The edges are jagged and sharp. The image is broken. A long time ago, the mirror reflected the smiling faces of a supposedly happy family: Dad, Mom, Jon, Lauris, Jimmy, and I.

1946–1954: the Sturbridge years. Everyone describes this time in our family as the good old days. But were they really? Where is my mother in all this? She's described in these glowing terms. Mom was our Pied Piper and we were swept along by her magical music. But it's hard not to notice what's laid down between the lines in these stories of our childhood. All these images of Mom: her leading parades over the exquisite antique furniture, Lauris's offering "Happiness Pills," Jim's describing the nannies as running "interference" for her, and Jon's pulling a knife suggest the cracks were already in the rigging.

Before every offshore voyage on my boat, I climb the mast in the bosun's chair. It's always a scary job to be hoisted 40 feet off the deck; I force myself to do it. I study each turnbuckle and fitting in the rigging, while trying not to notice how far down the deck seems to be. I look for hairline stress fractures that result from metal fatigue. My life depends on it. I can't risk losing the mast when I'm at sea.

But nobody in our family went up the mast. The Treadways just sailed on.

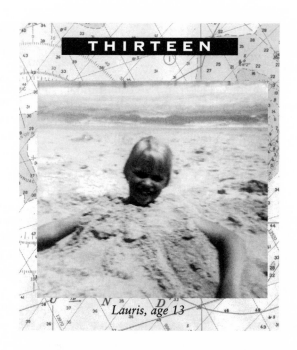

THIRTEEN

Lauris, age 13

SPARROWS

May 1991

"Don't you see clients anymore, Dad?" Michael asks me as I head up to the computer room and he packs his bag for school.

"Nope, I'm retired. I'm just working on my memoirs."

"Great, Dad, who's going to pay for college?"

"Relax, Mike, I'm just kidding."

I'm not exactly retired, but I have cut way back on my case load as I become more absorbed by this self-reclamation project. After immersing myself for years in my clients' stories, I find it oddly relieving to be finally confronting my own. The only patient I'm really worried about is Cindy, and fortunately I don't see her for a couple of days. I need a break from her desperation and despair.

I owe my sister a call.

"Hi, Lauris, it's David,"

"David, oh, this is a treat. I've been thinking about you lots all week. Is everything all right?"

"Sure. You know, after all these years, you still ask whether 'everything is all right' whenever I call."

"My heart jumps every time the phone rings."

"Anyway, this isn't a bad news call. I just wanted to touch base with you and also find out whether you had sent some more of your diaries. I know that you called a week or so ago. I'm sorry I didn't get back to you sooner. I've been traveling."

That's kind of a gray lie. I was only gone for one overnight, but I often put off returning my sister's calls. Even though our relationship has dramatically improved over recent years, I still dread that she will be crazy whenever I talk with her. It's been twenty-five years.

It started on the plane ride after burying Mom. It had been cold and overcast at the burial, but as the plane rose above the clouds, the sun suddenly appeared just outside our window. It bathed us in a warm glow. Lauris leaned over to me and said, "Look at the sun, David. It's God. He's telling me she's all right. He's holding her in his arms. Everything is going to be fine. She's happy now."

Lauris smiled at me. Her bright blue eyes were darting about in their sockets, sparkling with intense excitement. I remember shrinking away.

A few days later, her roommate called and told me Lauris had been hospitalized. Since returning, she hadn't slept or eaten. She had taken off most of her clothes and just paced the floor like a caged animal. Apparently she was hallucinating because she was talking incessantly with my mother. Her roommates tricked her into going into the hospital by convincing her she was going to work. Once in the hospital, she made several attempts to jump out the windows. She kept telling the guards, "The Mommie bird is hurt. She needs me. I have to fly to her."

Lauris was in and out of hospitals for years afterward. The doctors told us she would never recover. That was really helpful.

None of us wanted to give up on her, so I became my sister's keeper.

I remember a typical episode. She woke me up at 3:00 A.M., speaking in a harsh, rushed whisper.

"David, darling David, this is it. I can't go on anymore. The voices are calling. Your mother is calling. Can you hear her? You never listen. You hurt her so much. I'm the only one that listens. She needs me. She's lonely. She wants to explain. She misses all of us terribly. I have to go to her. Mommy, I'll be right there. I'm talking with David. Do you want to talk with him? He says you're not there. He says it's—"

"Lauris, listen to me, tell Mom you're needed here. You're the only contact between her and the rest of us. Without you we would all be lost. Tell her you've got to stay here for the 'little boys.' She'll understand."

"Did you hear that, Mother? I can't come now. David needs me. [pause] But David does care. He does. He's just a boy. Boys pretend they don't care. You know that." [pause] She says you're being selfish. You have a family and she is alone. You don't need me as much as she does."

"For God's sakes, tell her you've got all of eternity to be with her. It's too soon. Tell her it's too big a decision for now and that you need to sleep on it. Just ask her to give you until tomorrow night. Can you do that?"

We bartered back and forth. She finally agreed to wait until the next night. In the morning, I hospitalized her. I remember walking her into her bare little hospital room. It looked as spartan as a monk's cell. I held her hand and couldn't wait to go. I was late for work. I felt as smooth and sharp, hard and brittle, as a jagged piece of glass.

In the early eighties, it all came to a head when Lauris arrived unexpectedly on my doorstep. She was completely psychotic, vacillating between conversations with Mom or singing nonsense songs like Hamlet's lover, Ophelia. I tried to hospitilize her at Mount Auburn Hospital, where I was a family therapy consultant.

During the long wait in the emergency room, Lauris became progressively more agitated. Finally she insisted on leaving.

When I tried to hold her arm, she spun around and slugged me hard in the jaw. The hospital staff wrestled her to the ground. She screamed at me, "Stop them, David! Help me! They're raping me!" I watched as they carted her off in a stretcher. The nurse gave me some ice for my jaw.

I went home humiliated. I could just imagine my supervisees saying, "Did you hear that Dr. Treadway's sister cold cocked him in the emergency room? Sounds like he could use a good family therapist, the poor man [chuckle, chuckle]."

Spurred on by my embarrassment, I called a family therapist team I knew and we scheduled a weekend session for my entire family. I wanted out of my role as the in-house therapist once and for all. It seemed an auspicious time for the family to pull together around helping Lauris with her manic-depressive and periodic psychotic episodes.

It was only the third time that the whole family had been reunited since Mom died: my wedding in 1967, Dad's third wedding, and now this in 1984. We seemed to have spread across the globe ever since my mother died. We must have sensed unconciously that too much contact would lead us to the hurt.

The weekend went surprisingly well. Back on medication, Lauris was able to stay sane enough to participate. We barely mentioned my mother. The men in the group made it clear we weren't ready to deal with those issues. Bunny, the woman therapist, made a strong connection to Lauris around her pain of being the only woman left in the family and how much she seemed to be the holder of all the family's emotions. The men focused on planning a team effort to help Lauris when she went off her rocker again. Also, my family graciously accepted my retirement from my role as family therapist.

I was actually surprised that when Lauris broke down again, no one called me. The crisis was managed skillfully by my father and Jon. What's more, they were able to help her through a rough manic episode without hospitilizing her. Apparently Jon and Dad took turns just letting her babble on for the whole weekend. By Monday, they were all exhausted and she agreed to go see her shrink and get her medicine doubled. It worked. The family had managed quite well without the help of Dr. David

Treadway. I should have been relieved. Instead I felt left out. Who needed whom?

I remember the dinner at the Marriott. We were all sitting around the table swapping well-worn tales of childhood mischief and exploits. Most of our stories were wildly contradictory, and we were teasing and laughing about who knew the truth.

"I know Mother wishes she were here," said Lauris quietly. We stopped laughing. My first thought was, *Please, God, don't let her pull a nutty.*

"Actually, I don't know what Mom wishes. She's dead, you know. It's just I feel she would want to be here if she could be. She loved all of you so much."

I glanced around the table. Jon, Jim, and Dad all looked stricken. Their eyes were averted and they seemed to be holding their breath. Lauris seemed competely alone as she looked at the men in her family with a steady gaze.

I stared at my plate. Lauris had never spoken so sanely about Mother. She wasn't being crazy. She was speaking the simple truth. My eyes filled with tears.

Dad saved the day. "You're absolutely right, Lauris. I think we should have a toast." He raised his wine glass and said, "To your mother, may we all remember the touch of her love."

There was a pause. The silence was shattered by our banter and our clinking wine glasses. The awkward moment passed. I furtively wiped my eyes with my napkin. Fortunately, no one noticed.

Suddenly I realize that Lauris has been chattering along on the phone and I haven't been listening at all. "Gee, Laurie, sounds like a lot's going on. How are you doing with it all?" I ask while trying to find my place in the conversation.

"Now, David, this is how we always end up. Me just babbling on and never hearing anything about you. Why don't you tell me how you are?"

"I'm fine."

"Oh, my silly brother. Brother David's fine. His wife, Kate, is fine; his children are fine. His work is fine, and his play is fine. David's life is fine. Fine."

"Lauris, do I detect a slight note of sarcasm?" I say, playing along lightly. She has me dead to rights. In recent years all my family has made a much greater effort to engage me and even support me. I have responded in a very withholding manner, almost as if to say, "Well, it's all too little, too late." Usually, Lauris doesn't challenge me on it and I can comfortably slip into our normal conversation, where she talks on and on about herself, and I partially listen. I like her trying to push me a little. Maybe she's really interested.

"Well, actually I do have some things I need to check out with you. I'm in the middle of working on the family chapters for the book and I've been rereading Dad's biography of Mom. I can't get any sense of their relationship, except that they were in love and worked well as a team in the Treadway Inns. Dad seems to see the early years through rose-tinted glasses. Everything is so idyllic until the move to Boston in 1954."

"I think that's mostly true," she replies. "Certainly the years in Rockport and Sturbridge were happy years. It wasn't until we moved into 22 West Cedar Street that things fell apart. That's when the financial disaster from the Coonamesset Inn hit and Mom's drinking started to get really bad. But I guess there were early warnings even in Sturbridge. There was Jonny lighting fire to the garage when he was five or me rubbing poison ivy all over myself so that I could be sick. I was only seven years old. And then there was the time Jonny kept us up all night with the loaded gun."

"I don't remember that."

"Of course you remember. Mom and Dad were in Europe and the babysitter was that mean drunk. Jon convinced us she was going to come after us with a kitchen knife and so he got the gun, loaded it, and we stood guard all night, waiting."

"God, that sounds awful. I don't remember any of it."

"Actually, I think you just curled up and went to sleep. You never let the crazy things that happened bother you much."

"I know. I just checked out. Actually, one of the reasons why I started this book is that I don't remember anything. I just have glimmers. I don't remember the bad stuff and I don't remember much of the good old days either.

"On the other hand, Laurie, you always seemed to remember

everything. You were the only one who ever even mentioned Mom. You grieved for all of us. It used to just annoy me every-time you brought her up. Of course, the fact that you kept insist-ing that you were in direct and continuous conversation with her didn't help."

"Well, David, you may not believe that Mom's spirit is still alive, but she's still there for me. She'd like to be there for you, too, but I don't think you let her in."

Oh, oh, I don't want the conversation to go too far. "Anyway, I would like the rest of your stuff when you get a chance," I say, abruptly changing the subject.

> *"Slip sliding away, slip sliding aw-a-ay. My brother*
> *David's slip sliding away."*

Lauris sings slightly out of tune.

"All right, all right. I just don't like it when you start telling me what Mother thinks. I actually am trying to find my own way to remember her."

The conversation is disquieting. Both of us are working on breaking the old pattern of her being the sick one and my being the shrink, but it's touch and go. It's a step forward that I am asking her opinion about the family history. It is an even bigger step that I listen to her answer.

When we were kids, Laurie and I were close. She was my big sister then, always trying to protect me from my brother Jon's latest experiment in sibling torment. In recent years, as she's improved and I've tried to stop hiding behind my professional veneer, I've had glimpses of our old relationship. She still wants to look out for me. It's hard for me to let her.

During the twenty years that she was in and out of mental hospitals, the more she depended on me, the colder and more distant I became. Her melodramatic declarations of love blud-geoned me. For example:

TO MY BROTHER DAVID!

who saved my soul and my life more than once
and who continues to uplift and brave me
so that i too can save souls and lives!!

Need i say more. Yes, i need to say more. i always need to say more, especially to you, DAVID. And yes, this will be mushy, and sentimental and probably totally unacceptable to your adult, clinical, feelingless, psychological, doctorological, Mr. Spockish, side of your many selves. Therefore, as much as i adore that side of you, for the purpose of touching your exquisitely beautiful, diamond crystal, soft, tender, and bleeding red heart, i repeat to you the three most overused and abused words. Are you ready? i am now shouting them onto the page; screaming these words right into your small deaf ear. i Love YOU!!!!!!!!!!!!!!!!

Lauris was right. The more she turned up the volume, the less I bothered to listen. I copied this example of her gushing to show how overwhelming she was. But reading it over just saddens me. She offered up her heart and I just put it in a jar of formaldehyde, carefully labeled it, and hid it in my closet for safe keeping. She's right. I have been so "doctorological": hiding behind my professional role. And so afraid.

My sister has been writing volumes about Mom and the family for years. I have only skimmed the reams of pages she sent me. It's time to open my heart to the rawness of her pain. Once upon a time she was a little girl who rubbed poison ivy all over her body so that she could be sick.

I've been reading through her journals. This is a fragment of a letter to me written sometime in 1977. It saddens me that I don't know whether I've ever read it before.

Lauris

You were about three, David. I was, maybe, five. It was winter when I had this most special memory of all my small wee childhood. You may think it silly and unimportant, but in my heart this memory has sustained me through all the horrendous storms of my life; especially through the storm of Mom's death.

The memory is just this. Picture a cold, cold, blizzarding

moment in front of the Sturbridge house. I have no mittens. You have no mittens. I am holding your very small hand. My hand is freezing. Your tiny hand is warm and cozy in mine. To this day, David, I can feel that small warm hand in mine. To this day, it comforts me and I always know that I am not alone. Thanks kid.

I reread it out loud. Her words land on me like soft silent snowflakes.

11:00 A.M.

My morning's gone. The lump in my chest announces that my mourning has just begun. On the way to my mailbox, the perfection of the spring day grabs me. The sky is a deep royal blue, the color of the Gulf Stream. I remember when Mark, my minister friend, and I entered the Stream in the middle of a wild night. Suddenly the air was as wet and hot as a lover's breath. There were seabirds playing in the rigging and phosphorus glowing in the wake. The black night hung over us like a shroud and we were pelted by sizzling rain squalls. All around us, the lightning flashes split the sky. Finally a sliver of light on the horizon. Then the sapphire blue ocean began to sparkle in the shimmering light.

There are only bills, catalogs, and one letter. It's from Cindy.

Dear "Big Brother,"

I hope you don't mind my writing that. I know I am only a client. But you're as close to a big brother as I'm ever going to have. Anyway, I hope you don't mind my writing you in the first place. I just couldn't wait until Thursday. I'm dangling by the slenderest of threads and it's fraying before my eyes.

The harsh truth is that without you I'd be dead by now. But what's the point of living on a respirator. I give you money and you breathe hope into my lungs. How long can this go on?

My husband wants to take the kids with his whore. Now, he

*says I'm an unfit mother in addition to being a discarded wife.
I've cut way back on drinking as per your instructions and it's
not good enough. The bastard will be able to use the D.U.I.
against me.*

*Yesterday, I came upon a gnarled old apple tree. There were
only a few delicate, lonely blossoms remaining on the brittle
limbs. I reached inside a hole in the trunk. The wood was soft
and punky. Rotten. The tree is slowly dying from the inside out.
Soon it will be gone.*

Your struggling "little sister"
Cindy

The letter flattens me. Cindy's dying right before my eyes. I
hate it. She's just like my sister and my mother all wrapped up
into one. It seems as if I've been ministering to women in crisis
for twenty-five years, literally ever since my mother died. I suppose I'm doing some damn form of penance. Some of my colleagues would wonder how these desperate women serve an
underlying psychological need of mine. But right now, I don't
give a damn. I've just about had it. I don't know how long I'm
going to be able to hang in there with her.

I'm back at my desk, but I can't get to work. My mind drifts
back to that morning we entered the Gulf Stream. Amid the
seabirds, there was a surprising cheep. A little sparrow that had
been blown far out to sea was circling the rigging. It was obviously desperate to land and equally fearful. It circled and circled.
Finally it settled on the spreaders. In the morning, it was huddled
in the corner of the cockpit. When we came up to put out some
crumbs of bread and a little water, it panicked and flew away. It
started circling again. Finally, it found a safe spot up forward.
We kept putting bits of food and water out. We know it ate
some, but never while we were on deck. This went on for a couple of days. Sometime during the night before our landfall in
Bermuda, it took off. I've always hoped it flew south. I remember saying a prayer for its little soul. I like to think it made it.

Cindy's circling like that terrified sparrow. I keep putting the food out. I don't know whether she'll be able to take it. I wait and watch helplessly.

I retreat to the hammock in my backyard. Swaying under the cloudless blue canopy, I close my eyes and feel the rhythm of the *Crow* rolling to the beat of the waves toward the endless horizon.

"THERE MUST BE A HORSE IN THERE SOMEWHERE"

WHILE FLIPPING THROUGH A COPY OF *CRUISING WORLD* IN Barbara's waiting room, I'm still agitated about Cindy's note. "I'd rather be sailing" as the bumper sticker says, but my boat is two thousand miles away, swinging idly on its mooring under the hot tropical skies of the Virgin Islands and I'm here, waiting.

I begin our session reporting on all the work that I've been doing with my siblings and then I read her Cindy's letter.

"It sounds like she's on the brink. And I don't know what more I can do. I can't handle this stuff anymore."

"From what you've told me, David, it sounds like you're managing an extremely difficult case quite well. But there's a difference between being responsive and becoming responsible for her life."

"I know, I know." I wave off Barbara's comments. I don't want her to supervise me in my therapy session. But I'm not ready to deal with the flood of sadness that has built up inside me about my family either.

"It sounds like your contacts with your siblings and their writings have been emotionally wrenching, also," says Barbara, steering me into the heart of the matter.

"You know, for the first time I'm really beginning to deal with Jon and Lauris as people rather than as problems. Thinking about the reality of their lives shreds me: my sister tied to a hospital bed, my brother sipping on bourbon and watching old cowboy reruns at 3:00 A.M. What do I have to complain about? I've had a good career, good wife, great kids. Lauris and Jon's lives were shattered."

"I know the pain of your siblings must be wrenching for you, but as you go back to those times in Sturbridge, what do you feel about your own experience? It seems it's easier for you to feel connection to your siblings' struggle than to your own."

Barbara's steadfast eyes hold me.

I can't look at her. My chest tightens. I close my eyes to hold back the tears. Suddenly I can see the green pine boughs swaying above me under the clear blue sky. Then I'm sobbing with my head in my hands.

"I can't find me. It's not just that I don't remember my mother. I don't have any sense of myself. It's true I can feel deeply about my siblings or my clients. But I don't have any connection myself. I was a perfectly easygoing, charming nonentity. I just went along because I didn't want to make waves. I mean my brother had a damn noose around my neck and it never occurred to me to tell anyone. In the end I just acted like nothing happened. And that's me. I've been a chameleon shifting my coloring to blend into the background, hiding behind my smile.

"And I really haven't changed much. Every hour on the hour, all day long, I adjust myself to fit into the lives of other people. I put on slightly different personalities to match the variety of clients parading through my office. I am forever trying to be who they need me to be. I am always in character. Always on. Even with Kate and the boys. Maybe even in here. That's how it was in my family. Underneath it all, I've been afraid to be me all along."

I pause. I don't want to say the sentence that's flashing in my head.

"Maybe, there's really nobody home." I let my eyes meet Barbara's. She's leaning forward in her chair across from me. I feel embraced by her intent, gentle gaze as if she were holding me in her arms, stroking my hair, and rocking me back and forth.

"Know, David, that you were there and you are here. For many years, you needed to wear your charming smile like a suit of armor. But you are stronger now and you don't need to be alone to be yourself. You can bear the weight of your tears. So can the people who love you. Together, we will hold that lost little boy from long ago."

I'm able to let her comfort me. Somewhere along the line, I surrendered to her. Somewhere along the line, she became my missing Mom. I feel like a little boy. I want to climb up in her lap and tell her everything.

"It began with the pine trees in our backyard in Sturbridge. I remember being back there in the woods all by myself, and lying back on the wet ground and watching the clouds move across the sky through the branches. It seems like I could stay there for hours. Lying there, I wasn't lonely and I wasn't sad. I felt full of feelings. And it didn't matter what they were, because no one else was there. Do you have any idea what I'm talking about?"

"When you didn't have to worry about the response of others, you could savor all of your emotions freely."

"That's exactly right. 'Savor' is the perfect word. Yes. And then there was the sailing. Let me tell you about the sailing."

Back in my office, there are ten messages on my machine: several clients, a couple of speaking requests, and then three long-winded apologies from Cindy about her letter. She says she's afraid that it might have been "too, too grim" and she didn't want me to panic. I don't have the stomach for calling her back, but I know I will. The last call is from Bill Dunbar. I call him first.

"Remember when you said, a long time ago, David, that maybe it would be a good idea for me to have a session with my mother? Well, she's coming east this summer for a short visit and I think it might be helpful. I can't imagine ever really talking to her without some help."

I'm flabbergasted and very pleased. I never thought that our messy session last fall would lead to this.

"What would you be looking to get out of this kind of session, Bill?"

"Well, we've never talked about what happened in our family, about her leaving, and things. I've never heard her side. I never told her how it made me feel."

"These sessions can often be hard. No matter what your mother is able to say, it might seem like it's all too little or too late. I wouldn't want you to expect too much," I caution him.

We schedule the interview for the beginning of August. Bill certainly has come a long way from where we started. Therapy often takes many strange twists and turns. Sometimes when therapy works well, it seems more like a miraculous accident than a carefully constructed plan. Grace happens.

"So how did it go with Barbara today?" asks Kate as we clean up the kitchen together.

"Well, I think this therapy baloney is actually working. I was in tears almost the whole session today."

"Do you always have to put a sarcastic spin on it?"

"I know, I know. It's just hard for me. Frankly, I'm a little taken aback by how intensely I feel when I'm in there. I ought to buy stock in the Kleenex Corporation. What's weird is that I've never fully appreciated my clients' vulnerability. All these years I think I've felt so intensely connected to them and their pain. I have been right there with them, held their hands, and felt deeply compassionate. Actually, I think I was being compassionate for me as much as for them. But that's another story. Anyway, I never really had a clue how raw and exposed they must feel in front of me. After a session like today's when I bawl like a baby, I feel naked in front of her. I feel acutely dependent on her. It's probably how that suicidal client of mine feels toward me. It certainly doesn't always make me feel better. But I know it's good."

Kate looks at me. "I can't believe I'm hearing this from Mr. Solo Sailor himself. You always said you could never let yourself depend on anyone. Is this all worth it?"

"Beats the hell out of me. Lately, it seems like all I do is cry. I talked about the Sturbridge years and cried. I talked about being alone and cried. I ended up talking about Rockport, sailing, and my single-handed crossing of the Atlantic. And cried."

"I'll bet she never expected you to open up like this."

"Well, it's been a shock to me, too. It seems like sailing has always been my route into myself. It's where I've felt connected. So far in most of my siblings' stories, I feel like a trespasser peering into the windows of the Treadway family. I don't belong. Yet I can remember days and days on the water in Sandy Bay. Sailing was really mine. I think it held me together all those years."

"Is that why you've driven us all crazy dragging us on your sailing adventures for the last twenty years?" Kate teases.

"Katie, you missed your calling. You should have been a therapist. You're so nurturing."

"Check out how nurturing Barbara would be if every summer vacation she had to put up with pea soup fogs, howling gales, changing diapers while the boat's heeling, permanently wet sleeping bags, and Captain Bligh for a husband," Kate says with a surprising sharpness.

I'm taken aback. I go over to her at the sink and take her in my arms. I hold her tight and feel her breasts rising and falling against me. I can tell she's fighting back tears. I suddenly realize how hard it must be for her that I trot off to this other woman and bare my soul after all the years of my being emotionally distant in our marriage. Kate's been quietly standing by this therapy effort without asking for much in return, and I've been completely lost in my own self-absorption.

"You know, sweetie," I whisper in her ear, "I've put you through a lot. And you've hung in there. Being a sailing glutton isn't the only way that I've been a jerk. Trust me, I do understand. It's a lot easier for Barbara to listen to my story than it's been for you to live it."

"Sometimes I just wish you could have done this all twenty years ago. I think we missed out on a lot," she says softly.

"I know. All those years you used to complain about my 'not being there' or not being 'connected.' I was like so many of the men who are dragged into my office by their wives for intimacy lessons. I felt like an emotional retard because I never used to know what you were talking about. I guess I really haven't been much of a prize as a marriage partner."

Kate smiles. "When I was riding the other day, I heard a funny story about the little girl who was always optimistic. For years she wished to get a horse for her birthday. She lived on a dairy farm, and one year a big truckload of manure was dumped by accident next to their barn. All the way home from school, she had been hoping that this would be the year she would get the horse. When she got home she leapt for joy when she saw the pile of manure. Much to her parents' surprise, she started burrowing into the mess. 'What are you doing?' they called out. 'There must be a horse in here somewhere,' she said."

"Gee, Kate, I'm not entirely sure how I'm supposed to take this little anecdote."

Kate put her hand on my cheek. "I'm just saying that I always knew a horse was in there somewhere. I just wish we could have found it sooner."

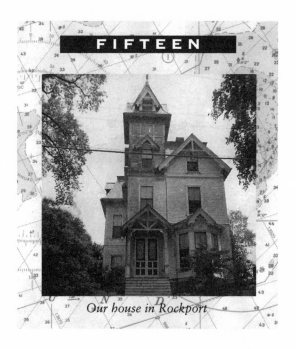

FIFTEEN

Our house in Rockport

THE ANCIENT MARINER

June 1991

Dad

The summer of 1947 Martha accepted my Aunt Ethel's invitation to join her for a month in Rockport, Mass. A flourishing and interesting art colony would be a further challenge to Martha's artistic instincts. To say that Martha fell in love with Rockport would be an understatement. With her energy, drive and enthusiasm, she convinced the rest of the family that's where we should be during summer vacations and "Daddy can come down on weekends."

In the spring of 1948, with Martha's help I bought a 10-room Victorian Gothic for $6,500.00 on Pleasant Street.

If Dad's date is right, then I must have been just three. My first real memory is the trip to Rockport with Mom. I assume we were meeting the realtor to go over the house. I was proud to be alone with her. The house seemed dark, gigantic, and scary. It smelled of mildew and the sea. Sheets covered everything. I wandered into one room by myself and saw a sheet-covered bureau that I thought was a ghost. I ran back to my mother and wrapped my arms around her legs tightly, burying my head in her skirt.

She pushed me away abruptly. "Big boys aren't afraid of ghosts," she snapped.

I felt so embarrassed that later when I had to make a bowel movement, I didn't dare bring it up. Perhaps big boys didn't need to make BMs? I held it back as long as I could and when it finally arrived, I remained silent and unobtrusive. But the smell betrayed me. She was mad. She didn't say a word. She yanked me off to the bathroom. Unfortunately, the water was shut off. She had to roll up the offending underwear in some old newspaper and stuff it into her purse.

The whole car ride home, we rode in silence.

I never realized before that I was only three. Mothers aren't supposed to be so mad when toddlers poop their pants. I always assumed I must have been five or six.

"Such a tragedy, tsk, tsk," I mutter. A week ago, a woman in my office described her experience of being anally penetrated by her father when she was four. She went on to describe being beaten by her mother because she couldn't control her bowels.

That woman's experience was a tragedy. Mine was a garden variety childhood experience of intemperate parenting. It's all the rage these days for people to heap blame on their parents for inflicting massive childhood trauma. Sometimes we sound like a culture of whiners, with us shrinks standing around like emotional vultures holding the hankies. The reality is that childhood hurts. Kids become resilient and competent in response to those hurts. No child should ever suffer what my client suffered. But all children have to learn how to survive being hurt.

Why this digression? I ask myself.

Because I hate the idea of coming across in these pages as a pity-pot-sitting, thumb-sucking, nit-picking whiner.

Then the image of sitting in Barbara's office flickers across my mind, her eyes holding me.

It's not about being a whiner. It's being afraid of feeling that little boy's shame; afraid of needing Barbara to be my missing Mom; afraid of not being safely alone anymore.

Dad

Every June, we would arrive with a car full of luggage, two horses in a trailer, and four excited children. Then we would be joined by Pop Chamberlin and Alice. Pop had purchased a sailboat and gave lessons to the children as they became old enough. David became the true sailor in the family. We hardly ever saw him all summer. I believe he won quite a few races as a crewman in little boats during those years.

In the late '70s, David sailed his 34' sloop alone from the Azores back to the Sandy Bay Yacht Club in Rockport. His wife, Kate, my grandson, Michael, and I went out to greet him upon his arrival. I shall never forget the lump in my throat and the tears in my eyes when I saw his little boat gradually appear on the horizon. How I wished that Martha might have been there with me at this particular moment in our family history.

I wish Mom had been there, too. I think she would have been proud of me.

It's odd reading how Dad distilled the essence of my childhood into a sentence or two. He even got most of the facts wrong. I won races as skipper of my own boat as a child, the *Crow* is 33 feet, not 34, and my solo transatlantic was in 1981.

I'm still feeling peevish. Where does the notion come from that my father owes me a complete and accurate memory of my childhood? The preceding paragraph is Dad's attempt to convey his pride in my accomplishment and my response is to nitpick it apart. Christ. Besides, who's to say that my memories are so accurate and complete anyway?

But I do remember Rockport.

Even before I opened my eyes, I would sniff the air. If there was fog in the harbor, the air would smell dank and seaweedy. I would listen for the sound of wind in the elm trees that stood at attention along the length of our street. The mornings were usually still, but sometimes you could hear the rustle in the leaves. Occasionally there would even be the clanging of a flag halyard on a distant pole that would promise a strong breeze, maybe even a small craft warning day: my kind of day.

Other smells came to me as I snuggled down into my bed. I could invariably pick up the promise of bacon frying, a residue of drying glue from our latest model boat, and even a whiff of Mom's oil paints. I could hear the radio playing softly in the kitchen, WBZ and Carl DeSuse's morning show. Mrs. Korpi, our cook, kept the radio turned down lest she wake anyone in the house while she cooked breakfast, but I could always make it out.

I loved being the first one up in the morning. The house felt as if it was mine. I even enjoyed having the corpulent, jolly Mrs. Korpi to myself. I'd throw on a pair of khaki shorts and a white T-shirt and slip quietly downstairs. Mrs. Korpi would greet me with a conspiratorial smile as she offered me an extra slice of bacon.

We always had the same conversation.

"And what might the ancient mariner like for breakfast today?"

I was all of nine or ten years old.

"Surprise me," I would reply.

"Well, let's see, how about two eggs over light made right; bacon, muffin, and extra butter?"

"Terrific."

There were never any surprises. I always had the same breakfast.

Each long, luxurious summer day promised its own special adventure. They truly began in the kitchen with Mrs. Korpi, breakfast, and the weather report. I didn't care about rain or shine. I wanted to know about the wind.

"Calm this morning, with a light southerly filling in. Southwesterly sea breezes this afternoon along the coast; building to 10 to 15 knots."

I could see the chart of Sandy Bay in my mind. Once I knew the wind direction, I could pick my course for the day. Maybe I'd head out to Thatcher's Island. It'd be a close reach in the southerly and not too bad a beat back.

Most mornings, I'd be on my bike and headed for the yacht club before the rest of the family got up. I'd have my paper bag with the peanut butter and marshmallow sandwich in one hand and my sweater bunched up in the other as I headed down the hill to the harbor.

The Sandy Bay Yacht Club is a ramshackle building resting on a rickety pier jutting out into Rockport Harbor. I have my mother's oil painting of the club hanging in my office. It was home to me.

If it was foggy, rainy, or a dead calm, I'd hang around on the porch. I'd sit in one of the rocking chairs and study all the boats in the harbor.

Rockport Harbor is tiny. On the left, a jumble of huge granite blocks curves like a lobster claw. At the end of it is a small red flasher. On the right, the hill rising above the town ends in slabs of rock jutting down into the water. There's a narrow entrance between. Boats were packed into the harbor like sardines in a can. On either side of the yacht club are the lobster boats with their high bluff bows, open cabins, and flat broad sterns. They are often given names like *Grace M.*, *Molly and Mike*, and *Annie B.* that speak of marriage and family, hopes and dreams. In the center of the harbor are the bigger boats, the day charters that take the tourists out to fish and get seasick, and the cruising yachts that I lusted after. Out near the breakwater are the day sailors and racing boats.

Except on the foggiest days, I could always make out my little Turnabout bobbing on its mooring as if it were nodding to me. It was pale green with a cream-colored deck and red bottom. To the casual eye, *Typhoon* probably looked like a bathtub with a mast in it, a child's toy. To me, it was a sleek pirate ship, a rugged ocean voyager, a slippery fast racing yacht, and my friend.

One day, when I was in my rocking chair waiting for the fog to lift, the harbormaster slipped up behind me and said in a classic down east accent, "Eh ya, I dare say you look like a retired old salt just settin' up there staring out at the water."

I don't remember what I said. I doubt I had a witty rejoinder. But I remember thinking that would be okay: I wouldn't mind being old, even too old to sail. If I could just sit on this porch, watch the boats, smell the ocean tang, and hear the low rumble of the surf breaking on Bearskin Neck.

Writing these last pages has been a race against more tears. But they are tears of relief. I'm flooded with memory. It feels like I could step backward in time and be in Rockport. I can close my eyes and see every detail of one of those long hot summer days.

The day's passage always began with checking out the rig. "The sea doesn't much care what happens to you out there. You take care of your boat and your boat will take care of you," my grandfather had warned me. I had a little checklist that I went over to make sure that everything was shipshape. I'm not sure that I would have even recognized a problem in the rigging back then, but going over the list gave me a sense of security.

As I cleared the breakwater, the wind always picked up and I could feel the boat surge forward into the long rolling ocean swell. The bow wave shifted from a gentle gurgling sound into an insistent chuckle. There would be the occasional sparkle of spray.

At first, I'd be alertly playing the tiller and the mainsheet for a little extra speed, practicing for the race days. But soon I'd settle into the rhythm of the boat. I would let the motion lull me into that gentle rocking place of daydreams, feelings, and fantasies. Sailing. Sailing alone. Sailing on and on. To England. And beyond.

SIXTEEN

Mom and me, sailing in Sandy Bay

THE LONG WAY HOME

I GLANCE UP FROM THE COMPUTER SCREEN AT THE FRAMED chart of the North Atlantic Ocean hanging on the wall. The northeastern coast of the United States and Canada on the left, England and the European coast on the right were depicted in a light gray. The broad expanse of ocean between the continents was a simple bland white with numbers scattered across it signifying the varying depths. Stretching from Rockport to the Azores, Ireland, Scotland, Spain, and back was a jagged line of color: my track, my voyage. Rockport to Scotland 1980. Scotland to Rockport 1981. My dream come true. Childhood's end.

I lost sailing when we sold the house in Rockport. I was thirteen; the family was beginning to unravel. We couldn't afford the Rockport house in addition to expensive private schools for the four children and the huge debt from my Dad's disastrous Coonamesset Inn investment. At first I pretended not to miss sailing much. Then I really didn't miss it. I replaced it with the pursuit of girls and the anesthesia of gin.

I didn't sail again until two years after Mom killed herself. Kate and I were in Manchester visiting Dad and his new wife, Sue. We got lost in the fog. Nevertheless, sailing those few miles in a rented boat brought back my childhood dream.

The next ten years of my life was devoted to plans and preparations to circumnavigate the North Atlantic. In 1976 I bought an old black Luders 33, a beautiful classic sloop with a great reputation for rugged seaworthiness. Imbued with the spirit of *Zen and the Art of Archery,* I wanted to have every aspect of my care and operation of the boat represent a commitment to excellence. Whether I was sailing the high seas, cleaning the bilges, or repairing the head, I wanted to approach each step with a calm mien and a sureness of purpose. In a moment of hubris, I named the boat *Arete,* which means "essence of quality."

Unfortunately, my ambition vastly outstripped my abilities, and within a short period I turned a variety of do-it-yourself projects into disasters. My commitment to excellence seemed likely to destroy the boat as my zen calm gave way to a cacophony of curses. The name *Arete* seemed a mockery. It hung around my neck like an albatross.

Casting about for a new name, I came across a book of poems by Ted Hughes. It was called *Crow.* The poems were built around the character of Crow, a scruffy, inelegant scavenger bird. Crow is ever-present at the great events of nature and history, but he's more concerned about the pedestrian tasks of finding and eating worms and grubs. He's just doing the best he can with what he's got.

Crow became the name on the transom of my boat. It seemed to befit the owner. Besides, it was a black boat.

What was I looking for anyway in those Atlantic crossings? Was it a trite variation on the standard "man alone in search for himself" theme? Was I seeking a romantized image of myself, the intrepid solo sailor living in harmony with the rhythm of sun, sea, and sky? Was David, the family therapist, running away from his own family; looking for the famous geographic cure?

Maybe it was just my insecure way of competing with Kate, who was going to medical school?

Yes. All of the above.

And what did I really get? I haven't thought about my transatlantic in years. Rather than continue with my family's writings, I impulsively drag out the audiotaped ship logs I made and start listening to them again. It'll be ten years next month since I made that passage.

AUDIO LOG

7/15/81

I'm alone in the harbor at Terceira in the Azores and very much in awe of the idea of sailing across the Atlantic alone. It's one thing to fantasize about this as a kid; it's quite another to be doing it.

Today I'm mostly feeling a jumpy, agitated kind of excitement mixed with a big dose of fear. This is an odd, unnecessary, yet seemingly irresistible quest. I suspect I'm looking for a meaningful epiphany, a momentous meeting with my true self. I've never been at a loss for grandiose notions.

I can't quite get it out of my head that I'm risking my life and the lives of the people most precious to me, particularly Kate and Michael. It all seems so self-indulgent, but feeling guilty about this is bullshit. Guilt's certainly not stopping me. So what the hell. Go for it, David.

7/18

Hello, I'm just sitting down to cocktails with my tape recorder. The Azores are 45 miles behind me. Rockport is about 1950 nautical miles over the western horizon.

Just to bring you up to date, I ran around Horta this morning like a chicken with my head cut off trying to finish up chores. By 0900, I hopped on board and shoved off. It was odd having nobody to say good-bye to. As I slipped out of the harbor and *Crow* took to the ocean swell, I couldn't help but wonder if I'd ever see land again.

Right now we're going along under full main and spinnaker, doing about four and a half knots. Pretty smooth sea. I've still got a lot of boat chores to do, but they'll wait. Mostly I'm mulling over what to cook for dinner. So this is it, man alone at sea. It mostly boils down to eating, sleeping, reading, boat chores, sun sights, and sail changes for the next twenty days or so.

7/21

Been a helluva day. I spent five hours sewing up the ripped main and trying to fix the halyard winch. Boat wasn't sailing anywhere, just sitting.

Finally got the main up, but was too tired and too lazy to change back to the big jib. So we just sailed along at 2½ knots while I brushed my teeth and tried to talk myself into going forward and changing sails. I hate sailing.

7/24

I shouldn't have complained about being bored yesterday. Big mistake. Today wasn't boring at all. A shitkicking cold front arrived and blasted the boat. At first it was just a gentle rain and I had stripped to take a freshwater shower. There I was buck naked except for my safety harness and all lathered up when a blast of wind hit. The boat heeled way over and I immediately had to start getting sails down. It must have looked comical, me scrambling around like a half-drowned monkey, fighting with the flapping sails, cursing the sea gods, and shivering from the torrents of cold spray. After I got the boat trimmed right, the wind changed direction and came in hard on the nose. That meant another sail change.

Now we're thrashing and bashing into the wind. The boat's hard over and laboring through the waves. I probably ought to go forward and drop the main entirely, but I can't stand the idea of getting doused again. Dear God, I promise never to complain about being bored again.

The wind's up to 40 knots. I'm tucked down into my bunk. I'm not sleeping. The boat's holding out okay, but she's taking a pounding. She's stripped down to the storm jib and we're running directly down wind.

I keep listening for something to break. I keep looking at my watch. It's only nine-thirty, but it's pitch black outside. The rain is tap dancing on the decks. Waves smack the side of the boat and send a shudder through the hull and me. There is a steady clatter throughout the cabin. Rising above the din is the occasional low moan in the rigging that sounds a little like the mournful whistle of a freight train. It feels like the train is bearing down on me.

Actually, all kidding aside, I'm scared. This isn't even a bad blow so far. It could get a lot worse. I've been to sea with the winds roaring past 50 knots. This is penny-ante stuff, but I am so scared. I wish I were home in bed with Kate.

It's going to be a long, long night. I keep waiting. The boat's riding well, but I keep waiting for the big one. I catch myself holding my breath as I feel the boat's stern rise to the wave. There's a moment's pause as the wave gathers under her, and then, whoosh, the boat goes screaming down the front of it. Then I wait for the next one. And the next one. Dawn's a long way over the horizon.

What the hell am I doing out here?

I stop the tape for a moment. "What the hell am I doing out here?" is still a good question ten years later.

At sea the motion never stops. Slowly your body develops a rhythm with the boat. Slowly your cluttered, busy, demanding world narrows to the simplicity of sky, wind, and sea. Slowly you become attuned to the play of dark and light, the shifting shades of blue, the sunrises and the sunsets. Slowly you become still.

That summer of '81, I put aside the ever-shifting, chameleon colors of my life with other people for a month of being alone with myself. I felt whole.

The solo transatlantic was foolhardy and selfish. I risked wreaking havoc with the lives of everyone I loved. Yet I needed to do it. It was my own version of being in therapy back then. It was a damn sight easier than what I'm doing now.

AUDIO LOG

7/25

I woke up this morning with the sun streaming through the portholes. The boat was gently rocking in the dying swell of last night's storm. We're hardly moving, because the wind's gone flat and I only have the storm jib up.

I am sitting on deck drinking a cup of coffee. I am feeling deliciously happy. I'm just going to sit in the sun for a while, curled up and purring like a cat.

7/28

Last night I was hand steering for the fun of it when I saw what looked like the glow of a huge city looming out of eastern horizon. It was a startlingly magnificent full moon breaking free from the sea. The water behind me turned into a shimmering silver, like an ocean of mercury, as the moon rose higher into the black sky.

I sat at the helm. I barely had to glance at the compass. I was steering by keeping a star lined up with the starboard shrouds. It's an old helmsman's trick that Pop taught me on our first overnight sail. I was on a course of 275 magnetic and I found a star to steer by just about 30 degrees above the western horizon.

I tracked my star as it slowly climbed the sky. I was lulled into a comfortable trance by the rhythm of the boat slipping down the face of the following seas and listening to the shush of the bow wave and the gurgling wake. I noticed tears streaming down my cheeks. They felt good.

I didn't know at the time why I was crying, but I do as I listen to the tape. In that moment, I had come home to myself again after a long time away.

AUDIO LOG

8/1

I motored all day. The sun was intense. I sat in the cockpit totally covered by a jury-rigged sunscreen and stared at the compass. 290 WNW. I have used up all but 5 gallons of fuel, which I have to save for emergencies when I'm in close to land.

Now I'm just sitting. There's not even a hint of wind, not a ripple on the water. The sea has that dense, heavy oiliness that makes it look like a huge undulating diesel slick.

Twenty minutes ago I finished *Heartsounds,* a book about the slow, painful unraveling of a doctor's life as he deals with his failing heart. It's told by his wife. He dies slowly before her eyes. Sitting out here on this empty ocean underneath this blue cloudless sky, I felt utterly alone. I put my hand over my heart and felt the soft steady beating. I felt like I was holding a trembling bird in the palm of my hand.

8/2

400 miles to go. I'm excited now. I can taste it.

8/6

I'm somewhere in Massachusetts Bay. I feel like I'm almost there. I'm home. I don't want to talk about it. I just want to get there. I love Kate and Michael so much.

8/7

0600. I'm in a dense fog just off the coast of Rockport. I can smell land. I talked to Kate on the ship-to-shore. She, Michael, and my Dad are going to be there to meet me at the dock. I should heave to and wait for the fog to burn off, but screw it, I've got to get in there. It'll just be dead reckoning from here on in. I haven't had an exact fix for a day and a half. I'll just work my way slowly and carefully, using the fathometer and listening for the fog horn on Thatcher's Island. I'm almost home. Rockport: where it all began. God, I hope the fog lifts.

Suddenly I know in my bones why I've been entranced by this reverie on sailing. I don't want to press on, either with Barbara or here on the page with the slow demise of my family in the Boston years. But I don't really have any choice. There's no turning back.

There was one morning in the middle of the transatlantic that I woke up and was just overcome with feeling alone. It was a near-perfect day; the sun was shining, the boat charging along in a nice breeze. But I was miserable. I studied the charts, and according to my calculations, I was almost one thousand miles from land in any direction. I was stuck. It would take me as long to go back as it would to go ahead. There was no stopping place: no place to run, no place to hide.

Understanding how sailing has been simultaneously a pathway to connecting to myself and an escape saddens me. I sigh deeply. There's something else that's been building up in me this morning, pushing its way into my conciousness. The big plan to sail to New Zealand is probably just more of the same old escapism. It's just another variation of running away to sea. I don't know that I should be dragging my family on another grand adventure. Sailing's not the answer and New Zealand's not the destination. Neither is being alone the way to find myself.

Sailing back to my childhood: That's what my twenty years of cruising oceans has been about. I just wanted to be that little boy in the bathtub boat; to be back in the time before things fell apart.

SEVENTEEN

The Richard Treadways, 1957

TOYS

July 1991

IT'S 6:00 A.M. ON A STEAMING SATURDAY MORNING. TENDRILS of fog slip through the trees outside my window. I'm sitting in front of my computer screen. Sam is ensconced next to me with the laptop. All week he's been looking forward to our writing time together. He's working on a book called *The Ant Family*. He says, "It's about a family of ants named Treadway. The three children raid a picnic and then they all get squished."

On the terminal in front of me, I have Dad's, Jimmy's, and Lauris's writing about the downhill slide of our family during the Boston years.

"Dad, Dad, you know what?"

"What, Sam?"

"Well, when I don't know what to say. I just write what's in my fingertips. Is that okay?"

I look at the little boy next to me. My son. He's wrapped in a bathrobe and his hair is a tousled mess. He looks sleepy but he made me promise I'd wake him up so that we could start our writing time together.

"Yes, Sam, I think that's great. I try to do that, too." I give him a big hug.

I turn back to face my terminal. 1954–1966: twelve years. My Treadway family also went to a picnic.

"Where were you, David?" I ask the face peering back at me between the lines on the computer screen.

My terminal responds with its normal Buddha-like hum.

1953–1959: The West Cedar Street Years

"David, DAVID! Where are you?" my mother was calling from the back porch. She was getting mad.

I decided not to hear her just yet. Lying back down under the pines, I took a deep breath and smelled the sweet scent of the needles cradling my head. The sky looked as blue as the ocean. The wind was rustling through the trees. I closed my eyes and memorized the moment. It was moving day.

> *Dad*
>
> Rockport in the summer and Sturbridge in the winter provided an idyllic life for the young Treadway family. Professionally and socially, we had become accustomed to our role of being pretty big frogs in a couple of relatively small ponds. It was Martha's restlessness and our shared love of challenges that led us to consider the adventure of politics and ultimately the move to Boston.
>
> I ran for the State Senate in 1954 and Martha proved to be my biggest secret weapon. She was a great campaigner with a knack for always saying the right thing at the right time. And she was gutsy. I'll never forget our showing up on the wrong night at a meeting of the American Legion. We didn't know a soul. At first we were pointedly ignored as if we were a cou-

ple of lepers. I was pretty much undone, but Marty seized the moment. She was the only woman there and when she hiked herself up on a chair, she turned every head in the room. There was a moment of dreadful silence and then she said, "Good evening, gentlemen. I'm Marty Treadway. My husband, Dick, wants to be the best senator this district's ever had but he needs to know what matters to you and he needs your help. So, how about it?" She threw them a winsome smile and suddenly they all clapped. The ice was broken and we spent the rest of the night swapping war stories and drinking highballs.

Martha and the Publick House gave a great party for our key supporters the night of the election. I won by 3,500 votes.

It was a magnificent evening. We were exhausted, full of champagne, and as happy as we had ever been. Martha, who had been such a vital and helpful part of the campaign, took as much satisfaction from the victory as I did. Our collective cups were running over.

Dad would have been thirty-nine. Mom was only thirty-four. They had four children, a thriving hotel business, and the State Senate victory. Dad was handsome, charming, and sincere. Mom was beautiful, charismatic, and talented. The sky was the limit for the Richard Treadways.

And then they flew too close to the sun.

It's been forty years since this moment of joyful triumph in my parents' life. I imagine them on that victory night: the young couple flushed with success, pride, and confidence. I am already eight years older than they were then. I wish I had known them. I wish I could have been there.

Dad

Life in the big city attracted Martha like a magnet. We had always been an ambitious duo. The social and cultural possibilities glistened before us. Unfortunately, we were extremely overconfident and financially naive when we bought a lovely town house at 22 West Cedar Street on Beacon Hill in Boston. Most of our living expenses in Sturbridge had been absorbed by the Publick House. Despite incurring considerable new debt, all of the good things that came from living in Boston might have been happily achieved if it had not been for our guaranteeing the lease of the Coonamesset Inn with all our personal assets.

The failure of the Coonamesset Inn and the high cost of living in Boston melted their wings. Then they fell from the sky. Is it any wonder that throughout my professional life, I have worried that someday I would face my own Coonamesset. I, too, came back to Boston with more professional stature than I had earned. I had worked at a world-renowned clinic in Philadelphia, and when we moved to Boston for Kate's internship at Mass General, I was welcomed like a conquering hero. I humbly accepted the role.

No wonder I have had a knot of fear in the pit of my stomach. Ample professional opportunities to be in the spotlight have been thrust my way. But I have shied away. David, the solo ocean sailor, has been scared of too much success. Whom have I been afraid of offending, the parents or the Gods?

My Dad has never forgiven himself for his financial disaster. Apparently each month's bills were a nightmare, as he sorted through what he could partially pay or had to ignore. But Dad put on a good front to all of us. "Someday our ship will come in" was his famous line and the family joke. The ship never made port.

Ironically, however, the "Martha and Dick Show" took the Boston social scene by storm. They were bright, beautiful, brand-new toys. Of course, the Boston Brahmins assumed that the Treadways were wealthy and came from an old established family in the western part of the state. My parents did nothing to dispel this image. They looked the part; they played the part— just as I have.

Their financial terrors were hidden in the haze of bright smiles, charming repartee, and tenacious optimism. Martinis before dinner, Bloody Marys on weekends, fine wines at each meal, and sipping sherry in the long afternoons kept the glow alive and the terror at bay. I suspect that it was in the dead of night, when they were both alone in their king-size bed, that the hollow desperate truth gnawed at them. I suspect they lay there together in silence, listening to each other's breathing, pretending to be asleep.

Dad

Despite our financial worries, life in Boston was perfectly marvelous for the family, with the exception of Jon and Lauris, who felt very much disrupted. David and Jim thoroughly enjoyed their school and Martha very shortly became a community leader, serving as a director at the Institute of Contemporary Art and founding the Spiral Art Gallery on Charles Street.

Martha was an outstanding social success even though she was always anxious. Martha developed her conversation skills into a finely honed art and had a knack of making guests feel warm, welcome, and important. She also had enormous spontaneity, which added to her appeal. Our collective knowledge of wine added to our stature as party givers.

Martha had an unfailing kindness and thoughtfulness when it came to lonely people. Christmas and Thanksgiving almost always included single people who had no place to go. Our children would always groan about entertaining "Mom's strays." But Martha was insistent. The children and I always found it easier to go along with her whims. Besides, she had a knack for making her lost souls feel welcome and included. I remember her saying once, "Now, dear, let's not forget that deep down we're all strays."

Martha's sense of humor was renowned and she could always poke fun at herself. She often told the story about the time she was seated at a dinner party next to Arthur Schlesinger, Jr. Martha had imbibed a little too much of the grape. In her efforts to make conversation, she turned to the distinguished guest and said, "And how old are your children?"

"About ten minutes older than the last time you asked" was his tart reply.

Our West Cedar House was the most attractive house we ever occupied. Martha was an innovative, free-spirited decorator. She had done such an outstanding job of furnishing our house that it was picked for a tour of interesting old homes in

Boston. After entertaining some of the ladies for a while, Martha decided that we should go on the tour ourselves. It was a disaster. Martha, much more sensitive and observant than I, noticed that despite her efforts, our house was by far the "humblest" of them all. Many of the other houses were brimming with distinguished paintings, elegant period pieces, etc. We, of course, had very little to compare. This caused immediate, though temporary, depression, which we ministered with dry martinis.

"Ministered with dry martinis?" I try not to judge Dad. This effort to write his story took courage. So what if he skims over some of the bad parts. I know how that goes. It's like being a skipping stone. You bounce off the still black water, once, twice, thrice. For a moment you think you're going to make it all the way across the pond. But you don't. You never do.

There was a massive underlying insecurity that drove my parents. They grew up in college towns in which they were seen as the "townies," the outsiders, "the lesser thans." Both were besieged by the need for a social stature that would prove they truly belonged. They were also anointed as the standard bearers for their families' aspirations. My Dad was the highly favored eldest son. My mother was the darling only daughter who could do no wrong. They were the couple designated to be the "most likely to succeed." But no success could ever satiate the insecurity behind their skillfully crafted social facade. I know a little about how that feels.

Just recently, a proper Boston dowager came into my office and asked at the beginning of the session whether I was related to Martha Treadway. I told her that she was my mother.

"The world has been a colder and darker place since she left us, young man. It was always a delight to know that the charming Treadways were going to be at a party. Martha's smile simply lit up the room."

I was startled by the sting of tears. What was the effort she made, the price she paid, to light up the room?

Did Mom skim over the bad parts too? Maybe she was one of those good skipping stones with a smooth flat surface that are small and light in the palm of your hand: one of the ones that give you six or seven long skips.

I wish I could remember the light of her smile.

During the West Cedar Street years, Jimmy and I were a family unto ourselves; the top floor was our turf. Dexter School, sports, model building, refighting WW II in the alley, and playing with toy soldiers was our life. We didn't make a lot of room for the rest of the family.

I remember throwing a ball once with Dad on Boston Common and Mom yelling at us daily for running up and down the stairs. I remember Mom being exasperated with our constant complaining about her culinary choices. She decided that we should eat earlier than the rest of the family.

"Since you boys fuss about everything I serve, I want you to choose one meal and that's what you'll have for one full year. And you will have your very own dinner hour, too," she said with a slice of a smile. "Maybe after a while you will develop some interest in expanding your menu."

We picked hamburgers, mashed potatos, and corn. We ate that meal until it came out of our ears. I don't remember whether we begged for mercy or she took pity on us, but after a long, long time we were allowed back into the main population for meals.

Actually, we preferred eating alone, and I suspect the parents were not pining away for our presence, either. After all, we were typically antsy little boys, barely suitable for a grown-up dinner table.

Oddly enough, Jim and I still do like hamburger, mashed pototoes, and corn. Occasionally.

My memory is so shrouded. I can still taste the hamburger and corn just as I can smell the tang of the salt air of sailing, but my mother is still lost to me.

Jim

We moved to 22 West Cedar Street and looked like and behaved like an all-American upper middle-class, maybe even upper class, family. Dad was a success in business and politics. Mom was successful as an artist, and as a gracious society hostess. Somehow the analogy about rearranging the deck chairs on the *Titanic* comes to mind when I think of our family in those days at West Cedar Street.

It was somewhere around third grade at Dexter that I became aware of Mom's drinking. There were tremendous mood swings. There was a coming-home-from-school ritual that included me getting a snack, usually ginger ale with a cube of sugar in it, and peanut butter and marshmallow fluff on Ritz crackers. Mom would enjoy some afternoon tea, quickly followed by a glass full of bourbon, usually chased by another glass full of bourbon. Sometimes she'd be happy and a real joy to be around. Other times she'd be an unbelievable bitch and someone from whom to hide. I must admit I got pretty good at reading her moods and being in the right place accordingly.

By the time we were nine or ten, Jimmy and I had learned that the best way of maintaining a good relationship with our mother was to avoid her as much as possible. No wonder she yelled at us for running up and down the stairs. Maybe she sensed we were running away from her.

I also relied on the Cheshire Cat's knack of disappearing while leaving behind a friendly charming smile and an easy manner of saying whatever she wanted to hear.

"David, have you done all your homework?"

"Sure, Mom," I would say. "I did it in study hall. What's for dinner?" Finessing the truth and changing the subject came easily to me. Somewhere along the line, I had stopped relating to her and begun treating her as an obstacle to get around. It didn't seem difficult at the time and I didn't know what I was missing. Fortunately for me, I was packed off to boarding school in 1959 and got to avoid seeing the slow, tortuous deterioration of my mother. Except on vacations.

Jim

1959–1964

When David went away to St. Mark's, I was in the sixth grade at Dexter, and during that year my world fell apart. I spent a lot of time on my own, lived on the top floor in constant fear of the house being burgled, Mom and Dad divorcing, someone in my family dying. I guess I had a lot of fears as I slept alone on the top floor of 22 West Cedar Street.

One would think that being the only child at home would allow for lots of quality time with one's parents. I hate to indict Mom and Dad, but it didn't feel that there was a lot of opportunity for quality time. But at least I had the use of David's toys that he had outgrown. I had all the toys any little kid could want.

Mom seemed to appreciate my sense of humor and athletic ability. She knew of my athletic achievements even though she never actually came to games. She would have wanted to but she was "sick" a fair amount of the time. It didn't matter. I still idolized her and felt drawn to her charismatic personality. In my mind, even to this day, she was extremely brilliant and powerful. One look from her could make your day. Or ruin it.

There is so much pain and loneliness laid down between the lines in Jim's casually dictated story. Yet, he has a high tensile resilience. Denial is not always a bad idea. Jon and Lauris grew up feeling the pain and it broke them. Jon survived with the help of the bottle. Lauris's mind snapped. Jim and I grew up wrapped in a little cocoon of benign neglect and have emerged relatively unscathed.

"Bullshit," I say to myself as I read that last line. Jimmy and I didn't get off unscathed. Our wounds were just tucked away in hidden places. The difference between us and our older siblings is that we learned how to act okay. "Fake it till you make it" has always been one of my favorite A.A. slogans. Now I know why.

It's also striking how consistently everyone describes Mom in such glowing terms as charismatic, powerful, brilliant. And yet I'm having trouble finding the woman behind the adjectives. I've resisted presenting my mother like a case study, a butterfly pinned to the wall. But I know she hasn't come to life in these pages. I hoped she would.

Jim

What was equally troubling were David's return visits on school vacations. He was quite the young preppie, developing physically into manhood while I was still a young schoolboy. I was experiencing a new distance between us and I was most anxious to get caught up by growing up and by going off to prep school myself.

I remember being jealous of Mom's affection for David. I always sensed that, of the two of us, he was the favorite. I remember one specific situation where Mom was admiring David's body. It was almost a sexual kind of thing and I was very jealous. As I recall, David didn't have much, if anything, on. I really had to fight to get under Mom's spotlight, it seemed.

The image of Mom admiring me in my jock strap penetrates me. I liked her looking over my body. This makes me queasy. Those moments under her spotlight stimulated me. Suddenly I can see her. Now, she's the seminude one. She's parading around her bedroom in a bra and transparent panties. I'm openly staring at the outline of her mysterious black triangle. She's nonchalantly pretending not to notice. Is she toying with me?

I remember lying in bed replaying the scene in my mind. Would she initiate me into manhood? Compelling images of my Mom introducing me to the magic of sex kept me up in the middle of the night. A little boy, hardened by desire.

I feel sorry for Jim being on the outside looking in. I feel sorry for David being on the inside looking out. And I even feel sorry for my mother, who was all over the place.

Once upon a time Mom was a young girl caught in the high beams of an older man's sexual desire. Did her heart quicken with fear and excitement like mine? Were her seductive overtures toward me drawn from the dark pulse of that time?

My fingers recoil from the keyboard. I just want to skip over these suddenly vivid memories. Writing these lines sinks me into a deep black pool of shame and arousal.

EIGHTEEN

David, age 17

THE LAST TIME

August 1991

Dad

In order to save money, we spent the summers of 1960 and 1961 at the Treadway Inn in Cooperstown, New York. Martha and I were refreshingly new faces on the social scene. There seemed to be a cocktail party every night of the week. We rationalized our attendance by feeling that it was good public relations for the hotel business.

In retrospect, it is now evident that Martha's drinking was gradually if imperceptibly increasing, and she was constantly looking for reasons to change what should have been a happy status quo. She was also increasing her pill intake and supplementing that with an occasional secretive drink.

Toward the end of 1959, she took on a lady psychiatrist in

Cambridge who seemed to be somewhat helpful. About this time, we jointly decided that the pills should be put under lock and key, which I did, keeping them in our document box with a combination lock.

From the late 1950s on, Mom knew she was in trouble with alcohol. But she was never treated for it. The psychiatrists, the internists, and the specialists, the best and the brightest of the Boston medical community, treated her for anxiety and somatic complaints. They treated her with a little therapy and a lot of drugs. Seconal to sleep with. Amphetamines to wake up with. Milltowns to relax with. Drugs to counteract the effect of the other drugs.

Alcoholics Anonymous was never suggested by anyone. I guess it would not have been proper to recommend A.A. to a proper Bostonian matron. I am painfully certain that my mother would be alive today if she had found a way into the program.

I'm mad: mad at the doctors, mad at my mother, mad at my father, mad at myself. Where was I?

Occasional images like that of my mother in her underwear seem to loom out of a pea soup fog like passing ships. I catch a glimpse of its ghostly shape and then it disappears again. Mostly, I can't make out anything through the impenetrable walls of gray. I feel clammy, cold, and scared. I am listening hard for the whistles, the fog horns, and the sound of breakers.

I was lost in the fog back then too. I was spared seeing the dangers surrounding me that I was powerless over. I wasn't afraid. Jimmy and Lauris were much more acutely aware of my mother's alcohol problems and my father's financial worries. I was oblivious to them, and in a way the fog protected me. It provided me with a gray cloak of invisibility. I couldn't see them and they couldn't see me.

My sister Lauris was the one who truly saw it all. No wonder it was too much for her.

Lauris

It was during high school that I remember becoming aware of Mom's drinking. She and Dad would have a few huge martinis before dinner without fail. My mother's personality suffered a major change. She would become supersensitive and paranoid, sometimes bursting into tears over a simple complaint about anything. I remember her running out of the room once when David asked for vanilla ice cream instead of strawberries for dessert.

My mother's behavior was predictably unpredictable. You never knew what she would do. Some of the time she was irrational and odd and then she would suddenly snap back to seeming like her old self. Even her gestures and facial expression took on an odd quality. I can't express how much I dreaded this side of Mother. I did not think she was drunk, but I knew the change had something to do with the few drinks she had. My mother's behavior embarrassed me, frightened me, and left me feeling helpless and more alone than ever. Nobody ever talked about this, except I may have mentioned it to Dad during the more severe incidences.

"What is wrong with her! Why is she like that?" I might have asked.

Dad would always make some kind of bland excuse like "She's had a bad day" or "She has her 'friend.'" It was a horrible situation and, yes, we all picked on her unmercifully during those irrational times, causing a bad situation to get worse. We fussed about the food. We displayed bad table manners. We never wanted to answer her questions about school and things. She didn't listen to the answers anyway. We weren't very good children. My mother frequently left the table in tears.

Suddenly, I can see the round dining-room table in a small dark room between the kitchen and the living room. We always ate by candlelight. Mom would be sitting nearest the kitchen. Lauris and Dad (if he was home) would be sitting across from Jimmy and me. Jon was off in boarding school. It would be after Mom had snapped at someone. Usually Jimmy was the culprit for fidgeting or dawdling over his food. She was always serving elegant meals that we hated like Coquille St. Jacques with sautéed eggplant. I remember a deafening silence.

We would all be looking down at our plates, even Dad. Mom would be eating slowly and staring blankly at the candles. Her face was cold and stony. Sometimes Jimmy and I would exchange knowing looks, even nervous smirks.

It could get worse. We never knew how bad it was going to get. You couldn't be excused until you had eaten everything on your plate. You just had to wait. Dessert would take forever. Sometimes I counted the ticks of the clock over the fireplace. Sometimes I practiced holding my breath. I got up to eighty-two seconds once.

I can remember the sound of forks scraping on china plates. I remember the tinkle of ice in glasses; even the occasional creak of the antique dining room chairs. I remember the waiting and the silence.

The atmosphere would get as thick and clammy as a hot, humid summer day. Finally there would be an outburst of anger like the crack and roll of thunder. She would flip into a tirade about our etiquette infractions or she would simply break down in tears and retreat from the table. Oddly enough, it was a relief when the storm finally hit. Much worse were the silence and the waiting.

I couldn't wait to get back to boarding school.

Lauris

It was in my 13th year that I started crying. Many nights a week I cried myself to sleep. I felt an aching loneliness and a sadness about the whole of creation. I do believe that some part of my soul had some forewarning of the tragedy that was to befall my mother and our family.

Somewhere in these years, Mom and Dad would "go on the wagon." It would seem that they were aware of a problem if they felt the need to stop drinking. I knew it was really for Mom's benefit and that Dad joined her to help. My Brothers Three were all sent off to boarding school at an early age. I don't know why. Maybe to protect her from them, or them from her. I am sure that Mom may have felt relieved to have the assistance of overnight schools in raising her boys. I'm not sure why I wasn't packed off. I guess I wasn't much bother back then.

I knew how deadly serious her drinking was once I was in college. She was in bed a lot. I remember my desperate loneliness. I wanted to ask her what was wrong, why was she drinking so much. We did not communicate.

One night she asked me, or I asked her, to sleep with her in the big bed. I think I was sick or she was. I don't remember sleeping the whole night. I don't think she did either. There was just a long, suffocating silence between us. I kept thinking she was dead.

The feeling of trying to doctor my mother through those years stabs me over and over. It was horrible. Throughout my life, I was forever switching roles back and forth with her. Often, I was the mother and she, the child. I also felt like a little Mom to my young brothers. Later I found myself dead smack in the middle between Mom and Dad when they were having problems. I would explain to Dad how Mom was feeling and what she needed. Then I would help her understand what was going on with Dad.

I'm feeling surprisingly jealous of Lauris. She obviously had a real relationship with Mom, even if it felt bad most of the time. For me, Mom was mostly a problem to be managed or avoided.

Lauris

The next incident that tore up my heart was a visit that Mom and Dad made to the religious camp where I was working. Mom was wearing a wig and looked so ridiculous I wanted to cry. She acted acutely uncomfortable inside herself and as usual our communication was next to nil. We both maintained our stiff upper lips, but I could feel her pain.

I even could feel her jealousy of me. She seemed to envy my youth, my determination to graduate from nursing school, my apparent success with men, and maybe even my golden hair— who knows? Mom stuffed her real feelings about everything. We said so much to each other totally nonverbally. I envied everything about her when she was well: her beauty, poise, artistic and creative nature. I compared myself to her and felt like a poor pitiful ugly duckling, the awkward foolish girl that would never amount to anything.

But after that summer-camp visit I knew she was in deep trouble, and that none of her gifts or talents comforted her. Her soul was turning to stone.

Lauris has put her finger on it. Mom died slowly, from the inside out. Lauris witnessed her demise. Jim and I were blessed by being at boarding school.

Jim

When I was thirteen, I escaped from 22 West Cedar Street. I was on my way to my first year at prep school, the very prestigious St. Paul's School. It was my home for six years. I had a wonderful time despite my inability to be a good student. I enjoyed the camaraderie, the structure, and the sports. I even enjoyed chapel and the religious orientation.

Summers were wonderful also because I spent them away from home, working.

During my teenage years, I became increasingly aware of Mom's health problems. She seemed to always be having a case of nerves, usually accompanied by diarrhea and lots of pills to wake her up and more pills to put her to sleep, and a constant diet of bourbon, beer, gin, or wine. She'd be lively and fun one day, then lay in bed the next, recovering from ailments that were totally foreign to all of us. Dad and Mom's bathroom was like a pharmacy. It was a place of great intrigue.

From 1959 on, Mom would be periodically hospitalized for "rest." None of us ever understood what her sickness was. Neither did her doctors.

Dad

On the whole, Martha coped with her children's difficult teenage development with understanding and often perceptive good humor. This was the summer that David discovered girls. It wasn't until much later that we found he routinely left his room via a convenient window after being checked in. It was a ground floor room, and David disappeared in the night into the arms of a number of Cooperstown girls.

Dad still doesn't know the half of it. That was also the summer that I drank everything I could get my hands on. One night I got whacked at a party and threw up all over my girlfiend on the car ride home. My parents cleaned her up as best they could and we drove home. When they opened the back-seat door, I rolled out onto the pavement. I looked up at them standing over me and began to laugh uproariously. They couldn't resist joining in the humor of it all, and it became one of the many David stories, like the one about my being caught in my underwear under my girlfriend's bed by her mother.

I never told anyone about the times I woke up drowning in my own vomit.

From 1959 until my mother died in 1966, I didn't have much to do with either of the parents. I emotionally left home when I went to boarding school at the age of thirteen.

My first year at St. Mark's when I was in the eighth grade, it was a rule that we write our parents weekly. The dorm prefects collected our letters every Sunday night. For that whole year, I sent home an empty envelope addressed to my parents. The parents joked about my technique for circumventing the school rules, but they never really complained about the lack of communication. My mother even gave me some postcards already addressed with stamps on them, but I don't remember using them. I was sure she didn't really care. Maybe she did.

Most of my adolescence was devoted to the sports of girl chasing and gin drinking. Although I had a reputation as an apprentice roué, debutante party devoté, and charming drunk, I must have been lost, and lonely. I just didn't know it at the time.

The feelings that I couldn't anesthetize with alcohol were expressed through falling in love, which I did constantly. As the product of all-male private schools, I had almost no contact with the opposite sex until puberty assaulted me. Other boys were known as good students or good athletes. I became known for being "good with girls." Girls were to be claimed as prizes in our struggle for status. They were to be groped in the dark and gossiped over in bull sessions. Yet even during the frenzied pursuit of "scoring," I was making the discovery that these mysterious creatures with alluring aromas, soft bumps, and strange crevices, clothed in odd items that you had to work through without a manual, were actually people. And I liked them. I enjoyed their company and conversation. They provided a relief from the constant "mine's bigger than yours" competition of the male world. I could talk to them.

Most of all, I loved being in love. It made me feel intensely alive, passionate, and connected. I would haunt my mailbox at St. Mark's, looking for a romantic missive from the latest fair maiden. I carefully mixed blue and red ink together in order to write my love letters in a passionate purple.

Being a romantic didn't deter my wanton pursuit of sex. I was a product of the fifties and fell in love with good girls and "did it" with the rest. My first time sums up my adolescence painfully well.

Clarkie Peterson, a fellow St. Marker, and I were fifteen and on the streets of New York. We were on the Lower East Side looking to score a whore.

We saw a young woman sauntering toward us. Her high heels were clicking on the pavement. She was dressed in a tight miniskirt and her breasts were peeking out of the top of her low-cut blouse. Clarkie nudged me. Even to our inexperienced eyes, she looked like a prime candidate for a business transaction.

As we drew close, I said to her, "Good evening, Ma'am, we're a couple of Dartmouth freshmen who have been cooped up in snowy New Hampshire all winter and we're looking for a good time."

"Oh, really. Dartmouth, huh? And what kind of good time do you 'men' have in mind?" she said with a bemused tolerance. She had a bit of an Irish brogue. Clarkie and I were both short and I know I didn't even look close to fifteen. But it was dark and we were horny and hopeful.

She took us to a dingy little hotel. Clarkie and I flipped a coin.

I won. He went and sat on a chair by the window. She and I went over toward the little single bed. She took off her skirt and her panties, but kept her stockings and heels on. Then she lay back on the bed. I thought getting into bed with your shoes on was very strange. I stood there like a statue watching these proceedings with my mouth hanging open. With the bedside table light on, she looked much older and I suspect that I looked much younger.

"Are you sure about this?" she asked.

"Oh yeah, sure," I said haltingly. My hands plucked nervously at my belt buckle.

"Well, come on aboard before you miss the train."

"What train?" I asked earnestly.

"Oh, brother," she said with a sigh. Then she patted the bed next to her. "This will work better if you come over here. Take your pants off, big guy."

I climbed aboard and she plugged me in. I came instantly. But being only fifteen, I kept sawing away, still as hard as a carbon fiber mast.

After a long while, she said, "Wait a minute, kid. Did you already come?"

"Uh huh," I said sheepishly.

"Well, get off then. This isn't a 'twofer,' my boy."

"I'm sorry, I didn't know what the time limit was."

"Oh, God spare the children," she laughed.

Poor Clarkie paid the price for my mistake. He came in a flash too, but she threw him off immediately.

It all seemed like a lark at the time.

Looking back on my adolescence, I don't like me at all. I was a self-centered, shallow, manipulative wastrel. All I cared about was getting drunk and getting laid. Truth is, I didn't give a shit about my mother or my family. Or, for that matter, myself.

At least, Lauris and Jim worried about Mom. I didn't. I thought she was a pain in the ass.

I remember one night in the living room at 22 West Cedar Street when I was about sixteen. I was there with some friends. We were drinking beer. Mom was drinking bourbon.

At first we all had a good time. She was being very funny and teasing us about how we were managing our "hyperactive hormones" and stuff like that. My friends thought she was a riot. As the night wore on, she began to slur her words and not make any sense. Everyone started getting embarrassed because she was clearly drunk. She wouldn't stop talking and she even began flirting with one of my friends. I was so ashamed of her.

Finally she announced that she was tired and was going to take a nap. She lay down on the floor in front of everybody, cradled her head in her arms, and promptly passed out. My friends started teasing me about my Mom's difficulty holding her booze. I couldn't stand it. I had to get her out of there. No matter how drunk she was, I didn't want my friends making fun of her. I remember yanking her up off the floor by the arm like she was a bag full of wet sails. She was a small woman, only 5 feet 2 inches. It wasn't hard to get her up. I put her arm over my shoulder and my arm around her waist. Her head flopped onto my chest.

My friends were stone silent. They were all looking away. I dragged her out of there. It was probably the last time I ever held my mother in my arms.

NINETEEN

Mom and me, skiing, 1959

SESSIONS

I'M JUST AS FIDGETY AS I USED TO BE DURING THE PRESTART maneuvers of a sailboat race. I never had much patience for the jockeying back and forth along the line. I just wanted to get going for the first mark. Today would be a hard race.

Later this morning, I'm meeting Cindy. It's time to force her to accept a hospitalization. Last week she blithely mentioned that she had bought a handgun that she's keeping in her lingerie drawer. Two days ago, she hinted that she's picked a date. Labor Day. That's this coming Sunday. I have to do something. She's desperate and I'm desperate.

But now I have to concentrate on my first clients. Bill Dunbar and his mother are sitting in the waiting room. They're probably nervous themselves. Bill said they've never really talked about what happened when his mother abruptly left the family. He reported to me that all he knew was that his mother fell in love with a woman friend and they ran away to California together. I suspect that there is more to the story than that.

With Cindy looming over me, I don't know how I'm going to do this session. I just have to keep my composure. Bill and his mother deserve all of my attention. This meeting is a big risk for them. What would it be like to sit down and have a talk with my mother?

Bill and his mother stand up in the same instant and smile in greeting. I'm immediately struck by how different they appear. Bill is dressed in a conservative olive green suit, button-down shirt, suspenders, and bow tie. He looks like a recruiting ad for the traditional blue-blooded Boston law firm. Eleanor Fitch looks like the epitome of artsy Sausalito. She has on a brightly colored, flowing summer dress. Her gray hair is long and pulled back into a pony tail. She's wearing large silver earrings and two big silver bracelets inlaid with turquoise stones.

Yet with all these fashion differences, the familial resemblance is remarkable. She has that same long thin face with the patrician nose that gives a slightly severe cast to their overall expression. Yet they both have broad and friendly smiles as we go through the normal exchange of pleasantries. I had expected the atmosphere between mother and son to be charged with high-voltage tension. They seem more relaxed than I am.

The session unfolds with Eleanor Fitch breezily describing her life in California. She's still teaching high school, is living with her woman partner of twenty years, is active in the lesbian political movement, and writes a column for the weekly newspaper. She reports having a rich, full life within a broad community of friends and acquaintances. Her only expressed regret is that she doesn't have more opportunities to see her children and grandchildren.

I catch a glimpse of Bill as I interview her. He's watching her like a hawk. I suspect that he's never paid as much attention to her. I wonder how he connects this bright, cheery lady with the Mom who left him when he was eleven years old.

It's time to bring the session into focus. These meetings are usually awkward. The parents are usually guarded, expecting they will be blamed for every imaginable difficulty in their child's life. My clients are nervous that I might be converted to their parents' perspective. Yet both clients and parents wish for some mutual understanding and even forgiveness. Invariably, these sessions are a bit of a letdown. One cannot assuage the wounds of a lifetime with words, or even tears. With this disappointment often comes the beginning of acceptance and healing.

"Well, let's talk a little about what you two hope to get out of this meeting," I say to open up the dialogue.

"Well, I'm here just to help Billy with whatever is troubling him. I was surprised and delighted that he would ask me because he's never been much of a talker. Besides, I know that he's always felt a little uncomfortable with my unconventional life-style," she says rather blithely.

"Now, Mother," jumps in Bill, "it's not your life-style. It's, ah, I don't know. We've never talked. Nobody ever told me anything. I didn't find out why you left until two years later. When David suggested that we have this meeting, I thought he was nuts. But I realized I'd never bring this stuff up to you without an extra push. Besides, I've discovered in this therapy process that I've had difficulty being trusting in relationships ever since things fell apart in our family. It's had a damaging effect on my marriage with Sarah."

The chipper smile fades from his mother's face. She looks down at the floor, and in a hushed voice says, "Oh, Billy, I hope you didn't bring me in here to tell me I ruined your life. It was so many years ago. You have no idea how badly I felt about what happened. I never meant to hurt you."

Bill shrugs his shoulders and looks away. There's a moment of silence. He's not ready for a quick "I'm sorry, son." I suspect that underneath her facile charm, Eleanor is wracked with guilt. She's not ready really to hear his pain. She may not have any room for it.

"This is the hard part," I say, jumping into the silence. "I know you both came in here with a mix of fear and hope. It takes considerable courage to try this. It might be a very hard conversation. But I know that you, Bill, don't want your mother to walk out of here feeling blamed and guilty. And Eleanor, I sense you came because you really would like to help Bill deal with the past, and maybe even develop a more comfortable relationship between the two of you."

I cross my fingers as I watch them shift uncomfortably in their seats. Without glancing at her, Bill says to me, "I guess I would just like it if she would tell her story about what happened."

"Well, Bill, your mother is right here. You can ask her yourself." I give him an encouraging nod in her direction.

Bill looks directly at his mother and says softly, "Why did you leave us, Mom?"

Eleanor talks openly and poignantly for the next half-hour while Bill and I sit and listen. She tells about her painful struggle to redirect her sexuality and her shame and self-loathing when she finally admitted to herself that she was a lesbian. She describes the horror of being found out by her husband and how he threatened her with exposure to ensure that she gave up custody of the children. With tears streaming down her face, she tells of that last night and tucking him into bed not knowing when she would see him again.

Now Bill is crying, too. "But why didn't you tell me? You didn't say good-bye. You should have said something. You just walked away. Nobody talked about it. Dad just said that you left because you wanted a different kind of life. I didn't know what he meant. I just thought it meant that you didn't want to have children anymore."

"Oh, Billy, I'm so sorry. I promised your Dad that I would just leave. He said it would be easier that way, instead of dragging you guys into it."

"You almost make it sound like it's all Dad's fault. That's not fair. He's the one who stood by us."

The conversation goes on. More tears are shed. There are no easy answers. Bill can't fully forgive his mother. Much to her credit, Eleanor accepts that Bill is still hurt and angry. Explanations don't heal wounds. The session doesn't end with a dramatic mother-son hug. But they both seem relieved and glad they came. The healing has begun.

"I wish we could have talked like this a long time ago," says Eleanor.

"Me, too."

As I watch them leave, I'm glad for them and sad for me. It was a good session. I wish I could have one with my mother.

Cindy is a disheveled mess. Her hair is dirty and uncombed and falls down in front of her face. She's painted herself with thick layers of mascara, rouge, and lipstick as if she were desperately trying to construct a mask to hide behind. She looks like a little girl who's been caught playing with her mother's makeup kit. She slumps in her chair and hangs her head. She won't make eye contact with me.

The silence squats over both of us. I've just told her that she has to go into the hospital or else I can't work with her anymore. I'm utterly helpless and defeated. So is she. In all this time, I haven't been able to completely reach her. Her drinking and her constant threat of suicide have blocked us from being able to do any meaningful therapy. I've been hog-tied by my fear.

I strongly suspect that she had a severely traumatic childhood, but she is adamant in her denial. She describes having had an "Ozzie and Harriet" family and it's all her fault that she can't make it. She's refused to let me meet with anyone in her family.

"You don't understand, Doc," she said, "I always knew that I came off the assembly line put together wrong. It just took a long time for the rest of the world to find out."

So here we are, after nine months of intensive therapy, and the woman in front of me is worse off than when she started.

I don't think she'll go voluntarily. I have the pink committal paper signed and ready. I've called the police and alerted them to be ready to pick her up at the end of the hour. I feel like a murderer. And yet I know there's really no choice.

"I'm so stupid," she whispers harshly. "Stupid! Stupid! I never should have told you about the gun. I should have known you'd quit on me. That's what everyone does. You're just like the rest. I knew you would be."

"What do you expect me to do? Watch?" My frustration and fear explode out of me. "Who do you think is going to explain this to your kids? What am I going to say? 'Oh, well, your Mom said she was going to kill herself, but she didn't want to go to a hospital, so I just stood by and let her do it.'"

"It's my life. I can do what I damn well please with it."

Suddenly, I wheel my chair right in front of her. "NO! It's not *just* your life. If you kill yourself you will be wrecking your kids' lives. You don't have a choice. You've got to stick it out!"

Cindy curls up in the chair and begins to sob. Then she sits up and glares at me. "I hate me! I hate me. I'm a disgusting fat drunk pig. You don't understand anything. Those children deserve better than this!"

She curls up in a ball and starts moaning like a wounded animal.

"You've got to let me go. I want to die!"

"I can't. I can't let you go." I'm suddenly crying uncontrollably. My whole body is shaking.

"Please, please, don't. Don't do it," I whisper. "You don't understand. Your kids need you. I know. My mother killed herself. It wrecked all of us."

There's a long pause. I can't look at her. I'm mortified that I've just dumped all over her. I can't believe I screamed at her, burst into tears, and then blurted out my story. I don't know what she'll do with this.

"Here," Cindy says gently leaning forward and offering me a tissue.

"Thanks."

"I didn't know."

"It's not appropriate for me to be hammering you with my story."

"I'm glad you did."

"You are?"

"Somehow it gives me an excuse to at least consider going to that damn hospital of yours."

She seems remarkably composed, almost chipper again. Now I'm the mess. She sees the surprise on my face.

"Now, don't get excited. I'm not making any promises. I'll need some time to think about it."

"Cindy, how do I know you won't just drive home and blow your brains out?"

"You don't. You're going to have to trust me that I wouldn't do it to you after what you just said."

"But you've been planning on doing it to your own children."

"When you were yelling, I suddenly imagined what it would be like if the kids were the ones to find me. Then I realized what this could do to them. It jolted the hell out of me. I don't know. I need time. Please trust me. It won't work if you make me go. Maybe I can do it on my own."

I don't know what to do. Is she manipulating me or for real? I feel lost. I lean toward her and look her straight in the eye.

"I can't let you go without a handshake and a promise that you'll either go to the hospital or come back here. If you need me to, I'll drive you over to the hospital. I'm going to try to trust you, but it scares the hell out of me."

After a long moment she takes my outstretched hand.

I burst into Barbara's office late. The session with Cindy ran overtime, and then I had to call off the police backup. I hope I made the right choice. I don't know what I'll do if she kills herself after this.

"I was completely out of control, Barbara. I screamed at her and then dissolved into tears. I'm lucky that she didn't run out of the room. What's going on here? I used to be a pretty careful and contained therapist. Now, I'm spilling my guts out as much as my clients."

Barbara pauses before responding, "I'm not sure you can hear this. It seems you never had the chance to struggle with your mother about her suicidal feelings. The feelings that welled up in you with Cindy must have been very powerful for her. She knows you care. Your anger and your tears seem to have reached Cindy when words weren't touching her."

"That's easy for you to say," I retort. "I'll bet you've never flipped out on a client."

Barbara lets slip a smile and then waits steadfastly. She's not going to let me divert attention to her story. I suspect she is shocked that I behaved that way but doesn't want me to punish myself over it. I know how that goes. Sometimes clients' confessions really jar me, too. I can't let her comfort me. I'm still too embarrassed. I'm still too scared.

After another ten minutes of ruminating about what I should have done differently, I finally say, "Well, it's in God's hands now."

Barbara looks at me with some surprise. I suppose it's the first time I've mentioned God in our work.

"I don't know what I mean by that. I don't know whether I even believe there is a God even though I keep showing up for that prayer group. We're even doing a retreat in a monastery this fall. Anyway, enough about Cindy and God. God didn't do much for my mother.

"This has been a hellacious day. I also had a session this morning between a mother and a son. It made me jealous. They really were able to relate like two adults. I can't imagine being able to talk to my mother like that."

"But it sounds like you wish you could."

"It's hard to talk to dead people." I retreat to my normal cavalier style. "Last week, you suggested that maybe I should bring in some pictures of me and my family during my teenage years. I rummaged through our photograph bureau. I was looking for one particular picture that I remember, one that shows me at a table with my mother and a group of people. I was about sixteen. In that picture, I appear to be half in the bag while I am trying to look cool, calm, and collected. There's a kind of sleepy half-smile playing on my face. It definitely shows me the way I was back then: numbed out and acting mellow. It reminds me of the dopey grin of the Alfred E. Newman character and the line 'What, me worry?' Anyway, I couldn't find that picture, but wait till you see what I came across."

I pull a black and white photo from my breast pocket and put it on the little stool between us. It's a picture of my mother and me when I was about thirteen. I think it was taken during the skiing trip that she and I went on by ourselves. We are standing hip to hip. She has her left arm around my waist. Her right hand is holding mine in place on her right shoulder. Her face is turned toward me and she's smiling at me. I am slouching next to her in a pose of studied casualness. I am not looking at her or the camera. I appear to be looking at the ground.

Barbara examines the picture for a while. I can't read on her face what she's thinking.

"What are your feelings about this picture, David?" she asks as she hands it back to me.

"I don't know. It's uncomfortable, um, I feel like the kid is all tangled up with the mother. She's got her arm around him, she's holding his hand, she's looking at him. I don't like looking at this picture. I can't connect to either of these people."

"It seems hard for you to relate to that boy as yourself. You're speaking about him in the third person."

"That's the problem, Barbara. Maybe it really was because I felt too much sexual tension toward the lady. I was so overloaded with feelings that my brain blew a fuse and everything was wiped out. I see this apparently warm mother-son picture and they look like strangers to me."

"Would you like to try to imagine yourself being inside that boy in that picture?"

"Sure. I do this kind of visualization with my clients all the time, but I don't know whether it will work for me. But give me a second. I'll see whether I can't get back inside the boy and then you talk with him. Okay?"

"That's fine. Take your time getting back there."

I close my eyes and sink down into an adolescent slouch. Images of being me in different places flash through my head. I see myself at St. Mark's, Dexter, and my room at West Cedar Street. Surprisingly quickly, I begin to feel like a kid again.

Without opening my eyes, I say, "I feel like I am back there, but I am jumping around between a bunch of places."

"Pick a place where you feel most comfortable and safe."

"I am in my room on the top floor of our house on West Cedar Street. I am younger than I expected to be. I am ten or eleven."

"Describe your room as you see it."

"Yes. I can see everything. Looking in from the doorway, my bureau is directly to the left and then there is my desk against the left wall. Directly across from the door is the big shelf in front of the row of half-windows. I have all of my toy soldiers lined up in march formation. There are almost two hundred of them. To the right of the windows is my bed, and then to my immediate right is the closet. I am sitting on the bed now, facing my desk."

"How do you feel about your room?" asks Barbara very quietly.

"I love my room. I can play in it for hours and I never get bored."

"Who else comes into your room?"

"Just Jimmy. We play together a lot, making forts and race car jumps, playing with soldiers, and building models. Jimmy and I always play in my room."

"Does anyone else come into your room?"

"No, it's just mine. That's the way I like it. After I do all my homework, I get into bed and read. I read Landmark books about important historical figures and I am always reading about Napoleon and French history. My soldiers are all Napoleonic period troops. At least, I pretend that they are. I fight every weekend with Lee Adams, who has a whole mess of British troops. Sometimes I just lie in bed thinking about strategies."

I stop talking and drift off into a reverie about my endless weekend wars.

Then somehow it changes. I'm still sitting on my bed but I am older now, probably about fifteen. I am holding an ashtray in front of me and smoking a Pall Mall. The toy soldiers aren't on the shelf anymore. My barbell set has replaced the fort that I used to keep set up on the floor.

"Where are you now, David?" Barbara must have sensed the change.

"I'm still in my room, but I'm older."

"And what are you feeling about being in your room now?"

At first, I can't respond. My chest begins to heave. My eyes fill.

"It doesn't feel like my room anymore," I said in a whisper. "I don't belong here. I don't like it here." I begin crying hard, holding myself with my arms as I rock back and forth. "I don't want to be here anymore."

"Things seem to have changed a lot. You seem so sad and scared." Barbara pauses. "How did things change?"

"It's not just my room. I don't want to be in this house. I hate this house. It's not my house anymore."

"You don't want to be in this house, not now."

"Everybody is messed up. My Mom is so messed up. I hate my family." Then I catch myself.

I suddenly say angrily to Barbara, "Why are you asking me these stupid questions?"

My eyes snap open and I'm back in the safety of Barbara's office and my adult self. I'm shaking. I'm feeling stung by her questions. My anger shocks me. Then seeing her there across from me, her hands folded in her lap, her body leaning toward me, and her eyes holding me gently calms me down. The tears well up in me.

"For a moment there, it seemed like you were trying to hurt me. I felt like jumping out of my skin. It's hard to believe that all this stuff was just barely under the surface when I was a kid. Nobody ever asked me how I felt about anything back then. Nobody ever said, 'How are you?' I didn't know I felt like this. I always thought I was just callous and cold."

"I believe you had much more feeling inside you than you realized."

"Exactly. It's actually a relief to know that I did care. I always assumed that I was so shallow and self-centered that none of it mattered. It makes me want to hug that kid sitting on the bed, puffing on his big grown-up cigarette and pretending to be tough. But he'd probably push me away, just as I pushed you away."

"Maybe you need to sit down on the bed next to him and just listen for a while."

TWENTY

Mom as a young mother, 1942

NIGHT WATCH

ON THE WAY HOME FROM THE SESSION, I FEEL EXHAUSTED AND exhilarated. First Bill and his mother, then Cindy, now this. I've been so ashamed of being such a callous and carousing adolescent. I simply obliterated my memories and denied myself any compassion or understanding. Now, I can imagine revisiting that boy from long ago. I can imagine sitting down beside him and just listening.

I walk into the kitchen of our house and there's Michael at the breakfast table eating a huge bowl of cereal. He's almost as tall as I am now and just in the last few months has begun to fill out into a handsome, well developed young man.

"Hi, Dad. How did your meeting go?" he asks.

"It was fine," I reply. Michael clearly thinks it's odd that his

Dad, the therapist, needs to see a shrink himself. Sometimes I think it's odd too. But I do need it. I have embarked on a journey that I never expected to make, but now that I am in the middle of it, there's no turning back. It is just like being in the middle of my transatlantic.

"By the way, Dad, do you know where your soldiers are? Jeff and I need them for our movie of the Boston Massacre for Social Studies."

"Yeah, I think I can find them. They're somewhere in the attic. I haven't had them out for a long, long time." Of all the days for Michael to bring up my toy soldiers. It makes me chuckle.

"Why don't you sell them, Dad? Aren't they really valuable?"

"Some of them are. But I couldn't possibly sell them. They're one of the few relics I have from my childhood."

"I thought you didn't like remembering your childhood."

"No, Michael, my childhood wasn't all bad just because in my teenage years my mother had a lot of problems and then she died."

"I thought she was an alcoholic and then she killed herself," Michael says in his typically blunt and direct manner.

"Well, Michael, that's exactly what happened. You're right to just put it out there. I've never really known how to talk about it with you or Sam." I've always been a little afraid to talk about the topic because I didn't want to put the idea of suicide into their heads. Suicide runs in families just like alcoholism does. I haven't wanted to introduce suicide as a viable alternative.

"Well, what really did happen? Why did she do it?"

"That's a big question, Mike. You want the long-winded clinical explanation or the short straight to the point one?"

"Better give me the short one. I want to listen to my C.D. for a while before I start my homework."

"Fair enough. It goes like this. My parents were undergoing a lot of financial stress. They both drank too much and slowly my Mom became an alcoholic. She was never properly treated by doctors, who made her much worse by giving her lots of drugs. By the time she killed herself she was really so depressed that she was mentally ill and believed in her heart that she would never get better."

"Sounds harsh," says Michael as he collects his books off the table. It seems like my short explanation was too long for him. It's just as well. Coming to terms with my mother isn't his job. It's mine. Besides even my short answer feels like a lot of hot air. I'm afraid the true answer is I still don't know why my Mom killed herself.

"Anyway, Dad, are we going to be able to have our talk later?"

"Sure."

Michael and I are having regular evening talks about the trials and tribulations of his adolescence. It surprises me how open he is. I wish I could have talked to someone when I was his age. It's odd being jealous of my son's relationship with his Dad. But I am.

I'm lying in bed. The house is creaking. I hear the cat padding up the stairs. Out on Route 20 there's the occasional whoosh of a car passing by. I can't sleep. All night I wanted to call Cindy. I keep thinking about the possibility that's she about to put a bullet in her brain. I have to let her go. I have to put it in God's hands. But I'm frightened.

The session with Barbara stirred me up, too. It felt good to be back in contact with that adolescent self. Despite all his pretensions, he was just a little boy dressed in grown-up clothes. I feel less ashamed of him.

That picture of my mother and me keeps coming into mind.

I just don't have a handle on her. She's still missing in action. After all this writing and therapy, I can only grasp slivers of memory of this woman who has dominated my life. I wish I could bring her into a therapy session with Barbara the way Bill brought in his mother.

Suddenly I remember her letters. I throw off the covers, put on my bathrobe and slippers, and head for the computer room. Next to my stacks of writing is a gold cardboard box. Lauris sent it to me six months ago. She got it from my Aunt Jane, who saved it all these years. It contained forty years' worth of letters from my mother. They were mostly letters to Dad's Mom, although there were some she had written to Lauris in the years before she died. I quickly scanned the letters when they first came, but found them boring. I had put them aside with the expectation that, at some future point, I'd be able to dig into them a little bit more. Now's the time. I'm wide awake. Just looking at her handwriting touches me.

As I begin reading, it's as if I were standing next to her watching her write them. I can almost see her long, thin, elegant hand holding the fountain pen.

Excerpts from four decades:

Mrs. Richard Treadway
82 Park Street
Canton, New York

December 16, 1939

Dearest Smokie,

I'm sitting straight up in bed with all my worries in the past, thinking about you and how sweet your letters have been, and how lucky I am to have a mother-in-law whom I adore. How nice it would be if you were here so that we could talk about the delivery and about Jonnie who's so darling, and about Dick who is terribly happy to be the father of a son—and of course about me—because I am a mother, at last.

It's quite an effort to become a mother, isn't it Smokie? You should know about that pretty well. How did you do it, anyway?

Would you like to hear about Jonnie? He looks just like a Jonnie—all boy with a very beautiful head, perfect in fact. Everyone says he looks exactly like Dick. He has golden skin, not pink and white but gold, and light brown hair in abundance and blue eyes and a beautiful Treadway rose bud mouth, a turned up nose and a perfect little body, not a mark of any kind, not even a mole. He eats plenty from my larder, which incidentally has been painful this week due to the great abundance of milk—and he cries only when he's hungry.

He's truly a miracle child.

Must tell you about Dick. Thursday night was the formal Xmas dinner at the dormitory he runs, and it turned out to be a glorious celebration in honor of Dick's new status as a father. In the middle of the dinner, the President called Dick up to the head table and made a speech about how much the boys liked him, etc., and presented him with a gift certificate in Jonnie's name for $25!! from the boys. They cheered for ten minutes and sang "For He's a Jolly Good Fellow." Dick was reduced to a completely amorphous state and wept real tears.

Smokie, our beloved Dick has landed on his feet at St. Lawrence. Never have I seen anyone so happy or have I ever been so thrilled.

Just two starry eyed kids!

Want to hear about me? Just a little and then I must lie down again. I will be going home Thursday. Dick has allowed me no visitors. Did he tell you? So I am getting a good start. I'm progressing beautifully and feeling no pain—just happiness.

Heaps of love to you and everyone
Marty

She was twenty years old, a starry-eyed kid, feeling no pain, just happiness. She was a brand new Mom basking in the glow of her perfect son and beloved husband. Her cup runneth over.

Was this ebullient young woman's future already written in the book of the Gods? Were the tiny black seeds of her disease already taking root deep between the joyful lines? I don't think so.

Of course, I could psychologize the letter to pieces: root out the perfectionism (emphasis on perfect child, etc.), codependency (focusing so much on Dad and child), low self-esteem ("Want to hear about me?"). But twenty-twenty hindsight is facile sleight of hand. It feels like it would be defacing this letter, this joyful moment in time, to pick it apart.

She was just a brand new Mom. Her future looked as golden and smooth as her baby son's cheek.

Dec. 26th, 1944

Dear Smokie and L.G.,

Dick and I are probably a couple of sentimental old fools but somehow Christmas almost meant too much this year. It was marvelous and it was sad; it was gay with eggnog and excited children and tearful with rememberance of Dick's lonely Xmas at Camp Lejeune last year and the possibility of a lonelier one next year if the war continues. And we were homesick. We tried to hide it from each other with no success.

Everything was for the children, despite the fact that we bickered amiably for a week on Xmas technique. Should we clean out the fireplace so Santa wouldn't get dirty? What should we have for Santa to eat or drink? Should Jonnie's note to Santa be removed, or should there be an answer written on the back in Santa's writing and so on and so forth ad infinitum.

If I do say so, we put on a good show (never forgetting the help from you folks). Smokie, your box was as usual thoughtful and generous. I could hardly enumerate the children's reactions to the separate items, but their mother can tell you how she reacted to the bathrobe, sweater, and the mittens in particular. She was thrilled. The bathrobe is an excellent fit and so grown-up that Jon seemed transformed before my eyes into a school age boy.

You know we wish we could have done more this year. It made us feel badly, but we thought you would understand better once you received the bottle of champagne and read the news about our little newcomer on the way. I hardly wanted you to know, Smokie, but if you had seen me you'd have known immediately. But at least I can say that I am well and contented (like all expectant female creatures should be) after three bad months. It's wonderful to feel well again and look forward to this baby with much pleasure. And I think Dick is particularly happy about it. And you, L. G., I suppose are nodding your head and muttering, "It's about time." It is indeed. It should have been last year, if our spacing scheme of one every two years could have been maintained. C'est la vie.

There's a great storm brewing through the window. I can see Jon's pup tent waving in the breezes, so I had better knock off and secure the house.

> *Ever so much love to both of you*
> *Martha*

I like your letters, Mom. You seem full of zest and spirit. You write well too. Was this the real you or was this your political self, carefully crafted to say the right thing, create the right impression? Are these perky charming letters your way of hiding behind a smile?

By the way, I'm the baby that you were carrying that Christmas of 1944. As you wrote these words, I was probably sleeping inside you, lulled by the steady comforting rhythm of your heartbeat.

22 West Cedar Street

December 28th, 1954

Dearest Smokie,

I can't begin to tell you about our Christmas until after I've gotten off one round of thank you notes. The main joy has been family participation to an astonishing degree. Jonnie shopped crazily daily. He, as a sort of grand finale, collected many dollars from the other three children and presented us with a clock radio. We were stunned and concerned for their financial solvency, but they were all very debonair and insisted that they wanted nothing so much as to disburse their funds completely for Christmas. Lauris did a beautiful job of selecting several small presents for everyone. Even the little boys shopped and wrapped.

My mother and dad came down and we put on quite a Christmas dinner with no help. However, Mother and I worked quite well as a team. But, you know, Christmas is the day of the year that never ends! Truly by four o'clock I didn't think I would last, so I mixed myself a potion, good and strong, and went into the seventh inning, exuberant.

There's so much to tell: Dick getting Christmasy on Friday

and sneaking a golf bag for me into the house, Christmas carol-
ing in Louisburg Square with a thousand people and a dozen
oddly assorted and quite discordant instruments, Dick stealing
off to make a tour of the open houses while I played busy elf
alone either wrapping or cooking, and so much laughter.

That boy of yours and mine is a miracle of joy and compo-
sure in difficult circumstances. As you know, nothing has
improved about the Coonamesset situation. Dick's had to take
out another huge personal loan. Anyway, when I'm about to
come unhinged from pressure, he smiles his confident green-
eyed smile, and I get so exasperated that the tension passes.

> *Well, darlings, a happy good New*
> *Year to you both. With love*
> *Mart*

1944 to 1954: What a difference a decade makes. One can sense
the storm brewing now. Christmas, "the day that *never* ends," "A
potion good and strong" to bring on the "exuberance," parties that
Dad gets to go to, but she can't because she's doing the cooking and
the wrapping "alone." Dad helping her with her anxiety by being so
cheerfully optimistic: "I get so *exasperated* that the tension passes."

It was still a good show. Much singing and laughter. Yet, I can
hear the discordant notes of instruments slightly out of tune. I
catch glimpses of a troubled heart between the lines.

The last letter is to my sister.

22 West Cedar Street

October 7, 1965

309 Central Bldg.
Deaconess Hospital

Dear Lauris,
I love your letters and your phone calls, and we miss you
and closer contact with you. Life seems to prevent us from

*appreciating what we have until we don't have it anymore. At
least it's always so with me.*

*I am sitting here in the Deaconess in the process of being
very scientifically admitted—for once and for all—to straighten
out the Martha drug cycles. Drs. Thornton and Blair are going
to consult and it shouldn't take long. So don't worry. I don't
belong in a hospital bed, but I can't seem to quite do it at home
midst politics, housework (you've noticed what a bore it is),
Treadway Inns, etc. Ironically I feel better than I have in
months. Tis ever thus.*

*Except for your many disappointments and problems,
which I hope are smoothing out—keep wanting to talk to you
to see if you have any new thoughts about your boyfriend situation and/or the life of womankind. You might stumble on a
truly great idea to resolve many niggling problems for young
women. One which occurs to me is to put yourself in one outfit (sort of a uniform) so you would never have to fuss about
clothes.*

Next day—midmorning. Wonderful hospital, strenuous!

Schedule—
Sleep 11:30 P.M.
5 A.M.—Urine Sample
7:20—Blood from arm
7:40—Insulin shot for appetite and pill for same
7:45—Blood from finger—pregnant technician, cute
8:00—Dr. Fleming
8:05—The Boston Herald
*9:00—Breakfast at last, coffee, orange juice, Cream of
Wheat, egg and toast. I enjoy it immensely.*

*Just now, darling Dr. Blain has left after directing me to
walk, eat 6 times a day and ordering up a bicycle for my room.*
*These times are all approximate because a good technique
that I learned from you is to be timeless, to put your watch*

away, and to take things as they come—can't do this at home, and you can.

The boys are all right. We have very little contact with them; a call on occasion would be appreciated.

Love you so very much. Think about you more than the boys because I was a girl and your problems seem familiar to me—whereas the boys' lives seem strange indeed. If you had one wish—wish to be a boy for a short time.

Love,

your mother

"Life seems to prevent us from appreciating what we have until we don't have it anymore." This seems so sad. The poor lost woman in the midst of being poked, peered at, and lectured is still relieved to be in hospital, momentarily free of her crushing feelings of responsibility and failure. "I feel better than I have in months. Tis ever thus."

And what is their idea of treatment for this woebegone woman? Exercise, rest, and pills to regulate her appetite, sleep, and mood. Why didn't they try bleeding her with leeches or drilling a hole in her head to let the evil vapors out? Maybe it would have worked better.

It's all so pathetic. Where did the vibrant, bright, ebullient woman of the other letters go? Here she is, reaching out to her only daughter from her hospital bed. She records her schedule dutifully to Lauris, the nurse in training. Her idea to help womankind is that one should wear a regular outfit so that one needn't "fuss" about clothes. She was so lost: so incapable of "taking things as they come."

And then the end of the letter. "The boys are all right but we have very little contact with them." I turned my back on her during those last years. It never occurred to me that my absence mattered to her.

"Love you so very much." Reading that makes me feel a sharp jagged pang of jealousy. Lauris got this letter. I didn't. My mother never wrote the words "I love you" to me. Or maybe she did? Would the cavalier boy that I used to be even have noticed or cared?

"If you had one wish, wish to be a boy for a short time" seems like such a plaintive wish to be able to connect. Yet, as I sense the intimate connection between her and my sister, I wonder whether it would have been different if I had been a girl. Maybe she would have felt close to me, too. Maybe I would have been able to reach out to her?

"Think about you more than the boys because I was a girl and your problems seem familiar to me. The boys' lives seem strange indeed." It was so true. Mom and I were strangers, slipping by each other in silence. It reminds me of ships passing at sea.

On the long night watches, you have to keep a look out for the running lights of other vessels. You watch the lights in your binoculars carefully. For a small sailboat, the other ships are dangerous company. Sometimes the huge oil tankers are on automatic pilot. They could slice you in half and they'd never feel the impact.

I'm always wary of ships at sea, but I'm also comforted by their presence. The ocean can be a lonely place. As I watch them pass by I wonder how their crew is faring. Are they tired, bored, even a little lonely, too?

I watch them carefully: the distant running lights of dark shapes moving silently across the horizon.

TWENTY-ONE

Mom in her studio, 1962

DEAD ENDS

DRIVING OVER TO BARBARA'S, I'M FEELING SO RELIEVED. THANK God. I took Cindy over to the hospital this morning and she signed herself in. There's no guarantee, but at least she's in a safe place for now. She even thanked me for our crazy session and said she knew now she couldn't do it to her kids. I apologized for yelling at her and she made one of her wisecracks, "Hey, I just needed to see if there was anyone home behind that Dr. Cool, Calm, and Collected mask of yours." I laughed uncomfortably. She sounded a little too on target, a little too much like my sister.

I glance at the cardboard box of letters sitting in the passenger seat. "Well, Mom, I guess this is as close as we're ever going to come to a session with my therapist. I hope you like her. And don't be afraid. I'm not out to nail you. I'm just trying to get to know you."

"What do you think of this lady?" I ask Barbara after reading the first three letters out loud.

"There's a lot there. I'd like to know how you feel reading her words, hearing her story in this way," Barbara replies.

"I like her. She seems spirited, considerate, and joyful. I wish I knew her. Listen to this last letter though."

I begin to read the letter my mother wrote from her hospital bed to my sister. Once again, the tears come. I keep reading. When I finish, I reach for the tissue box.

"You know, I think I'm going to invest in the Kleenex company now that I've become their number one consumer," I say ruefully.

Barbara looks at me for a moment and then says, "Yes, it's a very sad letter."

"In a way, it says it all. The lady really isn't a shrouded mystery. She was an ambitious and insecure woman married to an ambitious and insecure man. When their fabulous American dream turned into a nightmare, she cracked first. Being a fifties woman, she felt the load of feelings for both of them. Her being an emotional and physical wreck probably helped maintain him in the role of the big strong man.

"But she would have survived all that, except for the alcohol and the fucked up treatment she got. It makes me sick to think of that distraught woman sitting in her hospital bed being given shots to whet her appetite and an exercise bike. If somebody had only gotten her off to A.A."

Barbara looks at me for a moment and then says with some hesitation, "David, I'm sure you know that A.A. wasn't a very hospitable place for women back then."

Her comment pierces my shield of anger.

"I know, I know. It's so easy for me to blame. I blame Dad, the doctors, God, everybody. I know it's bullshit. I just don't know what to do with how bad I feel. I miss this woman. I was so jealous of my sister getting a letter like this. She had a relationship with her. I don't even remember her. Maybe we ought to try that technique we did last week of my going back into the past and seeing if I can locate her. She's got to be in there somewhere."

"David, she is in there, and whether you can find her today or not, know that you have already done the hard work of opening your heart to her. And her wish to be a boy expresses her own longing for a way to make contact with you, with her sons."

"I know that now. After I read the letter, I found myself having the fleeting wish that somehow, if I had been a girl, I would have been able to connect to her. Maybe she would have felt more comfortable with me. That seems so pathetic."

"There is nothing pathetic about your yearning to have some kind of closeness with your mother. Are you ready to go back there to see whether you can find her now?"

I instantly close my eyes, and like a scuba diver falling backward off the side of a boat, I plunge into my own deep and murky water.

At first I can't find anything. All I can see are images of my mother that seem as flat and lifeless as photographs. Then she's there at her writing desk.

"I see her."

"Tell me what you see."

"Well, she's in her studio. She's at her antique writing desk that has a row of cubbies on the top for bills and stuff and lots of little drawers. It's against the left wall. To her right is her painting area, in front of the big bay windows that provide plenty of natural light. There are two easels, one with a painting of a naked woman on it that she had been working on. There are paints, brushes, and stuff scattered everywhere."

"What is she wearing?"

"She's wearing a gray wool skirt and black crew-necked sweater, black stockings and black flats."

"What is she doing?"

"She's writing letters."

"Where are you?

"I'm standing in the open doorway between the kitchen and the studio. I'm looking at her."

"What are you wearing?"

"I'm wearing a blue blazer, striped shirt, club tie, khakis and loafers."

"You're dressed up for an occasion?"

"No, not really. We always wore a coat and tie to school, so these are my normal clothes."

"How old are you?"

"I'm about fifteen."

"Why are you in the doorway?"

"I need to ask her something, but I don't want to interrupt her. Wait a minute; there's something else I just noticed. On her desk, she has a full glass of Dubonnet on the rocks with a twist of lemon."

"How does seeing the glass make you feel?"

"Cautious, very cautious. It's why I don't want to interrupt her. It's early in the day, so it's probably going to still be okay. But I'm not ready for her to turn and look at me. I've got to ask her a question. If I didn't have to I wouldn't be there. I don't want her to look at me with her big fierce owl eyes that look right through me as if I weren't even there."

"That sounds like a scary look. How are you feeling right now?"

"I feel frightened and mad. Cold. I don't like standing here. . . . This is as far as I can go. This isn't what I wanted to be doing. Fuck this. She's pissing me off."

I open my eyes and stare at Barbara. "This isn't going anywhere. I didn't want the anger today. It's all old hat. I wanted to find my Mom, not the drunk. Her face looked like the one in the painting."

"You really hoped to find a different experience of your Mom today. Do you want to tell me about the painting?"

"Summer before she killed herself, she did this self-portrait that is almost too awful to look at. Her face is so cold and haughty. My mother was never your basic raging drunk but she could look so hateful it could turn you to stone. She caught that look on canvas. I think it was the last painting she ever did. I have it buried somewhere at home. Nobody wanted it. But I didn't want to deal with her drunk self today. I wanted to make a connection to the woman she used to be, the woman who wrote those earlier letters. This whole process always takes me back to the same old dead ends."

"The mother you're looking for was imprisoned inside the 'drunk,' a little like the boy in the doorway locked up inside his anger and his fear."

"We can't seem to reach each other."

"You will."

TWENTY-TWO

Dad holding Jon, 1940

TUR-A-LUR-A-LUR-A

September 1991

NATURALLY, THE DRIVE DOWN TO THE CAPE IS A HARROWING race to make the Nantucket ferry. Kate was delayed by a dying patient and was an hour and a half late getting home. I squeezed in an extra client on the foolhardy assumption that Kate would be home on time and we would do the packing together. I yelled at Kate, snapped at the boys, broke the speed limit, cursed the slow drivers, and now I'm reduced to muttering under my breath and glancing at my watch every thirty seconds or so. Kate ventures the possibility that I might be feeling a little tense about visiting my father.

"That's bullshit! If you had been home on time I wouldn't be so goddamn agitated. You know that if we miss the ferry, they'll be terribly upset."

She smiles right through my anger and takes my hand. After a moment's huff, I finally can't resist smiling back. "You're right. I really am nervous about this weekend. My defensive shield is down. I don't know why. I didn't used to care at all. Now that I've been worked over by Doctor B., I'm a bundle of nerves. This is one of the great benefits of therapy, I suppose."

"Well, what do you think is really bothering you?"

"Maybe I'm nervous about how he's going to respond to the first chapter of my book I sent him. God, I felt nervous even putting that innocuous piece of writing in the mail. But I don't really know why I'm so mad at him. I'm so caught up in angry feelings about the past. I'm like a nuclear waste dump with a radioactive half-life of five hundred years or so. In recent years, he's been trying really hard."

"I thought you weren't going to make excuses for him," Kate interjects.

"That's true, dear, but remember it's not up to you to express my feelings for me," I quickly remind her.

In the old days, before I started the work with Barbara, Kate would always be the one to express annoyance about my Dad's tendencies toward self-centeredness. He would invariably irritate her and then I would have the task of defending him. Blood is thicker than marriage. While loyally defending Dad, I wouldn't have to feel my own disappointment in him. Kate and I had agreed that it was time for her to retire from the job of feelings bearer. Therefore, I'm dreading this weekend. I don't really want to let myself feel how profoundly superficial my relationship with my father is.

"Well, I guess I will treat this weekend as yet another opportunity to deal with *feelings*. God, I get tired of this therapy stuff. I don't want to spend two days just being agitated and hiding behind my smile, and—"

"Dad?" interrupts Sam.

"Yes, Sam."

"Don't you like Granddad?"

"Of course I do," I say sharply. I can't believe that we forgot all about Sam in the backseat. Michael's sound asleep, but Sam has been all ears.

"You know, Sam, how sometimes I do things that get you mad like when I tell you to stop watching cartoons?"

"Yeah."

"Well, there are some things that happened between Granddad and me that used to make me a little mad. But that doesn't mean that I don't like him. I love my Dad a lot. And I know he loves me."

"What things?"

I laugh. "You'd have to ask, wouldn't you, Sam? It's hard to describe. Most of the things happened a long time ago when I was a little boy. My Dad was a very important guy and he wasn't home much. I suppose I wish he had been around more."

"You mean he went around to all the states giving presentions like you do."

"That's *presentations,* not 'presentions,' Sam. Besides I think he was away a good bit more than I am." I look at my watch again. "Dammit all. We don't have a prayer of making it."

Kate smiles knowingly. Sam accepts the change in subject.

"When are we going to be there, Dad?"

"I don't know, Sam. I just don't know."

I catch a glimpse of Sam's little face in the rearview mirror. I remember being little and riding somewhere with my Dad in his shiny new Pontiac. It was unusual for us to be alone in the car. It made me feel proud and important to be in the front seat of the car with him. I remember the squeaky clean smells of the upholstery and vinyl. I felt swallowed up by the big plush front seat. I could only see the sky over the dashboard. Dad was listening to Bing Crosby on the radio. I looked at the trees rushing by the window. I tried to think of something to say.

When the song ended, I said, "Gee, he's got a nice voice."

"You should hear him sing 'Tur-a-Lur-a-Lura.' "

"He sings our song?"

"No, David," Dad said with a chuckle, "we sing his song."

"Oh," I said. A new song came on. I looked out the window again. Dad hummed the tune. But, at least, we had talked a little. It felt good at the time.

"Tur-a-Lur-a-Lur-a" is an Irish lullaby that Dad used to sing to us on the occasions when he put us to bed. It was a favorite.

I used to sing it to my boys when they were younger. The first time I sang it to Michael was on the way home from the hospital. He was a tiny bundle in my arms. I cried like a baby.

I glance at Sam again. Will this wonderful moment with his cranky Dad be one of his memories?

We see Dad and his wife, Peggy, at the ferry dock as we pull in. There's a strong wind blowing in from the water. From high up on the ferry, the two of them look old and frail as they huddle close together. Their shoulders are hunched to the breeze and their windbreakers are flapping. They remind me of yellow autumn leaves being yanked at by a cold November northwester. I'm ashamed of my mean-spirited feelings.

"Dad, it's so good to see you." I give him a big hug. He gives me a good strong squeeze back. I note with interest that we both put a little extra oomph in the hug.

Their condo is right on the beach in front of Nantucket Harbor. It's quite small and it'll be a squeeze for them to accommodate the four of us. As Peggy shows Kate and the boys where they'll be sleeping, Dad takes me aside.

"I liked your chapter a lot," he smiles.

"Thanks, Dad." I'm glad he brought it up so quickly.

"The only question that I have about this book is who you're writing it for. Is this book for therapists or the public or what?"

"It's for a general audience."

"Well, it seems to me that if it's going to have a chance to make the *New York Times* best-seller list, you really ought to consider turning it into a novel. My friend Henry Tisbury, you know he won the Pulitzer Prize in 1954—told me that novels are what really sell."

I don't know what to say. I can't believe that Dad's immediate focus is on selling the book.

I smile. "Well, Dad. I really haven't been worrying too much about a marketing strategy. I haven't even bothered about getting a publisher yet. Are you sure you're not uncomfortable with my writing about our family?"

"Oh, no, I think it's just fine. Your mother's story needs to be told and many people will benefit from understanding her tragedy."

"I honestly don't know whether it will be helpful to others, but it's helping me. I'm finally facing my own shadow."

"Oh," he replies and then beats a hasty retreat to help Peggy with dinner.

Finally Kate and I are alone.

"Well, did he say anything to you about your writing?"

"It was typical. All he cared about was how to turn the book into a best-seller."

"How did that make you feel?"

"It didn't surprise me."

"But did it upset you?"

"For Christssake, Kate, would you stop therapizing me? One shrink is enough."

I get into bed in a huff. I'm such a jerk. I can't let Kate comfort me. I care too much what my Dad thinks. It annoys me that he still thinks the book is primarily a biography of Mom. What will it be like for him to read the whole thing? He'll probably be bored. Why should I care? I shouldn't still be needing his approval. But I do.

I lie still in the dark, listening to the surf breaking on the beach. My Dad's sleeping in the next room. He's seventy-nine years old. He's an old man lying in there with his eyes closed and his jaw slack. Is he curled up into a ball? Is he snoring? Maybe he is lying awake staring into the dark as I am?

In a blink of an eye, I'll be a tired and weathered old man. What bill of indictments will my sons nail to my front door someday? Will my parenting crimes get me a life sentence of blame, too?

The weekend unfolds according to plan: tennis, lunch, shopping, cocktails, dinner, bridge, sleep, breakfast, tennis, bridge, ride to the ferry. It's as well organized as Disneyland. Keep moving, keep doing, have fun. I dress appropriately for each event: tennis whites, blazer and lime green pants, khaki shorts and alligator shirt. Dad and I don't talk about the book again. He probably feels awkward. I do too.

I'm a wreck when the boys get to play tennis with Dad and Peggy. I want them to play well so that Dad and Peggy will be impressed. I also don't want to push the limits of Dad's patience. Sam can barely hit the ball at all. I can't believe I'm so worried about their performance.

On one of the trips back from the court, Dad and I drive alone. Dad says out of the blue, "You know, I wasn't the greatest father. I never had the kind of time that you take with your boys."

I'm taken aback. It was such a genuine, simple statement. I don't know how to respond. I'm annoyed instead of pleased. It seems somehow too little and too late. My sourness appalls me.

"Well, times were different back then, Dad. Fathers weren't expected to be all that involved with their kids," I say as graciously as I can to smooth over my jagged feelings. Then, suddenly, I remember the question I've been meaning to ask.

"By the way, Dad, this is sort of a jump shift here, but when I was talking with Aunt Jane about Mom, she told me that Mom intentionally overdosed on pills the summer before she killed herself. What happened?"

There's a long pause.

Then Dad says, "I don't remember her doing that. I mean sometimes she took too many pills, but I didn't think she really meant anything by it. We never talked about it."

For a moment, I can't breathe. His words choke me. I can't say anything.

"I'm sorry I can't remember more about it. It was a long time ago," Dad says.

On the car ride back to Weston, the tension in me spills out like an overheated radiator. I berate Michael unmercifully when I discover he hasn't begun his astronomy project.

Kate suggests that I'm overreacting.

I berate her.

I'm such an ass. Dealing with my mother is easier than with Dad. At least she's dead. Dad is very much alive and I'm pissed at him all the time. It's no wonder we hardly ever go to visit. It used to fill me with self-importance to work with him on managing the family. We were a team. But that was a long time ago.

The implication that Mom overdosed and no one did anything explodes inside of me like a dumdum shell.

No doubt Barbara will want me to "grieve" my relationship to my father. After all, it's one of the standard stations of the therapeutic cross. I can't wait.

"David, can we please slow down. You're driving over eighty."

"If you don't like it, why don't you drive? I'll walk."

"Please, Dad, don't get so upset?" asks Michael tentatively.

"Mind your own damn business," I snap.

The car becomes thick with silence.

I remember my mother spitting those same words at me.

I feel like ripping my face off.

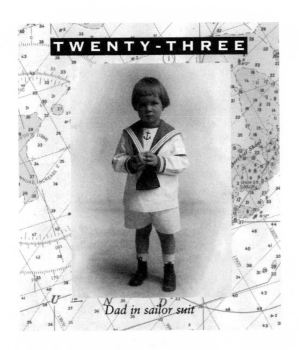

TWENTY-THREE

Dad in sailor suit

A FAR CRY

THE PLANE RISES OVER THE FIELDS CUT INTO NEAT SQUARES BY strips of road. A muddy stream is winding its way between the orderly patterns of cultivation. The stream's undulations are hidden from the roads and houses by a thin stand of trees along each side. Perhaps for the farm boys and girls it's a place of mystery, where they retreat from the parental glare on hot summer days for experiments in skinny-dipping and playing doctor.

Looking down from my window seat, the incongruous thought of Conrad's Kurtz working his way up the African river pops into my mind. Is this stream the local Congo where budding children explore their own hearts of darkness? From the 747, the stream looks as wispy as a loose thread on a plaid jacket.

I tilt my seat back and smile at myself. Perhaps my intensely self-absorbed journey into the dark recesses of my soul is just another adolescent adventure along the banks of a piddling stream in a forest ten trees deep. Was all of my current introspection just a variation of "playing doctor" with myself?

Of course, I want my therapeutic journey to be larger than life. I want my pain to be special, my story to be tragic. Maybe it's time I listen to what I often tell my audiences: "We all would like to be filet mignon, but in reality we're just meatballs."

I just completed a workshop in Fort Wayne, Indiana, called "To Thine Own Self Be True." It was fun and exhausting as collectively the audience and I explored how incompetent, confused, and insecure we feel as therapists; how much our responses are shaped by the limits of our gender, our current life compromises, and the crazy families we came from.

After all the theories are spoken, and all of the therapeutic techniques applied, the best of what we have to offer our clients is to share our own flawed humanity without shame. We are not all-knowing guides, marching fearlessly ahead of our clients as we lead them along the harrowing mountain trails. Yes, we do have pitons, rope, and hammers. Yes, many of us have made the climb before. We have maps and weather reports. It is good to have experience and equipment. But ultimately, our willingness to share the risk, to give gentle voice to the fear, and to hold the sweaty palms is the gift that heals.

At least that's how it feels on the good days. On the bad days, we're not much more than a "rent-a-friend," offering a less reliable result than your average escort service.

This was a good day. We all acknowledged our insecurities together. At least there are a lot of us on the same mountain. I'm glad I don't know what they all really thought when I acknowledged that I was undergoing my own therapy. Several participants told me during the break how much they appreciated my openness.

One young woman said, "To think that someone like *you* would admit that you still need to be in therapy means so much to me. I have been ashamed about going myself and wondering what my clients would think, if they knew."

I smiled at her weakly. The idea of my clients' reading this book made me shudder. I found her compliment unsettling. Through the miracle of therapy, I was now much more vulnerable than I used to be. Sounding open and vulnerable in front of two hundred people is quite different from *being* open and vulnerable.

"Undergoing therapy" is a good choice of words. I struggled with Barbara last week about my relationship with my father and the car ride back from Nantucket. I feel so bitter and blaming toward my old man. He doesn't deserve it. And I'm too old for it.

As the plane nears Boston, my thoughts turn to the upcoming retreat at the monastary. I can't believe that somehow I, Mr. Smug Agnostic himself, am dutifully heading off to an overnight meeting of my men's prayer group. It's all Mark's fault. I never should have taken the guy sailing with me. It made it impossible to turn him down when he asked me to join the prayer group after I had told him about wishing that I could genuinely believe in God and develop a meaningful spiritual commitment in my life.

Naturally I had screwed up the schedule. The meeting had started at six o'clock, with prayer followed by a silent dinner with the monks and then the first group discussion. I had completely forgotten that I would be flying in late from Indiana and would miss all of the evening program. What a shame, I mutter sarcastically. I'm thoroughly entrenched in my old familiar adolescent resistance.

Fortunately, the rest of the group of graying, middle-aged men seem to share the same difficulty in opening their hearts to God. Most of us have a problem with believing in the idea of God in the first place. What we share is a yearning for a meaningful spiritual life. We've been meeting monthly for almost a year with Father Tom from the monastery and Mark, our minister. So far we're still quite taken aback when Father Tom asks us questions like "Have you prayed to God about that?"

It's nine o'clock when the plane touches down. I drive like a wild man into Cambridge. I can't find the damn place. I drive around with the interior light on, reading and rereading the directions that I didn't write down carefully. It's dark. The streets are poorly lit. I can't read the street signs well. I feel stupid and wish I could get lost enough to justify heading for home.

Just as I'm about to give up, the street that I'm on dead-ends in front of a dark looming unlit shape. There's a gate. PLEASE DO NOT PARK IN FRONT OF THIS GATE, says the sign. To the right of the sign is a little gold plaque. I can barely read the small lettering, St. Paul's Monastary.

I wander around until I find the visitors' entrance and ring the door bell. Nobody answers. I ring it again. Nothing. Maybe nobody will answer and I can go home. Then the door swings wide and there's Mark, with a big grin underneath his handlebar mustache.

"Come in, come in," he whispers enthusiastically. "I thought it would be you."

"Why are we whispering?" I whisper.

"No reason," Mark replies in a low but normal tone of voice. "It's just that you get used to the silence around here, particularly when you're over on the residents' side or around the chapel. I'll show you your room and then I'll take you on a tour."

"How many residents are there?"

"About thirteen monks live here full time."

"Jeez, this is not exactly a booming growth industry, is it?"

Mark smiles. "Actually, given the status of the monastic life in our culture, this place is considered to be thriving. There are forty monks in the order spread among three different houses. Besides, it's like the Marines. God just needs a 'few good men.'" He winks at me.

Mark's saving grace is his utter conviction that God has room for everyone, including even the likes of me, and his ability to carry his deeply felt faith lightly.

We walk up the stairs of the guest house. The polished mahogany railing, the thick wine red carpet, and the navy blue floor-length drapes beside the lead paned windows contribute to an atmosphere that's heavy and still. There's a solid, masculine quality to the place as if it were the upstairs quarters of a stodgy British men's club.

We go down a narrow corridor by a series of numbered doors. Mark stops at number 12. My name is printed on a little card and inserted in a Plexiglas frame on the door: David Treadway. Seeing my name on the door is disconcerting. The room is a spare cubicle barely big enough to contain the dresser and the bed. It reminds me of my old Dorm C alcove at St. Mark's that I moved into in the eighth grade. That's appropriate. I'm feeling about thirteen.

I drop off my suitcase and Mark takes me over to the residents' side. The bare wood floors, the whitewashed brick walls, and the dim light make it seem like an ancient catacomb. Now we whisper in earnest.

"How much of the day do they spend 'in silence'?" I ask.

"They hold the silence from the 6:00 P.M. service until after breakfast."

"How many times a day do they go to the chapel?"

"There are five services a day, beginning with Matins at 6:00 A.M. and ending with Compline at 10:00 P.M."

Mark opens some thick oak doors and leads me into the chapel. It's a small chapel with bare walls and a marble floor. It seems stark and empty. At the altar is a statue of Christ on the cross. When I look at it closely, it surprises me. This Christ doesn't look as serene and God-like as some do. The face is contorted with pain. The shoulders look dislocated, as the full weight of his body sags earthward.

"I couldn't stand chapel once a day at St. Mark's. I can't imagine what it would be like to be doing this four or five hours a day for your whole life."

"I suspect that, like anything else you do, it just becomes part of everyday normality. Come on. I'll show you the dining hall."

The long mahogony tables and the black walnut straight back chairs in the dining room also remind me of boarding school. It's odd to think of all the silent munching that goes on in here. Can you ask for the salt? Or do you point? An irreverent image of cows endlessly chewing their cuds in collective yet solitary silence comes to mind.

"Two meals a day in silence seems almost as oppressive as five church services," I say.

"But, consider this," replies Mark. "At least nobody talks with his mouth full."

I laugh in spite of myself. "Well, I've got to get to my little cell and catch some ZZZs."

"I'm glad you made it, David."

"I'm sure God is thrilled."

"You never know."

"Right, that's the problem. You never know. Good night, Mark. See you in the morning."

I'm tired but I'm too out of my element to fall asleep. I pick up my novel, but I can't get into it. Then I notice the Bible by my bedside.

Leafing through the pages, I don't know what to read, even though Father Tom gave us a Bible study guide to read over the summer. I lost it. I'm just going to jump in somewhere. I come upon the Gospel According to St. Mark. This would make Mark chuckle, for openers.

I find myself in the section that describes the days leading up to the crucifixion. The story seems strikingly different from the way I remember it. Instead of approaching it as if I'm studying the WORD OF GOD, I'm reading it like a novel.

Christ seems more like a person. Obviously, he intuited his destiny and felt scared. There's a passage where he's clearly disappointed with the disciples and tells them all how they will each in turn betray him. Then he says, "My soul is exceedingly sorrowful unto death." He goes off to pray and says to God, "All things are possible unto thee; take away this cup from me."

Jesus seems scared, and quintessentially human in his moment of doubt and vulnerability. Is this truly God's gift to us; God's way of being with us, knowing us? So many others seem to have been able to grasp this idea. The glimmer of possibility cuts through me.

I've never been moved by reading the Bible before. As I reach over to turn off the light, I'm suddenly aware of feeling deeply calm, utterly still.

I remember the sunset in Christmas Cove on last year's cruise in Maine. We had pulled in there just as the light was fading. It was a rough passage from the Isle of Shoals with dense fog, a strong southeast wind, and occasional bouts of heavy rain. Everyone was tense as we worked our way from buoys to whistle. Kate and the kids were seasick.

We made harbor just as the sun broke through, showing a brilliant display of reds, oranges, and pinks through the clouds. We rounded the headland and suddenly we were out of wind. Inside the cove, the water was absolutely flat. Everything was still. In the distance, we could hear the crashing of the surf on the ledges outside, but tucked up into the head of the cove it was quiet.

For a moment, we sat in silence, breathing in the rich aroma of the pines and watching the sunset. We listened to the squabbling gulls. We were utterly still.

The memory rocks me to sleep.

I try reading the Bible again at dawn, but can't recapture the feeling. I try praying. It annoys me.

I don't know how to pray. I can pray for my clients like Cindy. I can express a depth of gratitude for the blessings of my life. I can even ask for His mercy for Kate and my childen. I can't imagine praying for myself. Tom teaches us that prayer is simply sitting down to a conversation with God, a kind of fireside chat. I'm far from that.

After dressing, I start to change the sheets as per the directions on the door. While I make up the bed for the next soul-weary pilgrim, I wonder why the idea of talking to God makes me angry.

Maybe this is the koan about the sound of one hand clapping. Maybe I'm afraid just to put my hand out. Overlapping images of God the Father and my Dad reverberate. I never talked to my parents about anything personal after I was about five or six years old. They had their life and I had mine. It wouldn't have occurred to me to share my innermost thoughts with them. I assumed they would be either uninterested, patronizing, or impatient. The absence of any intimate connection with either of my parents never even bothered me. I considered our parent-child relationship as normal as freezing weather during New England winters. "Don't complain about the cold, go skiing" would have been my credo.

As I tug the sheets straight on the bed, I realize that my

abortive attempts to relate to God have the same pro forma, superficial quality as my relationship with my father. I'm just going through the motions. I glibly blame Dad for our false relationship, but I'm no more honest with him than he is with me.

Someday I would be standing in front of Dad's coffin. What would I have to say for myself then? I remember Fran's last days, the joy of being able to express my love honestly, the sense of peaceful completion at the funeral. Would I feel that at Dad's burial?

"The hell with it, what have I got to lose?" I say out loud in my empty cubicle. It's high time I shoulder some responsibility for changing my relationship with Dad. Time to "stop sitting on the pity pot" as they say in A.A. Dad is seventy-nine years old.

I'll start writing him honest letters. I'm not interested in beating up on him. I just want to be direct and true. However he responds will be up to him. I'll be doing it for myself, without laying any expectations on him at all. I'll just thrust my one hand out. If we clap, fine. If not, not.

I'm suddenly shaken. I look around the spare little room. Many names have been placed in the door plate. Many tired bodies have lain in that bed. Many prayers have been spoken, many tears shed. I'm not alone. I'm not special. I'm just one among the many.

A prayer I was afraid to say feels suddenly answered.

"Thank you, God," I whisper.

The chapel is almost filled with the thirty or so people present. The monks dressed in black cassocks sit in the front row of chairs. Our group of guys and numerous other guests are sprinkled among the Brothers. We wait in silence. Father Mark had mentioned that the morning service was the celebration of the "Feast of the Cross." I had never heard of it, but I suspected that a longer than normal service was in the offing.

I smile at myself. Once again, I'm trying to cloak myself safely in my usual comfortable cynicism. But who am I kidding? Typical cynics aren't sitting in a monastary on a beautiful Saturday morning celebrating the Feast of the Cross with a group of guys in long black dresses who can't converse at most meals and who spend their lives praying. I'm kind of a closet supplicant, a spiritual virgin yearning to be swept away by the passion of faith. My cynicism is a thin veil indeed.

As the service unfolds, the hymns, lessons, and prayers direct our attention to Christ's last few days leading to his agony on the cross. "You sly dog, God," I mutter, having accidentally read about Christ on the cross the night before. It feels as if I've wandered into a spiritual "Twilight Zone." Much to my surprise, I'm relating to the words of the service as I recite them.

In his sermon, Father Brian tells a story that he heard from Elie Wiesel, the well-known survivor of the concentration camps:

It was dawn on a raw January morning. There had been some infractions the night before. Everyone knew there would be reprisals. They rousted us out of our beds, giving us no time to dress or even relieve ouselves. We were all herded together in a motley formation on the parade grounds. We were made to face a makeshift scaffold where there were three nooses dangling. Beneath the nooses stood three figures, two men and a little boy about nine years old. The men were known to me. They were part of the resistance. I hadn't seen the boy before.

As the nooses were fitted around their necks, the two men stood with their shoulders squared and their heads held high. Their silent, stony glare was dignified and defiant. The boy, on the other hand, was shaking all over. His face was contorted by panic as his eyes darted back and forth, watching the guards put the nooses on the men and then move over toward him. He started crying in loud wracking sobs. Then he started begging. "Please, please," he wailed.

This was too much for many of the women and I could hear many of them snuffling in the ragged lines behind me.

Then I heard a low, angry man's voice whispering bitterly, "Where is God? Where is God?" His question seared me because I still dared to believe in God. Even in this place.

After the guards had tightened the nooses, they stepped back and without further ado threw the lever that released the trapdoor under the feet of the three. They fell through like sacks of potatoes. The men died instantly. Their emaciated bodies hung still. Their pants were soiled with fresh waste. Their heads tilted at a grotesque angle.

The boy didn't die. He didn't weigh enough to have his neck broken by the drop. Instead he flopped about at the end of his rope like a sturgeon on the floor of a fisherman's skiff. He was gasping for breath.

Many of us averted our eyes, but the guards weren't finished. They made us march single file within touching distance of the three dangling bodies. Close up I could see the men's bulging eyes, their tongues, thick and protruding. I could smell the stench. The boy was still alive. His face was pink with exertion, but his twitching had slowed. It wouldn't be long now.

As we passed I heard that same low angry voice. "Where are you now, God!"

I spoke before thinking. My voice was almost a shout.

"God is that boy."

I sit utterly still as tears stream down my cheeks. God *is* that boy. Christ on the cross *is* that boy. God knows our fears and weaknesses, our desperate whimpers. "Father, Father, why hast thou forsaken me?" He's been there. He suffers with us. He doesn't avert his eyes. He is always there. God *was* there with my mother.

I don't brush away my tears. They are a gift.

The gathering of men is in the Undercroft. There are eight of us including Mark and Father Tom. I'm nervous as I wait for us to begin. I wonder whether anyone saw me crying. This is, after all, a bunch of proper New England Yankees, not a therapy group.

After a brief inquiry about how we all slept and enjoyed the services, we lapse into silence.

I look around the room. I'm not going to talk first. But I can't help it. "I feel as if I've been in the presence of God for the first time in my life," I blurt out. Suddenly everyone is staring at me.

I try to explain the jumble of thoughts and feelings I've been experiencing in the last twelve hours. I describe the way that my relationship to God mirrors my superficial, hollow relationship to my Dad, my determination to become more direct and honest with my Dad, and my tentative feeling of God's presence.

Trying to talk about the dying boy chokes me up. "It's the idea that God is the boy, suffering his experience as well as our own.

That God knows us for all our weakness and cruelty and loves us anyway. I could feel the possibility of such a God."

I pause, fighting the damn tears again.

"Maybe such a God could love me."

Some of the men shift uncomfortably in their chairs. I can hear the ticking of the grandfather clock. I can't look at anybody. Mercifully, Tom breaks the silence. "Thank you, David."

Many of the men look directly at me, showing some warmth and acceptance. I'm already less ashamed.

Then Mark fills the empty space.

"What you said, David, about feeling as if you relate to God the same way that you relate to your father struck a deep chord in me. I too noted that some of my feelings I chose not to share with God were the same kind of feelings that I wouldn't have discussed with my father. These are feelings I'm ashamed of. I wanted so much to have my Dad's approval that I hid from him for years all of the parts of me I was sure he couldn't accept. Believe me, there were some periods when I was hiding just about all of me. I think I do the same with God. I don't tell God about the things that I don't think are on his list of acceptable feelings. And here I am telling parishioners every day that God embraces all of us."

"The truth is, I think my father would have accepted all of me, too, if I had only had the guts to tell him. He's been dead now for four years, but sometimes I wake up in the middle of the night and I can almost feel him with me. I just want to put my arms around him. I want him to be there so badly."

Mark wipes his eye with his sleeve and then smiles at me. "So you better do it. Write to your old man; say what you've got to say. As that famous author might say, do it *Before It's Too Late.*" He gives me a broad wink as he twits me about the title of my book.

As the morning unfolds, the men talk progressively more comfortably about their relationship to God and to their fathers. I've touched a nerve. The commonality of our experience is comforting. Each of us expresses in our own halting manner the depth of our shame and our yearning. For once I'm not running the show. I'm just a member. I belong.

Toward the end of the meeting, I say, "You know, guys, this stuff about God is beginning to leak into my regular life. Just the other day, I was surprised to hear myself ask a client whether she had talked to God about her problem. The client looked surprised and uncomfortable, then politely ignored me, and went on with what she was saying. I felt embarrassed, as if I had just farted."

Everybody chuckles as we share our collective discomfort about acknowledging God.

"I suspect God even has room at his table for a bunch of confused middle-aged farts like us," says Mark.

When I get home, I want to hug Kate and each of my sons. Michael pushes me away with a mock scream, "Help, help! Police! I'm being mugged by my father."

Sam runs upstairs.

Kate assumes my hug was the precurser to a sexual initiative and quickly whispers in my ear that she's just gotten her period.

So much for being a prophet in one's own land.

For a moment, I thought the shimmering glow of joy that I brought home would burst like a child's delicate bubble when it lands on the grass. Pop. Gone.

But it doesn't.

I've decided to write to my Dad tonight. First I'm going to go back to that letter box. There are some letters that Dad wrote to his parents when he was a Dartmouth student, along with my mother's letters. It's a good time to read them.

The portrait of my Dad as a college student moves me. His letters are filled with earnest promises to study hard, soaring hopes about his social successes, worries about how his younger siblings are doing, and poignant declarations of appreciation for the love and support he felt from his parents.

Excerpt from one of my Dad's letters:

May 3, 1935

Dear Mother and Dad,

I would like to write you something that would cheer you up and strengthen your hope and confidence, but I am such a poor letter writer that my deep feelings for you at this time must of necessity be inarticulate. . . .

Everything is going well here in Hanover, and slowly but surely, day by day, I am learning to apply myself with more diligence. I won't make the mistake of crowing too soon as I suspect you will want to see the "proof in the pudding" at the end of the semester. . . .

Being elected to the club has made me happier than almost anything else that has ever happened to me. I'll tell you why if you promise not to laugh. Ever since I was a little boy I have ended my prayers at night by saying, "And please help me to make good when I get to Dartmouth for Mother and Dad. Amen."

So now you see how much it has meant to me.

      Love,
      Dick

P.S. I have met a most delightful member of the fair sex. She's the daughter of one of my professors. Her name is Marty Chamberlin. More about her, later.

My heart aches for that earnest, sweet college boy from long ago. Now it's my turn to write a letter.

Dear Dad,

It was great for all of us to see you and Peggy two weeks ago. I was particularly pleased by the interest you showed in my children around the tennis, etc. Your being their only grandparent makes your involvement very important to my kids. Kate and I want to extend our thanks to Peggy and you.

I've enclosed a couple pictures of us for the frame that I gave you for your birthday. Let me know if they're not the right size.

This past weekend I went on a prayer retreat with some other men from my church. We spent a night and a morning at an Episcopalian monastery.

One of the questions our spiritual director asked was why we don't share our feelings with God. I was making the bed in my little monastic cell, meditating on that question, when I realized that not being open with God was very similar to the way I'm not really open with you. Most of my relationship with God has just been going through the motions while feeling a lot of "who gives a damn" adolescent resistance. Unfortunately, how I relate to you is painfully similar.

In reflecting on all of this, I discovered that the heart of the reason why I don't open myself to God is that the silence of the response is too painful. It's the same reason why I don't open myself up to you.

When I was very little, I learned not to share who I was and what I felt with either you or Mom. You said at one point during our visit that you had come to realize that you and Mom weren't great parents. I think you're right. You weren't. I don't think you and Mom related to us kids as people. We were problems to be managed, bills to be paid. I don't think I ever came to you for advice, to talk about myself, or to be comforted. In retrospect, I know how much you loved us and how hard you worked to give us opportunities that you didn't have, but we didn't really have much of a relationship. I loved you and admired you from afar.

I felt close to you for the first time that summer of 1965 when you and I were in the house together and Mom was so depressed. I finally felt we connected because I could be helpful and supportive. I felt important.

For the next twenty years or so, our relationship evolved into an odd partnership in which we were close when I acted like your therapist. I also kept my own distance because I deeply resented your self-absorption in your painful struggle to recover after Mom's death and your lack of any demonstrable interest in my life. Just because I didn't go crazy or turn to booze doesn't mean I didn't experience my own pain about the destruction of our family in the wake of Mom's death. But I didn't share any of that with you, and you never asked.

I want to make clear the positive side of our relationship, too. I have felt deeply supported by your willingness to give me

*generous financial support at several critical periods of my life.
Plus, you have always been very appreciative of my support of
you with your problems managing your marriages as well as
the other family problems.*

*I feel like our partnership has been a mixed blessing that we
created together. I don't blame you for it.*

*Since the mid-eighties, our relationship has improved signifi-
cantly. I have mostly retired from my role as our family's therapist and you have become significantly more solicitous toward
me. You are careful about imposing on my time, nurturing
about my struggles with my knee, and supportive of my writing. I appreciate it.*

*Given how hard you've tried to improve our relationship, I
am surprised at how much difficulty I still have being open and
honest with you. In Nantucket, you expressed a desire to talk
more frequently and I came up with some lame excuse about
not liking to use the phone. That was bullshit. Sometimes I feel
like I'm being deliberately withholding to punish you. Maybe
it's because I am afraid of not getting a genuine response.
Maybe I'm afraid of the silence.*

*Sitting in my little cell, I realized I was fed up with going
through the motions of a father and son relationship. Life's too
short. I understand how difficult it is for you to know and
express your feelings after a lifetime of training in saying what
other people want to hear. Believe me, I've been a chip off the
old block. We're both natural politicians.*

*It may be difficult for you to respond to this letter. Whatever
you do with it is okay because I'm not trying to change you.
You don't owe me anything.*

*You weren't always a great parent. But guess what? Neither
am I. I know I have been profoundly hurtful to my sons. It's in
my own self-interest to find a way to forgive you for your fail-
ings, because I need forgiveness, too. We're both flawed fathers.
We're both sons.*

*Just before I started writing this, I read through letters that
you wrote your parents when you were at Dartmouth. They are*

filled with an earnest desire to do well and make your family proud of you. I felt moved and sad for the burdens and ultimately the tragedy that has befallen you. You did your best.

I don't want to end this letter on a whiny, critical note, but one of the reasons why I don't feel as close to you as I would wish is that I'm never honest with you about stuff that upsets me. I have to tell you that I was disappointed in your response to my chapter. You focused on marketing, and you didn't say anything about what I actually wrote. I didn't get any sense of what you really think about me doing this book. Do you even remember that grotesque mockery of cheerfulness we put on when we brought Mom her breakfast tray?

Well, Dad, I've got to go to work. I don't know what you'll do with this. That's up to you. I've decided to keep trying to write, no matter what. You're the only Dad I am ever going to have and I want to open my heart to you.

> *I love you (and I mean that)*
> *David*

P.S. The pathetic image of you and me trying to wheedle a smile out of Mom by acting like a couple of vaudeville clowns still makes me so sad. No wonder the lady turned her head away.

We blew it, Dad. We should have been yelling at her. "Don't do it! We love you. Don't leave us, damnit!"

TWENTY-FOUR

Mom's self-portrait, 1965

DATE OF DISCHARGE: FEBRUARY 5, 1966

April 1992

IT'S BEEN A COLD SPRING. LAST NIGHT, KATE WORRIED WHETHER the impatiens plants we bought would die. The temperature was supposed to get down into the high thirties.

The whole family has been working in the garden this year. Of course, we have to flog the boys into service, but this has been the first time that I haven't dragged my feet like a recalcitrant teenager myself. I have thoroughly enjoyed shopping for plants and bushes, digging and watering, even raking and weeding.

"Maybe all that money you're spending on therapy is working after all," said Kate. "I never thought I would see the day that you would volunteer to come with me to Russell's to look at rhododendrons and azaleas. What's going on?"

"I don't know. Somehow I feel that our home is more like my home now. Maybe I'm finally putting down some roots."

Kate chuckled, "Great. Talk about your basic 'late bloomer.' "

Today is a cool, crisp, sunny day. The cold front blew through in the night and there's a dying northwester riffling the bright newly minted leaves in the trees. Outside my window, the chirping birds compete noisily with the hum of my computer. I'd rather be out back planting the azaleas.

Perhaps April really is the "cruelest month." Maybe that's why my mother didn't risk waiting until spring. Maybe she didn't want to be tricked by another season of false hopes, seduced back into life by the ephemeral beauty of tulips, daffodils, and magnolias. She picked early February, the dead of winter.

I knew when I started writing about my family that I didn't want to write this chapter on the last months of my mother's life. I was afraid of going through the feelings. I was afraid I wouldn't feel anything at all.

In the last few months, the work with Barbara has been slow and difficult. I continued to bang away on the walls that kept me from myself, the past, and my mother. I often felt as helplessly doomed as a sailor locked in an airtight compartment tapping on the hull of his sunken ship. But I knew Barbara was there. She never lost patience. She never pushed. She trusted me and trusted our work.

In my search to find a way of connecting to my mother, I even took my mother's self-portrait to a session. I propped it up on a chair between Barbara and me.

"I know this is weird, but I can't engage with this lady after all the reading about her, talking about her, and writing about her. This picture shows her crazy, bitchy side that could slice you in half with a look. I never dealt with her at all during those last years, Barbara. Just look at that cold, icy stare."

Barbara sat still and looked at the picture for a long time. Finally, she turned back to me and asked, "David, who is she looking at with that 'cold, icy stare'?"

I looked back at the painting. I looked into my mother's eyes and then I got it. "My God, she's looking at herself." I blurted out, "She obviously must have been looking in a mirror when she painted this. This is what she saw. It's so filled with hate and self-loathing. All these years, whenever I've looked at this, I self-centeredly related to the picture as if she were looking at me. I didn't understand it at all. This angry, cold woman is what she saw, who she thought she was. This is how she felt about herself. The poor woman. You have to be riddled with self-hatred in order to be able to kill yourself, and it's all here. It's all in this painting."

I pause for a long time. "I know that look, Barbara. I see it sometimes when I look at myself in the mirror. The same damn cold stare."

After the session with the painting, I knew it was time to address my mother's descent into suicide. I kept wanting to keep her at arm's length. I didn't want to feel the depths of her desperation and pain. During the last months of her life, I virtually had nothing to do with her. I was away at school and out of touch. I had turned my back on her. Here it was twenty-six years later and I still had the same response. I couldn't face the woman.

This is going to be a hard week. I've cut back on my clients. I have scheduled four writing mornings, a follow-up phone call with my Uncle Tiger, and two sessions with Barbara. I have the writings of my Dad and my siblings spread around the computer. We're all here, present and accounted for. Let the drum roll begin. Forward march.

Dad

The fall of 1965 was a hazy one from a memory point of view. Martha was struggling to maintain her mental equilibrium, struggling to get out of bed in the morning to go to her art class, struggling to maintain her interest and morale during the class, and struggling to be a good wife to me during my new beginnings in the insurance business. We had already realized that selling the Treadway Inns had been a terrible mistake. She blamed herself for that, too, like everything else.

Dad has never forgiven himself for the sale of Treadway Inns. I asked him about it a few days ago on the telephone.

Dad explained that he had just run out of steam after so many years of crushing debt. He couldn't resist the offer to sell out even though his own family, who all worked in the business, really opposed it. He was the eldest son and company president. Everyone had always deferred to his judgment, and so everyone in his family reluctantly accepted the sale. Mom had encouraged him in this decision. She had been complaining about the difficulties of sustaining the family business for years. However, shortly after the sale, Mom's depression and drinking became dramatically worse. She told Dad it was the worst decision of their lives.

"Suddenly she had nothing to do," Dad explained. "The inns were always her other children. She had such an important role in every part of the business. You kids were all away and she was alone. I wasn't there either because I was hustling to get my insurance business off the ground. Day after day, she was home alone with nothing to do."

I heard the pain in Dad's voice. His guilt was still eating at him.

"You know, Dad, she pushed for it. She wanted it more than you did. You just did the best you could."

Dad didn't even seem to hear my reassurance. "If only I hadn't left her at home with nothing to do. Maybe we could have bought an old resort hotel and fixed it up together. She could have thrown herself into the redecorating and hiring the staff. It would have been starting over again. It could have been like the Publick House."

The possibility Mom and Dad actually might have pulled out of their tailspin is more than I can bear. I imagine her in the kitchen puttering away at dinner. I can visualize her with gray hair and a wrinkled face. I can see her smile. She would have been seventy-three this year.

Dad

Martha spent that fall painting and then repainting a very poignant self-portrait, which literally cried out with despair, a portrait which I really cannot bear to see. Several times I would personally escort her to the subway to make sure she went to the art school. On several occasions, when I checked by calling the house, I would discover that she had turned around and taken the next subway car back and had gone back to bed.

Most of each weekend was spent in bed, most of the time reading, but other times staring at the ceiling. I was at my wit's end.

Christmas, 1965 limped along its merry way. It was full of psychological confusion with only an occasional happy moment. The children were home for Christmas at West Cedar Street. It should have been a very happy time. But Martha's eccentric behavior was noticeable to all, and in fact she was so fragile that the traditional Christmas dinner, which she would normally prepare, was moved over to the Parker House. Needless to say we did not add any strays to this dinner.

Jon

To tell you the truth, David, I don't remember much about that Christmas. At the time, you may recall, I was in an intimate relationship with Jack Daniels. I remember the family trooping over to the Parker House for that rather dismal lunch. I particularly liked the rolls. I think I stuffed a few in my jacket to eat later.

Jon's still quite cavalier about Mom's suicide, but twenty-five years of Jack Daniels hasn't been able to wash away the pain. I hear it in his voice. He still loves her and misses her. He just doesn't want to know it. I know how he feels.

Lauris

1965 in December (not a year of our Lord for me!!!!) Christmastime in New York City is a pretty and jolly time to the many who love the city, love themselves, their families, their lives. For me, living in New York back then was a daily/nightly nightmare. My mother's illness invaded every corner of my existence. Every piece of furniture that she gave me for my first apartment screamed at me to do something to relieve her suffering in far, far-away Boston town.

"Mommy, Mommy, Mommy," I cried. "I can't help you, Mommy. I can't. I can't help myself." I wandered around my apartment crying like a lost child.

At least, I'm going home for Christmas with David and Jimmy. She'll be better, I know. And I'll feel better. It's got to be different this time.

These two bright, handsome, jovial brothers have always lifted my spirits since our smallness in early childhood. My love for David and Jimmy was stronger, purer, and happier than any love I felt toward the rest of the family. I fantasized that I was their little mother and that it was my responsibility to take care of them, protect them, nurture them, secretly. I guess I felt that our real mother did a rather sloppy job in all these areas, what with all her varied interests, absences, and personal problems, physical, mental, marital, spiritual, but especially nurtural (new word, dear? yes a new word).

Please understand that the writings of these honest and brutal feelings must also include the dialogue I have simultaneously with my dead mother, who has graciously consented to be an active part in the family healing and yes, I am quite certain she has been with me all along, comforting me and guiding me across the live wires of insanity that I wouldn't have survived alone, okay. So what if I have chosen Ma to be my higher power, to sponsor me in the program, to cheer me on through life, one day at a time. Whatever floats your boat, right, Ma?

Ma, this seems the appropriate moment to let you know that I am aware of the wickedness of myself. I competed with you in every area of your existence. My love for you was passionate and wild. But deep inside I hated you, you hot and cold Mama, you hurt me. Hurt me so, too critical Mama. Your artist, perfection, eye, nothing ever right enough, my hair, my nose, the way I wear my clothes, my lips, my voice. Maybe I was one of the children only a mother could love. That you loved me more deeply, maybe even more than the others, maybe even more than you loved yourself, has never completely removed the pain or the scars from your kind of rose bush, barbed love.

Oh, dearest, hot and cold Mama. I envied you, your beauty, your talents, your ability to enchant others.

Ma, I wonder if I was ever a child. It seemed I was a grown-up since birth. Either I felt like an angel or the devil's child, either your best friend or your arch enemy, wolf dressed in sheep's clothing. Was it I who killed you????? Nope, no, I didn't do it. It wasn't me. Don't lock me up again. Don't turn the key. I am innocent. Stop blaming me. Don't you see you killed yourself? You judged yourself, sentenced yourself, executed yourself. The penalty for murder is death so death is what you got. But damn you, you were never satisfied with anything, not even with death. Or Dad, you ate him alive with your negativity. Your final statement was soooooo negative. You loosed all the demons in hell on your family.

Oh, Ma, you know this is the dark talk. You know and I know, we both have agreed that dragging the dark out into the light is the greatest power we have against evil!!!!!!!!

Bad Mom, good Mom, angel mother of my heart, thank you for allowing me to use you as the scapegoat for my negativity. Only those who knew you and loved you know how truly special you were, how bravely you fought to save your life and ours. 'Tis but for the grace of God that it is me living to write about us.

"Lauris, this is your mother speaking. Do you understand the meaning of OVERKILL??? Don't bother looking it up in your teeny, tiny dictionary. It's not in there. It means to kill your mother over and over and over and over again. I agreed to be here with you while you're writing because you promised that it wouldn't be all the same old tiresome tale of woe. I am losing patience with all your self-centered pain, and if you don't start tempering your remarks with laughs and jollies, I will take my good humored dead soul elsewhere and let you dry right up."

"Oh mother, you are sooo correct. And with a grain of salt still left from the rivers of tears cried so long ago, I rejoice to have your criticism, wisdom, and most of all your teasing humor here. Yes, it's not all black. Perhaps you are trying to steer me back to the story. Yes, where was I. Christmas. 1965."

Twas the day before the night before Christmas. My protective pattern of sleeping away all my free time before and after work was pleasantly and boldly interrupted by my brothers' visit. Whatever was my constant sleep protecting, my sanity? Of course, I was in a miserable state of depression, Mom and me, both. I found out later that, while I was sleeping full time to avoid the living, Mom was unable to sleep at all. No, I didn't take her sleep from her. I didn't I DIDN'T!!! I didn't even know she wasn't sleeping.

"Hush child," Ma says softly. "Everything is okay now, tell about your brothers."

David and Jimmy came bouncing into my bedroom together, cheering loudly. "Up, up, up, Lauris. Time to eat, drink and be merry. We're going to take you out to a party."

"There is nothing, zero, zilch in your refrigerator," said Jim loudly in my tuned out ear. "You're clearly a hopeless case, Sis."

They tickled my toes and squeaked my nose until I screamed for mercy and a cup of coffee. David bowed deeply and politely addressed me, "Madam Queen, Black? A bit of cream? One sugar or two?"

I pulled the covers over my head and moaned muffly into the pillow, "Black, Black, Black and make it snappy, brave knave, or I will go back to sleep."

"Yes, Madam, at your royal service," said David as he bowed with an exaggerated flourish.

I found myself all warm and smiling at the backs of the two boy/men as they retreated from my room to fetch the coffee. On the way out, David couldn't resist checking out his gorgeous self in the mirror. Ever since he was little, David had a thing about mirrors. We always teased him about it. I suspect it was his way of looking to see if he was there.

The little boys' enthusiastic effort to jolly me up touched me deeply. It felt so surprisingly good to be happy for a moment that I couldn't wait for the coffee. I got up and put on my best uniform, which was only slightly stained with blood and baby spit-up.

Both brothers are charmers, but David was more apt at flattery and diplomacy. He said, "Gee, you look terrific, Lauris. Ummm, is that a new uniform? Wouldn't you prefer to put something else on for the party and change into your uniform before your shift starts? Actually, where we're going everyone will be dressed to kill."

Jim piped in and said bluntly, "That uniform isn't even clean. You've got stains all over it."

The truth hurts, and I started to do what I am most famous for in the family. I started to blubber again. Sniveling and sobbing, I whined, "But I don't have a clean uniform, and I don't have a pretty dress for a fancy party. I haven't eaten for two days. Where are we going, anyway? I can't handle trying to find something else to wear. Can't I go like this? I have a really pretty coat. I promise, I won't take it off."

"There, there," David there, thered me, patting me gently. "Don't worry, be happy. We're off to the party. It's being given by a girl I kind of like named Kathy Kennedy. No one will mind what you wear. After all, the booze has been flowing for hours. We'll have a blast. We'll definitely get into the Christmas spirits."

Lauris knew and was suffering side by side with Mother. I didn't let myself know. I was in the Christmas spirits. I don't remember the last few days that I was home with my mother. We didn't even show up at West Cedar Street until Christmas Eve, two days late, and we never called to tell the parents. None of us wanted to go home. Mother must have been wracked with anxiety, waiting for us to arrive at any moment for two days.

It was awful at home. My father was trying to jolly everyone up and my mother wandered around dressed in a bathrobe with a vacant, dead look in her eyes. I didn't know at the time how whacked she was on Dr. Blair's prescriptions.

Dad

On February 1st, my brother John, who is my closest friend, spent the night with us. Even though Martha was terribly fond of John, she was so depressed she refused to see him.

I was really worried. The following morning I went to my office and immediately called Martha's psychiatrist, a very pleasant lady who lived in Cambridge. I told her that Martha was extremely depressed and urged her to contact her right away. She said, "I'm seeing her tomorrow."

In the meantime, I asked a housekeeper who Martha liked to come in everyday to do some light work and perhaps provide Martha some much needed companionship. When she agreed, I impulsively decided to go home early because I couldn't wait to tell Martha. It was two-fifteen. I remember calling up the stairs to her, "Guess what? I've got some good news."

Martha was lying in our bed in a coma.

I immediately went to the locked document box where I kept my Seconal which I was taking for insomnia due to my anxiety. I discovered she had, by a tremendous exertion, torn the hasps from the box and taken 30 Seconal.

She must have been so fiercely determined. I've seen that box she ripped open. It wouldn't have been easy to do. Thirty pills. Clearly she was committed to doing it right. What does it feel like to take thirty pills? You can't do more than four or five at a time. So you stand at the sink with a glass of water and you just keep shoving them in. Making sure that you don't gag and throw them all up. You see yourself doing it in the mirror. Maybe you have doubts, but you shake them off. You force them all down. You can feel the glutinous lump in your stomach. You feel bloated. It's not too late to throw them up. But you don't. You walk into your bedroom. Your eyes must take in every detail of the room. Your head begins to feel heavy. Your thoughts must begin to thicken.

What was she feeling as she pulled back the covers? How long did she lie there, conscious? What was she thinking about before the poison finally snuffed her out?

I remember Cindy telling me that what stayed her hand was the thought of one of her children finding her body. What the hell did Mom think it would be like for Dad to come home and find her?

Dad

I called the doctor and ambulance immediately. She was taken to Mass General Hospital. I remember riding to the hospital with her and praying.

From that Wednesday until Saturday noon, I went about my business and visited the hospital once or twice a day. I spent considerable time in its chapel. Martha was in a coma being fed intravenously. I was not encouraged to think that she might come out of the coma. I didn't tell anyone about her hospitalization. I reasoned, however, that it would be better for her if no one knew about her suicide attempt, when and if she rejoined us.

On Friday night I was at the hospital talking to a young intern who was a personal friend of ours. He said, "I don't care what the other doctors say, there's absolutely no hope." I called my brother, John, and asked him to come down from Williamstown.

He came and we went over to the hospital at noon Saturday, February 4th, at which time I gave the doctors permission to yank out the tubes and let her die.

It is a sad end to a happy, beautiful, and useful life and I do not have the ability to put into appropriate words how much she meant to me and our children.

Despite the funeral service being held at 3 PM on a Monday afternoon, the ground floor of Trinity Church was filled and Dr. Ferris, the Rector, did a magnificent job in his very personalized prayer of Thanksgiving for the life of Martha Treadway.

On Wednesday, Lauris, her friend Corny, David, and I picked up her ashes and took them to Williamstown for a brief service at Westlawn Cemetery where they were interred in the beautiful family plot.

I have since carried with me the deep and abiding hope that her beautiful soul will finally rest in peace.

I stare at the computer screen for what seems like a long time. Dad carried so much on his shoulders. Those hours must have suffocated him. The poor bastard. He tried to be a hero to the bitter end. He went through it alone. Living in the house, sleeping in their bed, going to work, sitting by her for hours, and praying in the hospital chapel.

And did she find peace?

I pull out the medical records again.

The last admission has a discharge summary on top:

adm/date	time	name
02/02/66	2:55 P	Treadway, Mrs Martha

Date of Discharge: Feb 5, 1966

Principal Diagnosis: Barbiturate Intoxication

Condition on Discharge: DEAD

The words are simple and stark. The rest of the record simply fleshes out the bare bones. She was truly dead on arrival. But they hooked her up to the machines anyway. They did their best to keep her heart beating and Dad's hope alive.

As I read through the bland medical entries of each day, I'm smacked by the image of this dead woman with a respirator pushing air into her lungs like a bellows. I can imagine her chest moving up and down under her nightgown.

I pause and listen to the sound of my own breathing and watch the rise and fall of my chest.

TWENTY-FIVE

Merry Christmas from the Treadways

Christmas card photo, 1962

CLOSE REACHING

CINDY'S TWO CHILDREN SEEM SCARED. MY ATTEMPTS TO PUT them at ease don't seem to help. Jack is six and Claire is four. They're towheads just as Jimmy and I were at that age. They've squeezed together in the easy chair leaving Cindy alone on the sofa. Claire's sucking her fingers.

This past year must have been terryifying for them. I suggested that Cindy bring them in for some sessions a long time ago, but when she was at her worst she was adamant in her refusal to include the kids. Now that she's been sober and doing much better, the kids have been coming apart. Jack's been acting out in school and Claire's been wetting the bed.

The session is awkward as I encourage Cindy to acknowledge

all the difficulties of the past year and how hard it's been on them. The kids are silent. It's much too grown-up for them.

"Hey, do you two play with guys?" I ask. Clearly straight talk won't be the way for these cute little clams to open up.

They both nod shyly.

"Would you like to play with some of my son's toys?"

Finally Cindy, the kids, and I are on the floor and we're playing house with Sam's G.I. Joes. At first the kids pretend that it's a perfectly harmonious little household, but quickly it deteriorates into a more normal jostling and conflictual scene.

Suddenly little Claire says, "Let's 'tend the mommy's sleeping so hard we can't wake her up."

She lays the mommy down and then Jack and she take turns trying to wake her. They yell at her, pull at her, and finally hit her. Cindy looks at me over their heads. Her eyes are filled with tears. I nod at her.

"Can I be the mommy doll?" Cindy asks the kids. "You can go ahead and try to wake her up."

This time Cindy has the doll sit up and say, "Oh dear, I've been sleeping so long that you children must be very hungry. I'm so glad you woke me up because I think it's time for a big breakfast. I'm *never* going to sleep that long again."

As the G.I. Joe family argues over home-cooked versus McDonald's breakfast, Cindy gives me a wink. It's been a long haul. And we still have a way to go. But thank God, we made it this far.

11:00 A.M.

Just finished with Bill and Sarah. The work with Bill's Mom has brought them even closer together. Their relationship has improved now that, as Bill says, "We've exorcised the parents."

I'm jealous of them. I'm more in Cindy's position. I still have a long way to go. I've got the whole middle of the day off to work on my stuff, beginning with a scheduled phone call to my Uncle Tiger and Aunt Cynthia and ending with another session with Barbara.

Cynthia begins by telling about the last time she saw my mother.

"We didn't know that Marty was in bad shape until about three months before the end. But that last visit was so awful. Your mother seemed to be feeling just terrible, but she wouldn't talk about it. She wouldn't let you get near her. It was as if she were a trapped and wounded animal. As far as I could tell, she wasn't talking to anyone. I would be surprised if she was telling the truth to her psychiatrist. And I suspect that she felt absolutely dreadful that she couldn't be her normal gracious and charming self. She spent most of the visit in bed."

Both Tiger and Cynthia talk at length about what a "star" Mom was and how the role was, perhaps, a burden for her. Neither of them had been aware of the severity of the drinking problem.

Cynthia goes on to say, "I think that one of the most difficult things for your mother was that she was basically honest and straightforward for all of her enormous social skills. She had a truly penetrating clarity. She saw through people's pretension and illusions. I think toward the end she looked hard at herself and her life and found it simply unacceptable. She was much harsher on herself than others. I think she must have felt trapped inside a life she lost faith in."

"That was one thing that she didn't have that was always a comfort to Dad and me. She didn't have a true faith in God," adds Tiger.

"Well, in the last months of her life, I know she turned to God," I reply. "But I guess she really didn't find any comfort there."

"Well, Marty's death sure was a test of my faith. I don't think Cynthia and I would have joined our Evangelical movement if it hadn't been for your mother's death. Marty's death just shattered me. I remember feeling like I was the straw that broke the camel's back. She was terribly worried about me that last week because I was in the hospital being tested for cancer. Your mother was absolutely terrified that the tests would be positive. Sometime during the beginning of that week, she managed to go out and buy a little portable radio that she sent with a get well card. She wanted me to have it while I was still in the hospital. She was gone before the tests came back. She never knew I was okay."

There's a long pause on the phone. I can't tell whether Tiger is crying. I feel bad for him. He seems to have a little shard of guilt still lodged inside, too.

It feels like a storm at sea. Everybody's story hits me like the steady thumping of huge waves smacking the side of the boat. I feel as if I'm close reaching: clawing my way against the wind. But I'm getting there.

Sitting in front of Barbara, I pull out Jim's letter. Reading out loud to her is a direct pipeline to my tears.

Jim

It was February, 1966. We were halfway through a very good freshman hockey season. We had a good team and we were kicking ass and having a lot of fun all along the way. It was on a Saturday. Sometime around noon, Rick Billings, my roommate, told me that I had to call home immediately, as there was a family emergency. I ran all the way across the Green to some pay phones by the student dining room. I called home and got Dad and as best he could, he told me that Mom died that morning.

I completely fell apart but managed to ask on the phone whether or not I should come home right away or stay and play the hockey game, which was about to begin. Dad was adamant that I stay and play the game. He said that I owed it to the team and that it would be good for me.

The game was a disaster, as was I. Somehow, Lauris and Mom's mom showed up at the beginning of the game as spectators, both of them aware of her death. Baba, at her advanced age, was unable to absorb the significance, I'm sure, as she seemed to be fairly normal. Lauris was acting strangely, but nowhere near as strange as I was acting on the ice. My approach to the game of hockey that day was almost comical. I felt the need to be everywhere that puck was. I also had extraordinary energy and strength, much to the dismay of my teammates. Everybody had great difficulty separating me from the puck, even when it was to our team's advantage that the puck be with someone else.

At the end of the first period we were in the locker room. As soon as we all got in the room, the coach and about five of my teammates all had the same question. It went something like this: "Treadway, what the fuck are you doing out there?" I was beside myself with my grief, but I wasn't showing it.

Rick Billings, my roommate, was a defenseman on the team, and he knew what was going on so he got the coach aside and told Coach that I'd just learned of my mother's death. He spread the word quickly to the team and everybody felt like real heels for being so unpleasantly aggressive about my bad play. The rest of the game I did whatever the hell I wanted to.

The next thing I remember is being in Baba's car, driving south to Boston after the game. I'd had a couple of beers and was kind of in a fog, just anxious to get home. Lauris was doing a good job of trying to console me, and Baba was there physically, but didn't seem to be all there mentally.

We got to Boston that night, and then, quite frankly, I don't remember anything clearly. I recall everyone drinking a lot, and a lot of crying and a lot of love being expressed. Jon was in a perpetual state of being anesthetized by bourbon, Dad was more manic than depressive, and he, too, spent most of the time totally shit-faced. Aunt Jane was mothering the hell out of all of us, which at the time I appreciated. David was being the essence of cool, and Lauris was experiencing a lot of difficulties, although I didn't understand what they were or why.

My reaction was to cry a lot initially and get a little stronger every day thereafter. If memory serves me correctly, Bob Gordon, Jane's husband, who killed himself a couple of years later, was around as well.

On Monday a memorial service was held at Trinity Church. It was really hard for me to sit through that. I just wanted to lie down on the pew and bawl. Somehow it was over and we got back to the Bloody Marys.

Interestingly, I was back in Boston in early June of this year and, while touring the city on foot with a couple of colleagues, I took them into Trinity Church, my first time in that edifice since February, 1966. It was much too much for me, and I started to cry and ran out, leaving my friends behind. Perhaps my memory of Mom's death is not that distant, after all.

A day or two later we all went our separate ways. I went back to Dartmouth in a daze, using my mother's death as an excuse to sleep more, drink more, and study even less, if that was possible. The faculty seemed sympathetic, and I know I took advantage of that sympathy. I really only cared about having a good time, being with my friends, and playing good hockey. Weeks later, I learned of Dad's flipping out and being committed to an institution. Also, Lauris was hospitalized in New York while Jon went back to Miami. Jane was our rallying point and tried to keep things together as best she could.

David and I seemed to be doing the best of everybody so we started traveling separately and together to visit Dad and Lauris in the loony bin.

I suppose I could go on through the next several years, but there's not much point, as we would get off the subject matter, which is supposed to be Jim and Mom.

I dealt with Mom's death in what turned out to be, in my opinion, a fairly healthy fashion. My grief at the time of her death was intense and gradually subsided with time. Each day after her death I spent less and less time thinking about her, until a couple of years after her death I'd pretty much put her out of my mind altogether.

Occasionally, I have dreams that include her, which are bizarre. Sometimes I recall some of the strange moments in my relationship with Mom, like the time she came to Martha's Vineyard wearing a horrible greenish brown wig and came into the main dining room of the Harbor View Hotel where I was a waiter. She did not acknowledge me, and I did a double-take when I saw her. I was certain it was my mother, but for some reason she seemed to be a stranger. I finally went over to her table and I said, "Is that you, Mom?" and she said, "Yes, it is. How are you, Jim?" I said, "Fine." It was like she was in a different world. She explained, sort of lamely, that she was just taking a couple of days off to get away from it all and was staying at the hotel and pretty much wanted to be left alone. I obliged.

Then there was the other time in her bedroom at 22 West Cedar Street. We were talking and she asked me very seriously and sincerely if I felt I was grown-up and able to handle life, and what the future might hold for me. It was late '65 when this conversation took place. At the time, I felt a little bit strange and awkward, and now, in retrospect, I think she was having a conversation that somehow fit in to her premeditated suicide plans. I think she needed to hear from me that I was okay and that I could get on without her. It was a strange conversation that I really didn't understand until after she killed herself.

Let me close by saying that as dramatic as some of all this may sound, my early years weren't too traumatic. I had a lot of fun and ended up being quite independent and self-sufficient, traits by which I've done well in later years. I loved each member of our family quite a lot, but was closest to David and Mom.

I can't think of too much else to say right now, and I really do have to get back to work.

I reach for the tissue box after reading Jim's writings. I glance at Barbara and shake my head, "Jim's surprise at being emotionally overcome by his return to Trinity Church is much like mine as I work my way through this book and therapy. I would have said that I had dealt with all this stuff a long time ago too. After all, according to him, I was 'the essence of cool.' "

"What touched you the most today?"

"Well, the two scenes he casually mentions at the end of the piece about my mother in the wig and her asking him whether he's going to be okay both grabbed me.

"I found myself feeling left out because she never asked me whether I was going to be all right. Maybe she thought there would be no point in asking because I wouldn't have given her an honest answer, anyway. I just would have said whatever I thought she needed to hear.

"I definitely remember that wig. Lauris mentioned it too. I was so embarrassed to see her wearing it. The wig looked like a dead animal lying on top of her head. She looked so bizarre. Maybe it was her way of showing how desperate she felt on the inside: her way of baring herself. I couldn't stand the idea that she barely seemed to recognize Jim. I remember feeling like that in those last years. It's like she wasn't there. Like she was already dead.

"I wasn't the slightest bit surprised when Dad called that Saturday with the news. He got on the phone and the first thing he said was, 'David, your mother passed away this morning.'

" 'Oh, that's terrible,' I said, but I didn't feel anything. 'What did she die of?'

" 'She took an overdose of pills.'

"Then I said something inane like 'Oh, that's too bad. Are you all right?'

" 'I'll be okay,' Dad said. And that was the whole conversation. The only other memory I have was of calling the airport to get on a plane and deciding that the situation was awful enough to warrant my reserving a first-class seat. The next few days, I was in the same pea soup fog as Jimmy. Maybe it would be more accurate to call it a bourbon haze."

"Do you want to go back there in the way that you have before?" Barbara asks.

"Nope, not in the slightest. I didn't feel anything then and I don't much want to feel anything now."

Barbara looks surprised.

"Just kidding," I say quickly. "This stuff really gets to be a little much, that's all."

"David, you don't need to force yourself," she says firmly, "You may still need some of the protection you get from being in the fog."

"No, I'm really ready. I just don't want to, that's all."

I slouch down in my chair and close my eyes. I am quickly back in my dorm room at school. I can see myself lying on my bed, reading, when the phone across the room rings. When I hear my Dad's voice, I know it's going to be bad news. I can't go any further.

"What's happening, David? Are you okay?"

"Yes, I'm on the phone and Dad's telling me. Then I put the phone down and I go to the window and I look out on Spruce Street. There are all these kids going to classes. They are all bundled up because of the cold. There's slushy snow on the ground. It's sooty with city dirt. It's been raining hard all morning."

"David, what are you feeling?"

"I'm not feeling anything. I'm just looking out the window. She doesn't mean anything to me. I'm just pissed off. Why did she pull this fucking stunt? I knew she was going to do it. I knew it. What the fuck was the matter with her!"

My anger snaps me back to the present. I open my eyes and I am relieved to see Barbara leaning toward me.

"David, let the anger come. Don't be afraid. I'm here."

I close my eyes again. I find myself in another scene.

"I'm in my mother's bedroom where she died. It's dark. Only the light by her side of the bed is on. My Dad is sitting on the bed with his head in his hands. He is sobbing. Lauris is sitting next to him with her arms around him. She's crying. I'm standing there. I'm just looking at them. I don't know what to say."

"What are you feeling?"

"I think, ah, I don't know. I guess I'm wondering why nobody is hugging me. But I know I don't want to join them on the bed. Somebody already tried to hug me when I got home. Maybe it was my sister or my aunt, but I just went through the motions. I feel nothing. I feel so alone.

"Wait a second, I'm still standing there, but now I'm looking past Lauris and Dad. I can see Mom lying there in bed. She's got a nightgown on and a bed jacket. It's a pink quilted bed jacket with a little lace across the front and tied at the neck with a bow. I can see it clearly. I don't know why it's important. I think Jimmy and I gave it to her for a Christmas present one year. She's sort of sitting up, propped up with pillows, but her eyes are closed. Her arms are down at her side. She's dead.

"And that's how I feel as I look at her. I feel dead inside," I say as I open my eyes again. Barbara is right there.

"This is the part of me that I have hated and been ashamed of all these years. The part of me that just feels cold and dead. I like it better when I cry; when I feel like I care. I hate this. I feel so empty. I've been trying to cover this feeling up ever since it happened. At one point, in that weekend, Lauris got mad at me because I hadn't seemed to be upset at all.

"She lashed out, 'What's the matter with you, David? You're acting like nothing's happened. Aren't you even a little sad? She was your mother, too.'

"I said something like, 'Of course, I'm sad. It's just not my style to go around blubbering.'

"That shut Lauris up, but I didn't really know what to say. I didn't know why I wasn't upset. I just went through those few days watching what was happening like I was sitting in the back row of a movie theater."

"Lauris was sad. You were mad. You didn't have a way to get closer to more of your feelings then. I think you felt jammed up by your anger, maybe even in shock."

"I didn't feel jammed. I felt cold and heartless. I didn't give a damn about her or anyone else. Listen, Barbara, I'm getting lost in the anger right now. I'm just feeling pissed off. Let me switch gears and read something that my sister wrote. I found it this morning. It might help me get past this wall of anger. It's a poem that Lauris wrote a long time ago that's so raw and connected to my mother. As bizarre as it sounds I'm jealous of her pain and her ability to express it. Listen to this."

SUICIDE
by
Lauris

The anger of the mother, the child, the wife
took her life.
In the dark of her soul's suffering
came a strengthness of hand
reaching for, breaking open
the locked, black, painted box of the death
of her choosing.
The large-boned, long-fingered, wide-knuckled veiny hand
poured capsule, after capsule, after capsule
down the willing throat.

Was she winning?
Was she losing?
None is quite sure.
Did she have regret?
> *Maybe many or*
> *no not any?*
> > *We will never know.*
Did she have to go?
Was it willed so?
> *We will never know.*

Then what?
She lay back down on the double bed
death thoughts swirling around her head
pleasant at first like soft rain, flowers, fields, and trees.
Her death in her lonely, warped mind
would be the gift of oblivion.
Death would mean she would no longer suffer
> *aliveness.*
Death would mean freedom from endless depressions,
> *fear-filled obsessions.*
Death would release family from the terminal care
> *burdens*
> > *of the many years dying, lost mother.*
The cost—only the price of the Seconal:
debts, perhaps a few. —credits, zero will do.
Everyone must die, why not I?
No tears left to cry, what else to do, but die.
She did this dying thing alone,
talked to no one on the phone.
It was midday,
upon the bed she lay in shuttered room,
close to her religious books.
Eyes closed, she waited for the dear death,
Odd peculiar patterns flashed like pictures in her brain.
Small voices called her name.
Spiraling sensations of inward, inward—

amoeba-like floating sensations,
floating in black waters.
Inward she goes
but where she goes
nobody knows.
She is somewhere in the labyrinth
of her inner ear, perhaps.
There is a time lapse, centuries,
maybe just two hours.
Does she?
Yes, she does, but no she doesn't, want to hear
the dear Richard, the wicked Richard calling,
calling her name, "Martha,
Martha."

The he of the she, Martha,
says inwardly to the her of the him, Richard,
"I'm not the same Martha.
It's not a game, Richard
I am dead, dying, dead Martha.
Soul sighing
Can't you see?"
Finally,
me.

The children, four, were not called
    to the deathness door of their mother;
not called to sit by the bed of the still breathing
    bride of their father;
not called until it was finally finished;
    all hope was sealed, locked away in the dead body.
not called until the Martha cells had marched away
    carrying with them the tiny soul
of Mrs "I don't care" / Mrs "I cared too much."

I put the pages down. I feel drained beyond tears. "Poor Lauris was like my mother. She didn't have any protection from her pain. She had the courage to care and it broke her. She's suffered so unfairly, twenty years worth of psychiatric hospitalizations doesn't begin to tell the story of the shit she's been through.

"As for me, I was a coward. I didn't give a damn about my mother or anyone else. I'm just a selfish shit with a smooth good-guy act."

Barbara leans toward me with outstretched hands. For a moment, she doesn't say anything. Her eyes are filled with concern.

"David, you may have been distant and self-centered, but you weren't empty and you weren't cold. When you were little, you tucked your feelings deep inside you for safekeeping. The boy under the pines, the boy in the sailboat was full of feelings.

"It's not that you didn't care enough, it's that you cared more than you could bear. Your 'cool' protected you. It was your life preserver."

Her words reach me. For once, I'm able to stay with her. I don't flinch from the warmth of her steady gaze. I remember the little boy under the pine trees, the little boy in the sailboat. I remember the studiously nonchalant teenager slouching through his mother's funeral. I want to go to him. I want to tell him he's not really bad. I would put my arm around him and tell him, "It's not your fault. It's really not your fault."

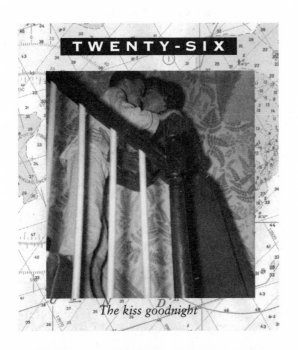

TWENTY-SIX

The kiss goodnight

MINIATURE ROSES

May 1992

ALTHOUGH IT CLEARLY SAID STURBRIDGE: NEXT RIGHT, I almost drove by the exit. That would be an inauspicious start to this therapeutic adventure, I thought. I finally had decided on a visit to my Mom's grave. I wasn't sure what I was hoping for. But for eighteen years, I have spoken the language of grieving and promoted healing rituals from the safety of the therapist's chair. Now it's probably time to practice what I preach.

As I pull off the Mass. Pike, I'm surprised by how little Sturbridge has changed. I go by the Publick House. Memories of our regular Sunday meals at the inn wash over me as I drive by. My younger brother, Jimmy, and I always had the roast beef, mashed potatoes, and more than our share of the breadbasket filled with corn sticks, garlic bread, and sticky buns. Being the owners' children always meant that the waitresses treated us like visiting royalty.

On the other side of town, I make the turn to go up the hill. It has been been thirty-five years since I last drove up Fisk Hill Road. As I pull into the driveway, I notice, with a small stab of disappointment, that our old house is now brick red instead of the bluish gray of my childhood. The barn where we kept our horses, the home base of the Fisk Hill Cavalry, is gone.

It's odd to be renting a room for the night in my childhood home, but our house now provides additional rooms for the Inn. I wanted to rent my old bedroom, but it was occupied. I turned down the offer of the master bedroom. I knew I didn't particularly want to end up in my parents' double bed. I chose my older brother's room.

As I walk through the living room, it's striking how little has changed. It seems like a museum. The TV is in the same place where we ate popcorn and watched "The Lone Ranger" and "Howdy Doody." The glass-topped coffee table with the magazines is still there. I wouldn't be surprised if they were the same magazines. Even the striped chintz living room chairs look like the same ones that my mother led us charging up and over in the parade when I was six.

It had been a rainy Sunday afternoon and my mother was bored. We were too. Mom decided we should play follow the leader. She called it a parade. We each had to wear something exotic on our head. I wore one of her hats with a veil, my sister wore one of Dad's fedoras, Jim had on a pointed clown's hat, and Mom had a *Life* magazine split over her head with the pages coming down over her ears. She marched us around the whole house, over all the fine furniture, including the dining room table. She got us singing and laughing as if we were the Von Trapp family. She could do that kind of thing. She used to be a lot of fun in the Sturbridge days.

After unpacking, I call Kate.

"I'm here."

"How is it?"

"Feels a little anticlimatic, so far. I think I might have spilled all the feelings I have left in Barbara's office."

"How are you feeling about the trip to the cemetery tomorrow?"

"I'm afraid that I won't feel anything. But I tell my clients that it's good enough just to do it and not expect they're supposed to have some kind of cathartic epiphany. I guess the same goes for me."

I eat dinner at the inn in the room called the Barn. For one hundred years, it has been the horse barn for the inn's guests. I sit at a table not far away from the mock stall where my family always ate our Sunday lunches.

I'm suddenly very tired. Being in this old house has unleashed a torrent of memories. It surprises me how many good feelings came back: skating down on the pond past the horse pasture; diving for pennies in the swimming pool; the first moments of pedaling beyond my father's supporting hands on my brand-new two-wheeler; playing the endless games of toy soldiers with Jon, and building block castles with Jimmy.

I crawl into bed, but can't fall asleep. I reach for Dad's manuscript and turn to his epilogue.

Dad
  Why did Martha kill herself? She wanted to. Her anxiety and depression had become unbearable. Her prescription drug–filled mind had rationalized itself to the point where she felt she was doing me and our children a favor by bowing out.

I put the page down and stare at my face in the black window across from me. I really have been better off since she died. I was just floundering before that, chasing girls and good times. Then my mother took her thirty Seconal and Lauris and Dad got sent to their respective mental hospitals and Jon retreated into alcoholism. That left me to pick up the pieces. I became the head of the family. I might have ended up a drunk myself if she had lived. Instead I became a specialist in treating families with addictions.

Suddenly I know it's time for me to quit drinking entirely. I should end my little self-control mind-games. More than anything else, alcohol killed my Mom. It could have killed me. I still don't drink in a healthy way. I never have.

Dad

As Sherlock Holmes would be quick to point out, there are many factors to this bizarre and intricate puzzle. Each of us who knew her intimately would bring to the puzzle a personal and unique reaction. There is really no easy or neat answer to the question of why this beautiful, talented, and loving woman took her life.

Probably it was a cumulative wearing-down process: the financial worries, the sale of the hotels, prescription drugs, anxieties about the children, emotional insecurity, and last, but not least, a frustrating husband.

If Martha were with us today, I feel she would be proud of us. I would also welcome the opportunity to convince her of the importance and worth of her 47 years amongst us.

I ache for my seventy-nine-year-old Dad writing those words. He still loves her.

I wake up to the sound of a driving rainstorm: not a great day for an outing. Weeks ago I had decided to write a letter to my mother to read out loud. I hadn't been able to find the right time to do it. It was now or never, but as soon as I sit at the desk to write the letter, I click on the TV. I tilt back in my chair and put my feet up on the desk like an adolescent. I channel surf. It doesn't work. I'm well past the point of being able to blot her out of my mind with "Good Morning America."

I turn to the blank page.

Dear Mom,

I'm writing in the old Sturbridge house, Jon's bedroom. Soon I'll be leaving for Williamstown and I'm trying to figure out what I want to say to you after all these years. Thinking about you still jams me up with feeling mad and sad and guilty.

I guess the time has come for me to forgive you for killing yourself. I've spent years romanticizing your death into a noble tragedy with you the forlorn heroine. Other times I've been angry and blamed you for destroying the family with your singularly selfish choice. I've also felt so guilty because I avoided

*you like the plague for the last few years of your life, and I
really didn't feel anything at all when you killed yourself.*

*I've never allowed myself to know how awful you must have
felt. It's in the last self-portrait you painted. Your self-loathing
is brutal to behold, the cold disdain in your eyes. Toward the
end, I imagine that you lay in bed filleting yourself with hatred:
exaggerating every mistake or flaw, dismissing every accomplishment or talent, and blaming yourself for everything that
ever went wrong in our family. You must have felt a desperate
craving for utter oblivion.*

*For years I felt that I had forgiven you for murdering your-
self. That was bullshit. Beneath the smoothly polished facade of
forgiveness, I was dead inside. I hated you and I hated me for
hating you. And I felt nothing at all.*

*It's been twenty-six years now. For most of that time, I never
gave you a second thought. Now, I can't get you out of my
mind. This is progress?*

*Mom, I think it's time to really forgive you, and maybe even
me. But I'm still mad. I just don't know how to let go of it.
Believe it or not, I've been trying to pray about it. I've also
begun to write it all down. It's a form of prayer, too.*

But I don't really know what I'm doing. I'm just here.

*I've never said thank you, Mom. I've never really acknowl-
edged how much love and joy you gave all of us. How much
the best part of me comes from the best part of you. I am
proud to have been in your parade.*

*I am blessed with a wonderful wife. You would like Kate. She
doesn't buy any of my bullshit, and she loves me anyway. I also
have two sons who fill my heart with joy and gratitude. (Not all
the time, of course.) I wish you could meet them. I wish they
could have met you. It's hard to explain suicide to them.*

*I finally did sail the Atlantic. I think you would have been
proud of me. It's going to have to be enough though. I've
decided not to cross the Pacific. I'm too old. I have learned to
care enough to be afraid. I am the same age you were when
you died.*

By the way, I've decided to quit drinking. I don't drink that much, but the way I think about drinking is deadly. It's been like sipping poison my whole life. It's time.

There's really not much more to say. I'm sorry I've been so angry. I'm glad you were my Mom. You still are. I wish you were here.

Good-bye,
David

The day clears as I leave the inn. The sunlight shimmers on the wet leaves and grass; the countryside is lush and green. I'm too agitated to appreciate the scenery. Thinking of the ease with which I had sent clients off to visit their parents' graves with reassuring murmurings about "grief," "healing," and "recovery" makes me feel slightly queasy.

I turn off the Mass. Pike toward Williamstown and suddenly remember the flowers. I planned to plant some at the gravesite and to bury my mother's wedding ring under them, too. My sister, Lauris, gave it to me and said, "Take it. I can't stand having it anymore. It's killing me." Burying it with the flowers seems fitting even if it is a little melodramatic.

I pull the ring out of my pocket. It's a wide silver band carved to look like a floral wreath. My mother designed it with her usual artistic flare.

Mom was nineteen when she married Dad. Twenty-eight years later, Dad bent over her hospital bedside, kissed her forehead, and said good-bye.

I put the ring back in my pocket. It's definitely time to focus on finding a flower shop. Robinson's Flower Emporium appears in the corner of my eye and I swing the car around. The store's packed with people buying flowers. Why are all these people here in the middle of a Friday morning? Suddenly, I realize my pilgrimage to the grave coincides with Mother's Day weekend. This is altogether too cute.

"May I help you, sir?" asks the friendly old lady behind the counter.

"I just want to plant something that won't need a lot of tending. I like these things right here. What are they?"

"Well, that's a very nice choice. They're called miniature roses. But you wouldn't want to plant them until the end of the month."

"Actually, I was going to plant them today. What's the problem?"

"At this time of year, you still have to worry about a frost killing them. Most people will keep them inside for a few more weeks."

"Well, that's a good tip. I'll take them."

"Do you want a card? We have quite a selection of Mother's Day cards."

"No thanks, I don't need a card. The flowers will say it all."

I like my choice. The blood red buds are small, delicate, and beautiful. I hope they won't be too intrusive at the gravesite. The idea of them growing there through the summer feels good. But if a frost kills them, so be it.

Williamstown is the epitome of bucolic New England—white colonial houses, neatly tended lawns, and a town green with a Civil War monument. This was my Dad's hometown. What was it like for him to drive back here with my mother's ashes in the backseat of his car?

I'm sure I won't have any difficulty finding the grave. The family plot is marked by a marble bench. How many of those can there be? I remember seeing the bench when they buried Mom's ashes. It was situated so that there was a compelling view of Mount Greylock looming over the valley.

I go all the way around the graveyard twice before I find the bench. I've forgotten how many relatives are buried here. My Dad's parents, my great aunt, two people I've never heard of, and my Aunt Jane's third husband, Bob.

My mother's little marker is off to the left. I remember when Dad buried the cardboard box. The procedure seemed so banal at the time. There was a little tiny hole dug in the frozen ground and my father knelt down and lowered the cardboard box filled with her ashes down into the hole. And that was that. I don't know whether anyone said a prayer. Someone must have said something. All I remember is Dad in his winter overcoat, on his knees, lowering the box.

I stand in front of the flat rectangular stone.

MARTHA CHAMBERLIN TREADWAY
1918–1966

"Died by her own hand" crosses my mind as a possible epitaph. I shake it off. I'm not experiencing any of the emotions I hoped to have. I'm just feeling awkward and self-conscious, not really wanting to be here at all.

I relax a little. Mom's marker is filthy. I don't have anything to clean with, but I start scraping dirt off the marker with my shoe.

I walk over to the marble bench and read the inscription.

> *Tarry, neighbor, God's good work to behold.*
> *Open your heart to the healing power*
> *Of the everlasting purple hills.*

I sit down on the bench. There aren't any purple hills—a stand of scrub trees has grown up on the other side of the road, obscuring the view of the mountains. So much for the healing power of the everlasting purple hills.

I pull out my letter to Mom and start reading it aloud. I'm distracted by a car that drives up to a grave a hundred yards south of me. Sitting there on the bench and reading the letter seems hopelessly foolish, but I push through it.

Afterward, I sit for a while listening to the songs of the birds doing their mating calls. There's also a harsh whine of a chain saw, probably a farmer clearing some land for spring planting. I remind myself that just because I'm not overcome with grief doesn't mean I'm a heartless person. The warm breeze and noonday sun feel good and so I just sit still for a moment.

Back at the car, I see the roses. I don't care much about following through with the planting ritual. I even forgot to bring a little spade, so the windshield scraper would have to do.

Kneeling on the damp earth to dig, I realize with annoyance that I'm going to get my freshly cleaned slacks dirty. Great. I had envisioned this scene as providing a profound moment of love and connection with the woman who gave birth to me. Instead, I'm worried about spotting my pants.

Suddenly, I remember the parade. The only time she came to life that last Christmas was when she decided to set up the Christmas parade. When we were little, she had always put a column of tiny animals on the mantlepiece. They marched behind a black wooden sloop that was filled with little make-believe Christmas packages. She had made each package by carefully wrapping wooden Scrabble pieces in white tissues and tying them with red ribbon. After dinner, she announced she wanted to make the parade and sent us all through the house looking for the animals and the boat. We found them, but we couldn't find the tiny presents. So she insisted that we sit down with another Scrabble set and make up a new batch of miniature packages.

My brother Jim and I could tell it was going to be a difficult scene so we fortified ourselves with a jolt of bourbon while my father and sister tried to make a go of it. A fire was lit and Bing Crosby's Christmas album was put on. Jim and I wisecracked about what a nice Hallmark card scene we seemed to be, while my mother and sister sat in front of the fire with the Scrabble pieces and the tissue paper, and Dad drifted off to the kitchen to freshen everyone's drink.

I noticed that Mom's hands were shaking so badly that she couldn't wrap any of the squares. Nobody said anything. Lauris worked away and amassed a little pile of packages while Mom struggled intently with her first one. She fussed with the tissue and ribbon over and over again, but somehow her twitching fingers kept defeating her.

We just sat and watched her. Finally, she put the piece down and said to no one in particular, "Well, this was a wonderful idea. It's so nice to have everyone home at last. But I'm very tired and I really must go to bed."

It wasn't until she was at the door that I noticed tears streaming down her cheeks. After she left, we packed away the animals and the boat. Not even Lauris had the patience to finish the project. Jim and I grabbed the bourbon and went down to the basement to join our brother, Jon, in front of the TV. We didn't say a word to each other.

Now I'm kneeling at my mother's grave and feeling the same emptiness that I had that Christmas. I just want to get away from there. I fumble for the ring in my pocket. Burying the damn thing is definitely melodramatic, but I know I don't want to take it home. I drop it into the little hole.

Then I plop the flowers into the hole, brush off my pants, and march off to my car without looking back.

Leaving Williamstown, I head up into the mountains to the east of the town. I race the car through the hairpin turns and past the scenic overlooks while barely noticing the lush green beauty of the mountains. Only the broad trails of a ski area catch my eye. The swaths of green cut into the mountainside look like scars.

I'm in a hurry to get home. I don't won't to be late for Sam's first Little League game. I know Kate's rushing through her day at the hospital to get there, too. I'll be so glad to see her.

The anticlimactic moment in the cemetery seems both comical and disappointing. Did I expect that she was going to appear before me? Maybe. Sit down on the bench and ask me how my life was going? Maybe say she was sorry, after all?

Feeling hungry, I start keeping an eye out for a quick fix burger place. For once, I'm going to indulge in a double cheeseburger, large fries, and vanilla shake without sweating the calories and the cholesterol.

Sitting in the McDonald's parking lot, I pause and close my eyes. Suddenly there she is.

I'm standing on the stairs in my PJs. She's all dressed up for a night on the town. I'm frightened about being left home with a new babysitter. An incandescent warmth comes from the depths of her brown eyes as she gazes at me. She bends toward me, putting her hands on my shoulders, and nuzzles me nose to nose, doing our Eskimo kiss. A slight smile plays on her lips. "There, there, sweetheart, I won't be gone too long. Keep your chin up. I love you, David."

"I love you, too, Mom."

My eyes fill. The soothing tears flow down my cheeks. Then I imagine sitting on the sofa in our old living room that Christmas Eve. I'm seeing that poor, pathetic woman struggling with the ribbon and the tissue paper. Suddenly, I just want to be back there. I want to get down on my knees and help my Mom wrap the Scrabble piece and fill the black schooner with presents. I want to help her make the parade. I want to put my arms around her and tell her that I love her. I wish I could say I was sorry. Sorry for coming home late. Sorry for everything.

I hear myself whisper out loud, "I hope you like the roses, Mom."

Mom's watercolor of Rockport, 1953

EPILOGUE

October 1993

THE FOG SQUATS HEAVILY OVER THE HARBOR. OVERHEAD THE gulls screech at each other as they squabble over bits of dead bait chucked by the lobstermen. In the distance, I can hear the low moan of the foghorn off Milk Island. It's as steady as a heartbeat.

It feels good rowing out to the *Crow* this morning. As I pull away from the Sandy Bay Yacht Club, carefully feathering my oars just the way Pop taught me, I am my ten-year-old self heading out to my Turnabout for a day of sailing.

The *Crow* is one of the last sailboats in Rockport. It's late October and most people have pulled their boats for the winter. Later in the day, I'm going to take the boat around to Gloucester to get her hauled. I've thoroughly enjoyed having this time in the harbor of my childhood. There have been many days I've slipped out here to work on finishing this book. I've been grateful for the silence and the solitude, for the gentle lapping of water along the hull and the slight rocking motion. I've been grateful for the return of memories, even those that make my heart ache.

Every time I drive into Rockport, I take a short detour down Pleasant Street. The elm trees are all gone, but not much else has changed. Our old house is high above the street and still towers over its neighbors. The house is freshly painted and seems well cared for by its current family. I hope they love it as much as we did. My mother was happy here. We all were.

Now I can really remember our Sunday excursions to the rocks off Halibut Point where we steamed lobsters and clams. We watched the waves beat against the rocks and the golden arc of the sun slipping into the sea. In the gathering twilight, Mom led us all in singing rounds and telling ghost stories around the fire. She was funny. I can hear her rich laughter amidst the sound of the breakers.

This morning I stopped in front of the house and for a moment I could see Jimmy and I sitting on the back porch playing Scrabble with her. It made me smile.

After awhile I continued on down the street to the cemetery where Jimmy and I used to ride our bikes. It was always cool, shady, and quiet in the graveyard. We would often go down there to get away from the hustle and bustle of the town and the tourists. Sometimes we would make up lurid tales of murder and mayhem about the lives of the people buried around us and we would wonder whose tortured souls might still be lurking about.

Wending my way through the cemetery, I was surprised to see how many names on the headstones I remembered: Knowlton, Thatcher, Barnes, Crenshaw. They were all solid, ordinary Yankee names. Treadway would fit right in here.

As I row toward the *Crow,* the light taping of the main halyard on the mast guides me. I pull alongside her sleek black hull and freshly varnished toe rail and feel a lump in my throat. The *Crow* is at home in Rockport Harbor. At last. It feels as if I've been at sea a long, long time.

The boat is a mess. The gulls have been using it for an outhouse. When I crank up the engine, I discover the batteries are dead, so I can't use my portable computer. Oh, well, life on the *Crow.*

Somehow, it seems fitting that I'm writing these last few lines in my illegible schoolboy handwriting scrunched up in a corner of my cockpit. It's cold and damp, but overhead, I can see the pale sun poking through the cloud cover. The fog appears to be lifting.

I sent a draft of this book to my siblings and my father last spring, and then we all got together for a surprise eightieth birthday party for my Dad. I was nervous about how they'd respond but they've been strongly supportive. I feel cradled by them.

It's odd none of us drinks anymore. Each in our own fashion has concluded that drinking is playing with fire. We're all grateful to be done with it.

Although I'm no longer the in-house family therapist to my own family, I couldn't resist asking for the four of us siblings to break away from the groups of spouses and kids so that we could be alone for a moment.

We crowded into a small, spare bedroom in my brother Jon's house.

"If this is going to be a touchy-feely session, I'm out of here," said Jon, playfully.

"Now, Jon," admonished Lauris, "we can do this for David."

"Don't worry, guys," I said. "I just wanted a moment for us to talk about Mom. We've never really done it before all together."

"Well, it had been a long time since I had given her a passing thought until your damn book stirred me up," said Jon. "I was surprised by some of the anger you seem to have held onto, David. I let her off the hook years ago."

The conversation unfolded. We talked about the book, our feelings, our memories.

"Your book didn't say anything about them moving into the Parker House the day after Christmas. Don't you remember?" Lauris asked me. "We didn't just have Christmas lunch there. Mom and Dad actually checked in for a couple of days because we were all so rowdy. I remember her calling me up to invite me over for a 'just us girls' lunch. I was so embarrassed about how badly behaved we had been, I couldn't face her. I just said 'no thank you, Mommy' in a wee small voice. I never got another chance to see her."

Jimmy, Jon, and I sat, frozen. As usual, Lauris had been the one to cut to the heart of the matter.

Finally, I said, "I don't think any of us saw her again. We just left. I can't believe I forgot about them moving over to the Parker House. What the hell was going on with us? After all this work, there's still so much I don't understand or even remember."

"Sounds like you need another decade of therapy," teased Jim, breaking the tension.

Then we began swapping stories again. We laughed. We cried.

I looked at the other three. Our faces were lined. Our heads were graying and balding. Each of us had our own version of a middle-aged paunch. Jon is struggling successfully with a lifetime of addiction. After years of mental illness, Lauris is managing being a single parent and pursuing her artwork. Jim has remarried and is a successful hotel executive. And I've specialized in taking care of other people. We've all been scarred. Some of the scars show and some don't. We are all survivors in our fashion.

After a while, the conversation began to slow down. It was time to end.

"One last thing, and then I'll leave you alone," I said, "I know it sounds hokey, but I'd like us to all hold hands and pray for her."

There were some groans, but we moved closer, and with some awkward smiles, we took each other's hands.

"Dear God," I began. "Please comfort the soul of our mother, Martha Treadway. Tell her we're all okay. Tell her we love her and we're doing the best we can."

I couldn't say any more. We sat in silence.

Then Lauris said softly, "And, Mom, we wish you were here."

ACKNOWLEDGMENTS

A SOLO PASSAGE IS NEVER TRULY TAKEN ALONE. ONE IS TETHERED to those who share the risks and the waiting. One is buoyed by those who helped prepare the craft and sharpen the sailor's skills.

This book has been a six-year voyage. Without the constant support of my circle of family and friends, I would have foundered long ago. I want to thank:

Kate, Michael, and Sam for their patience and their love. They worked beside me through every hour of this journey.

Dad, Jon, Lauris, and Jim, who are truly my coauthors and whose support for this undertaking has been as steady as a heartbeat.

Aunt Jane, the keeper of the cuddle, Uncle Tiger, and Aunt Cynthia.

Dr. Barbara Greenspan, my therapist, who encouraged and challenged me every page of the way.

Barry Dym, Holly Robinson, Michael Glenn, and Jay Lappin, who skillfully critiqued each draft with care and patience.

Grace Doyle, who provided all the logistical support.

Beth Vessel, JoAnn Miller, and my editor, Juliana Nocker, for their trust and commitment to excellence.

All my clients—past, present, and future—you have always been a gift to me.

And finally, I'd like especially to thank my Dad, Richard Treadway. Throughout the writing of this manuscript, he has been a constant and loving supporter. He has been mentor, confidant, and friend to me. He has fathered me.

Thank you, Dad. I'm proud to be your son.